KV-241-440

WEST SUSSEX INSTITUTE OF
HIGHER EDUCATION LIBRARY

AUTHOR

—

WS 2106575 6

TITLE
EDUCATION

371.97

DEC94

Education for cultural diversity

What do we mean by 'anti-racist' or 'multicultural' education? How does racism affect children's achievements? How do teachers – circumscribed as they are by the national curriculum – meet the needs of all children in all schools?

In examining these questions, this book continues the debate begun in 1985, with the Swann Report *Education for All*. Following a unique personal view from the late Lord Swann, contributors examine the legacy of his report and suggest ways of meeting the educational needs of a society that is growing ever more culturally diverse.

Although not a record of its proceedings, this book grew out of a conference held in 1989 by Hampshire LEA and the University of Southampton. It illustrates the action that can be taken and looks at the impact of government policies, not least the Education Reform Act.

Alec Fyfe is currently Senior Research Officer working in Child Labour at the International Labour Organization, Geneva. He was formerly County General Inspector for Intercultural Education, Hampshire, and was a member of both the National Curriculum Council's Task Group on Multicultural Education and its Whole Curriculum Committee. During 1991–2 he was responsible for developing a special project on the European dimension of education for Hampshire in conjunction with regions in France, Germany and Italy. His publications include *Child Labour* (Polity Press 1989).

Peter Figueroa is a Jamaican settled in Britain. He is a Senior Lecturer in the School of Education at the University of Southampton. He has lectured and carried out research since 1968 in colleges and universities around the world and has published widely on issues of education and race. His most recent book is *Education and the Social Construction of 'Race'* (Routledge 1991).

Key contributors include: James A. Banks, Professor of Education at the University of Washington, Seattle; John Eggleston, Professor of Education at the University of Warwick; Professor Christopher Brumfit and Dr Rosamond Mitchell of the University of Southampton; Carlton Duncan, Headteacher of George Dixon Comprehensive School, Edgbaston; Maggie Semple, Head of Education Unit at the Arts Council of Great Britain; Mitchell Marland, Headteacher of North Westminster Community School, London and Professor of Education, University of Warwick.

Education for Cultural Diversity

The challenge for a new era

Edited by
Alec Fyfe and Peter Figueroa

London and New York

W. SUSSEX INSTITUTE
OF
HIGHER EDUCATION
LIBRARY

First published 1993
by Routledge
11 New Fetter Lane, London EC4P 4EE

Simultaneously published in the USA and Canada
by Routledge
29 West 35th Street, New York, NY 10001

© Hampshire County Council, Alec Fyfe, Peter Figueroa
and contributors 1993
Education for All: A Personal View © 1993
Introduction © Peter Rabbett 1993
Chapters 1, 14 © Peter Figueroa 1993
Chapters 2, 19:1, 21, Introduction to Part 2 © Alec Fyfe 1993
Chapter 3 © James A. Banks 1993
Chapter 4 © Carlton Duncan 1993
Chapter 5 © Maggie Semple 1993
Chapter 6 © Alistair Black 1993
Chapter 7 © Nell White 1993
Chapter 8 © Sue Watts 1993
Chapter 9 © Michael Marland 1993
Chapter 10 © John Fines 1993
Chapter 11 © Geoff Dinkle 1993
Chapter 12 © Rosamond Mitchell and Christopher Brumfit 1993
Chapter 13 © David Naylor 1993
Chapter 15 © Pat Holmes 1993
Chapter 16 © John Eggleston 1993
Chapter 17 © Paul Zec 1993
Chapter 18:1 © Beverley Naidoo 1993
Chapter 18:2 © Len Garrison 1993
Chapter 18:3 © Anne Marley 1993
Chapter 19:2 © Clare Brown 1993
Chapter 19:3 © John Evans 1993
Chapter 20 © Alec Roberts and Ian Massey 1993

Printed and bound in Great Britain by
T.J. Press (Padstow) Ltd., Padstow, Cornwall

All rights reserved. No part of this book may be reprinted or
reproduced or utilized in any form or by any electronic,
mechanical, or other means, now known or hereafter
invented, including photocopying and recording, or in any
information storage or retrieval system, without permission in
writing from the publishers.

British Library Cataloguing in Publication Data
A catalogue reference for this book is available from the British Library

ISBN 0–415–08385–0 (cloth)

Library of Congress Cataloging in Publication Data
has been applied for.

ISBN 0–415–08385–0 (cloth)

It is with great pleasure but a deep sense of loss that we dedicate this book to the memory of the Right Honourable the Lord Swann. *Education for All*, the Report of the Committee of Enquiry, which he chaired after Anthony Rampton OBE, represents a watershed in the terrain explored by this book.

Contents

Contributors

Dr Peter Figueroa, Senior Lecturer, School of Education, University of Southampton

Alec Fyfe is currently Senior Research Officer working in child labour at the International Labour Organization, Geneva. He was formerly County General Inspector for Intercultural Education, Hampshire, and was a member of both the National Curriculum Council's Task Group on Multicultural Education and its Whole Curriculum Committee.

Professor James A. Banks, Professor of Education, University of Washington, Seattle, USA

Alistair Black, County General Inspector for Drama and Media Education, Hampshire

Clare Brown, Co-ordinator for Equal Opportunities Education, Cumbria

Professor Christopher Brumfit, Dean of the Faculty of Educational Studies and Director of the Centre for Language in Education, University of Southampton

Geoff Dinkele, County General Inspector for Geography, Hampshire

Carlton Duncan, Headteacher, George Dixon Comprehensive School, Edgbaston

Professor John Eggleston, Professor of Education and Chairman of the Department of Education, University of Warwick

John Evans, Executive Director with Kirklees Metropolitan Council; formerly Director of Education for Derbyshire

John Fines, Head of History, West Sussex Institute of Higher Education

Len Garrison, ACER Project Director 1976–88; currently Education, Cultural and Study Centre Director, Association of Caribbean Families and Friends (ACFF)

Pat Holmes, Co-ordinator, Head of Service, West Midlands Education Authorities Education Service for Travelling Children

Professor Michael Marland, Headteacher, North Westminster Community School and Professor of Education, University of Warwick

Anne Marley, Senior Librarian, Children's and Schools' Services; formerly Resources Development Officer for Intercultural Education, Hampshire

Ian Massey, Teacher/Adviser for Intercultural Education for Hampshire Education Authority: formerly Head of Social Studies, Frogmore School, Hampshire

Dr Rosamond Mitchell, Lecturer in Education, Centre for Language in Education, University of Southampton

Beverley Naidoo, Author and Advisory Teacher, Dorset

David Naylor, General Inspector (Secondary) for north-east Hampshire; formerly General Adviser for Religious Education, Hampshire

Peter Rabbett, Senior Adviser, Curriculum and Professional Development for West Sussex; formerly County General Inspector for the Management of Learning, Hampshire

Alec Roberts, Deputy Headteacher, Park Community School, Havant, Hampshire; formerly Head of English, Bohunt School, Hampshire

Maggie Semple, Head of the Education Unit, Arts Council of Great Britain; formerly Director of Arts Education for a Multicultural Society (AEMS)

Sue Watts, Deputy Headteacher, Aylwin School, Southwark, London; formerly Advisory Teacher with the Secondary Curriculum Development Unit for Multi-ethnic and Anti-racist Education, ILEA

Nell White, Senior Curriculum Development and Resources Officer, the Commonwealth Institute, London; formerly Project Leader, Wiltshire ESG Project 'Education for All', 1986–89

Paul Zec, Head of Department of Educational Studies, Christ Church College of Higher Education, Canterbury

Acknowledgements

The authors and publishers wish to thank the following who have kindly given permission for the use of copyright material.

'Epilogue' by Grace Nichols from *i is a long memoried woman* © Karnak House 1983/1991 reprinted by permission of the publishers Karnak House; Rangoli and Islamic patterns © Wiltshire County Council 1987 reproduced from *Maths For All* published by Wiltshire County Council price £5.00; Extracts from *Mathematics in the National Curriculum* reproduced by permission of the Controller of HMSO; Diagram 'Confluent education' © Oxford University Press 1983 from Chapter 4 'Humanistic Geography' by John Fien in John Huckle (ed.) *Geographical Education; Reflection and Action*, by permission of Oxford University Press; Extracts from *Religious Education in Hampshire's Schools* © Hampshire County Council 1978; Examination results table 1 adapted and reproduced by permission of the Controller of HMSO; Examination results table 2 and Average performance scores table 3 adapted from tables in *Educational Research* 30.2 (June 1988) pp. 84, 85. *Educational Research* is published for the NFER by the NFER-NELSON Publishing Company Limited; Examination results table 4 and Average performance scores table 5 © London Residuary Body, reproduced by kind permission of the London Residuary Body; Figure 'Living in Cumbria . . . living in Britain . . . living in the world' © Cumbria Local Education Authority 1987 reproduced from *The Curriculum 4–19: Cumbria LEA. Curriculum Paper No. 14: Education for Life in a Multicultural Society* published by Cumbria Local Education Authority.

Abbreviations

ACER – Afro-Caribbean Educational Resource Project
AEMS – Arts Education for a Multicultural Society
CATE – Council for the Accreditation of Teacher Education
CNAA – Council for National Academic Awards
CRE – Commission for Racial Equality
CSE – Certificate of Secondary Education
DES – Department of Education and Science
DHSS – Department of Health and Social Security
ERA – Education Reform Act 1988
ESG – Education Support Grant
ESL – English as a second language
ESN – educationally subnormal
ESW – English, Scottish and Welsh
ESWI – English, Scottish, Welsh and Irish
GCE – General Certificate of Education
GCSE – General Certificate of Secondary Education
GRIST – Grant Related In-Service Training
HMI – Her Majesty's Inspectorate
HMSO – Her Majesty's Stationery Office
INSET – In-Service Education of Teachers
ILEA – Inner London Education Authority
KS – Key Stage
LEA – Local Education Authority
LMS – Local Management of Schools
MARN – Multilingual Action Research Network
NCC – National Curriculum Council
NAME – National Anti-Racist Movement in Education (previously National Association for Multi-Racial Education)
NCATE – National Council for Accreditation of Teachers (US)
NUT – National Union of Teachers

PGCE –   Postgraduate Certificate in Education
PSE –   personal and social education
PSI –   Policy Studies Institute
RAT –   Racism Awareness Training
RE –   religious education
3Rs –   reading, writing and arithmetic
SACRE –   Standing Advisory Council on Religious Education
SATs –   Standardised Attainment Tasks
SCDC –   School Curriculum Development Committee
SEAC –   School Examinations and Assessment Council
TIE –   Theatre in Education
TVEI –   Technical and Vocational Education Initiative
TA –   Training Agency
VR –   verbal reasoning
YTS –   Youth Training Scheme

Education for All: A Personal View by Lord Swann

Editors' note:

This book has grown out of a conference organised in September 1989 by Hampshire Education Authority and the University of Southampton. Lord Swann kindly agreed to give a personal view of Education for All *as the opening key-note lecture of the conference. After Lord Swann's sudden death in September 1990, Lady Swann readily agreed to the publication in this volume of an edited version of that lecture, the last on the topic given by Lord Swann. In this edited version we have made several cuts, but have paraphrased or added nothing – except for some minor clarifications in square brackets. We have taken great care not in any way to alter or distort the thought of Lord Swann.*

Over the years I have chaired five government committees charged with reporting on difficult problems, and I am all too familiar with what a trial this is . . . [Of the five Reports] four were Reports on scientific problems. The fifth, *Education for All*, dealt with something quite different, namely, sensitive social and political problems which are inherently far more difficult, and where objective evidence and guidance is much harder to come by. . . .

The committee was originally set up by Shirley Williams in 1979, towards the end of the last Labour Administration. . . the chairman was Anthony Rampton, but the membership was not completed until after the ensuing General Election. The committee was asked to produce, as soon as possible, an Interim Report, dealing particularly with the educational needs and attainments of children of West Indian origin. . . .

The bulk of the evidence the committee received from the West Indian community . . . pointed to racism within schools as very much the principal cause of underachievement, and because there was not time to assess other possible factors the [Interim] Report was seen, perhaps unfairly, to be dismissing them as unimportant.

In addition . . . the Report's statistics on underachievement . . . made it very clear that, by and large, Asian children were achieving very much on a level with white children. And since Asian children are certainly subject, like West Indian children, to racism, the explanation of underachievement as being solely or very largely due to racism in schools, was immediately suspect. . . .

The Government all but ignored the Interim Report, and though I was not on the committee at the time, I fear that this must have been profoundly upsetting to both Chairman and members. Be this as it may, Anthony Rampton ultimately resigned, as did a number of members. I don't know whether Mark Carlisle, Secretary of State for Education in the new Conservative Government, considered letting the committee lapse at this stage but, if so, he decided against it in the end, and he approached me with the suggestion that I take it on. . . .

A variety of thoughts went through my head. I didn't know much about the problems in question; a rather outspoken friend of mine who had earlier been involved in the problems of race relations, and who likes making shocking remarks, said it would drive me crazy and if I wasn't careful it would turn me into a flaming racist.

I thought that perhaps, given a chance to help in a good cause . . . I ought to do something. And having recently become a Life Peer I thought I ought at least to show some sense of social responsibility. So, for better or worse, I said yes to Mark Carlisle and became Chairman. . . .

My main immediate concern was to do something about the widespread allegations that followed the publication of the Interim Report, namely that the true cause of West Indian underachievement was simply that as a race they had a low IQ. . . .

Since the problem involves difficult and complex psychological and statistical issues, I looked for a distinguished scientist with an open mind, who had political sensitivity and who had not become embroiled in the long-running and heated debate. I was fortunate in enlisting the help of Nicholas Mackintosh, Professor of Psychology at Cambridge University. He, together with his colleague Dr Mascie Taylor, reviewed all the scientific literature, made some fresh analyses of their own, and wrote a long, scholarly but nevertheless eminently readable and sensitive paper which was published in full as an Annex to the [Swann] Report. I believe that anyone who wants to know the truth of the matter should read it with care. In brief, the authors show that much of the difference in average IQ scores between West Indian and white children is related to differences between them in matters of socio-economic status.

It is not generally realised that these factors are related to IQ among whites, and when they are taken into account, the differences between West Indian and white children are sharply reduced. As the authors point out, the difference may well be of no more significance than the well-known average difference in IQ scores between twins and single-tons within a white family. They go on to make the telling comment:

> We do not think that this matters, and we should rightly question the good sense or good will of anyone who claimed that it did.

. . . I have seen no more mention of low West Indian IQs from that day to this. I sometimes think this was one of the more significant things we managed to do.

Since our IQ finding carried with itself the clear implication that socio-economic status was an important factor in West Indian underachievement, and indeed underachievement in any other ethnic minority, we turned naturally to thinking about it, but not about it alone. . . .

There is much research evidence that the poor socio-economic status to be found in all the minorities is due, at least in part, to racial discrimination, over housing and over jobs. We did not attempt to prescribe detailed solutions to these problems, which fell rather outside our terms of reference. . . . But we did of course pick up the obvious and familiar conclusion that if things are to get better, then the educational system must pay just as much attention to the educa-tion of the white majority as it does to the education of the ethnic minorities. Hence, of course, the ultimate title of the Report, namely *Education for All*.

The concept of Education for All is not new – far from it, but the title is new, and is one that we hoped would catch on. Has it, I wonder? Some say yes, some say no. Certainly I fear it has not caught on as we had hoped in the all-white areas. . . . In a government Report one can only hope to sketch out a general plan, and this we did at some length in Chapters 6 and 9.

I shall not go into detail over the educational concept, but summarise as follows what we thought to be the necessary administrat-ive steps, in the Guide to the Report. . . .

> The Committee is in no doubt that progress will be slow unless the thinking behind the concept permeates the whole structure of teacher training. . . . Among many recommendations, the Committee hopes to see greater attention to multicultural issues,

as well as optional specialist courses relating to such issues, both in PGCE and B.Ed courses. They would like all students to be given the opportunity to gain some practical experience in a multiracial school. They hope that both the CNAA and the universities will take active steps to promote the pluralist perspective throughout teacher education. They would like to see more in-service training reflecting a multicultural approach. They recommend the development of a number of teacher training institutions as acknowledged centres of specialism, giving long and short courses, undertaking research and fostering curriculum development. And they would like to see pilot projects in 'all-white' areas, and teacher exchange between such areas and multiracial schools.

The Committee is also much concerned at the very small number of ethnic minority teachers, and make a number of recommendations. While they do not support positive discrimination and quotas, and do not wish to see any diminution in standards, they believe that much could and should be done to overcome the prejudice and discrimination which they believe to be the major obstacle to the employment and advancement of would-be ethnic minority teachers.

. . . It was my hope that, having had one success in research, we might have another. I myself spent a good deal of a summer holiday, helped by various people, and drafted a chapter of the Report (Chapter 3) which attempted to summarise what general lessons we might learn from research. . . . I have already touched on socio-economic matters where there is indeed objective evidence. But I found no objective evidence on the inadequacies, if any, of the West Indian family. Indeed, my general conclusion was that they are as concerned for their children's success as any. The Committee had received a lot of oral evidence from the ethnic minority community on the inadequacies of schools and teachers, but there is little objective research evidence. This does not necessarily mean that all is well, but it does perhaps mean that the situation is more complex than is generally supposed. . . . We examined a range of other problems, amongst them language and language education, religious education, separate schools and the concerns of the smaller ethnic minority groups.

Looking to the future, we asked Professor Cornford to write a lengthy Annex on the research that needed doing and that we hoped would be supported by the Government in due course. But alas the recommendations ultimately fell on deaf ears. It is true that Sir Keith Joseph, speaking in the Commons on the day of publication of our report, said:

> . . . We badly need more hard information about the effect on achievement of factors in and out of school. I intend to commission research which will look at these factors and at the extent to which they contribute to underachievement among pupils of all backgrounds. Ethnic minority pupils would be one part of such a study.

One such project, concerned in part with ethnic minorities, of which more later, was in fact already in progress but, as far as I am aware, only one new project was discussed in Sir Keith's fairly brief time as Secretary of State, and his successor Kenneth Baker decided that he was not interested in any further research in this area. Indeed he withdrew support from the only new project that had been mooted. Fortunately it has been taken over by one of the well-known trusts, but bearing in mind that the amount of money the DES had allocated for research at the beginning of 1988 was about £14 million, one can only describe the situation as disgraceful.

It will be evident that we set much store by further research, believing that we needed to know far more than we do about all the factors in school and out of it that bear on achievement and underachievement, and the creation of a better and fairer society for our ethnic minorities.

. . . I come then to the aftermath of the Report. . . . What matters more than the immediate response is the later considered response, and later still the acid test of whether the Report has led to changes of practice that put to right the ills that the Report aimed to correct. . . .

I was . . . very interested to read a recent book edited by a member of the committee, Dr Gajendra Verma, entitled *Education for All: A Landmark in Pluralism*. It contains a dozen or more essays written by a very diverse group of experts, and it seems to me a valuable touchstone. Frankly I was surprised, indeed touched, at the extent of approval of the Report. In my gloomier moments I feared that we had made little impact. . . .

I do want . . . to say a little about the long-term response of the Government. Once Sir Keith Joseph, who had been a stout supporter, had moved to the House of Lords, and Kenneth Baker had arrived as Secretary of State, things changed. I mentioned earlier that Baker rapidly turned off the tap so far as support for research was involved. But I was further dismayed to learn what one of his Junior Ministers, Mrs Angela Rumbold, had said on the radio. Not surprisingly I failed to get the details from the DES, but my old organisation, the BBC, keeps a tape from which I quote:

In essence the Government has taken on board Swann's recommendations, but it feels that the way in which one deals with the whole of this problem is perhaps changing with time and one perhaps cannot go back to something which was thought through . . . and presented in a time and an era which is very different from today. One of the Government's main thrusts has been to tackle inner city problems, and that is one of the more effective ways . . . for many of the suggestions that came through in the Swann Committee.

Perhaps one shouldn't be too censorious about off-the-cuff remarks made on the radio, but they have, so far as I know, never been disowned by Mrs Rumbold or anyone else. What in heaven's name she means by the Report stemming from a past era when she spoke a mere three and a half years after the Report was published defeats me. As to inner city problems, yes, if the Government's initiatives have actually raised the socio-economic status of the inhabitants, they may have raised that of the ethnic minorities in proportion. But they may not and, in any event, poverty is a relative matter. Does the Government have any relevant research evidence? Not to my knowledge.

Such remarks as these suggest that the Government thinks somehow or other that it need worry no longer about the problems of the ethnic minorities. . . .

I have been puzzled for some time past at Mr Baker's determination to renege on Sir Keith Joseph's promise to support more research on the problems of our ethnic minorities, and at Mrs Rumbold's extraordinary remarks, assuming that there must have been some more or less rational basis behind them. It now seems to me that it may have something to do with a lengthy and valuable Report by the Policy Studies Institute, submitted quite a long time ago, finally published last June and entitled *The School Effect: A Study of Multi-Racial Comprehensives* (Smith and Tomlinson, 1989).

At a somewhat casual reading of the Report, two things stand out which might indicate that all was well and that further research on the education of ethnic minority children was unnecessary. Firstly, the Report shows that good schools manage to raise the levels of achievement of all children, both from the white majority and the ethnic minorities. Secondly, questioning of parents showed that very few indeed complained of racism within schools.

But a closer reading reveals that there are a number of important matters that the Report did not explore or attempt to explain, and which make one think again. For example:

1   There are numerous differences in the levels of achievement of the different minority groups when they enter secondary school. Why is this? Two years later there is a widening of these differences. Why is this?

2   West Indian and Asian children tend to stay on longer at school than whites in order to get better qualifications, and are more likely to follow further studies after leaving. Nevertheless the proportion of West Indian children going on to get degree-level qualifications is much lower than for whites and Asians. Why is this? Surely it should be matter of much concern?

3   The Report found that very few parents indeed complained of racial hostility or prejudice at school, either on the part of the pupils or teachers. On the face of things this is surprising in the light of much evidence in our own Report and others. One must doubt whether regular questioning of parents within a small community is a wholly reliable guide. And one must also ask whether the subtler forms of discrimination are always to be discovered by asking parents about racial hostility and prejudice. I suspect that more elaborate and sophisticated research is still needed.

4   The Report has by no means fully explored the factors that make for success in the good schools.

5   Lastly the Report has not addressed itself to the admittedly very difficult but crucial element of *Education for All*, namely, can one discover what elements in education help to reduce the degree of racial prejudice and discrimination on the part of white children in after-school life?

   I don't want to sound critical, the Report is a very valuable one, and one can't expect any research project to cover everything. But it is clear to me that only at a casual reading could one possibly conclude that the Report has rendered further research on the problems of the ethnic minorities unnecessary, or relegated our Report to a past and irrelevant era. . . .

References

Department of Education and Science. (1981) *West Indian Children in Our Schools* (Rampton Report). HMSO
  (1985) *Education for All* (Swann Report). HMSO
Smith, D.J. and Tomlinson, S. (1989) *The School Effect: A Study of Multi-Racial Comprehensives.* Policy Studies Institute
Verma, G. (ed.) (1989) *Education for All: A Landmark in Pluralism.* Falmer Press

Introduction

Peter Rabbett

'There is still much to be done'

Some years on from the publication of the Swann Report, *Education for All* (DES, 1985), we read daily of publications and events which confirm the enormity of the task still facing the educational world. We have much to do to raise the levels of achievement, combat racism and promote the values which support a multi-ethnic society. *Education for All* played an important role in raising public consciousness and giving affirmation to the wealth of work which had opened up the debate within schools and their local communities but, according to Lord Swann himself, it has been since publication substantially disregarded by Education Ministers and the Department of Education and Science.

The steamroller of educational reform, powered by the Education Reform Act of 1988 (ERA), has shifted our attention and introduced countervailing pressures on schools. Offering a chimera of parental choice, ERA has encouraged an upsurge in tension over the character of schools. Bradford and Dewsbury are notable case studies, with new disputes over school placement being supported by pressure groups. Religion is frequently cited as a factor either in support of the creation of schools for children from minority faiths, or in favour of government policy which enshrines in statute the Christian character of schools and makes compulsory a corporate act of Christian worship. The Commission for Racial Equality's Report, *Schools of Faith* (1990), sought to open up the debate on the purpose of religious schools and whether they are likely to foster division or equality and diversity. It was criticised for its secular tone by a broad spectrum of religious groups yet it supports one of the Swann Report's recommendations in arguing that schools should be more sensitive to the dress and dietary requirements of minority faiths. In doing so the CRE believe that pressure for more denominational schools will diminish. Religious groups are calling for a less secular education for their children, imposing instead a closer focus on religious instruction to support a religious community. Such beliefs may lead to fragmentation.

At the heart of the debate over denominational schools lies the question of what schools are for and the impact that they might realistically have on individual belief and behaviour. Can they encourage a respect for cultural diversity? Can schools promote the values which will counter racism? Can schools become institutions in which all learners are valued equally?

Much work has taken place in schools and local education authorities where there are significant multicultural communities, but the post-Swann era has seen little development in all-white areas. So often, the 'no problem here' excuse is cited.

Education for Cultural Diversity – the conference

It was in this context that in September 1989 Hampshire LEA and the University of Southampton organised the conference 'Education for Cultural Diversity'. It aimed to bring together the key actors nationally and internationally. It was an opportunity to celebrate achievements as participants could share good practice and refocus attention on neglected areas. It did stimulate fresh thinking and helped to establish priorities for action within our communities.

This book is not a record of the conference but contains papers which have been drawn from the work of conference contributors and participants. It attempts to look at the opportunities and conflict created by the Education Reform Act 1988, to look at other government policies which promote or discourage action for equality and to encourage activity at all levels of the education service to exploit those opportunities for development.

It was fitting that Lord Swann opened the conference, for his message echoes throughout the book. His personal view of the impact of the Report confirms the need for renewed vigour. In lamenting the current DES view that *Education for All* is no longer relevant to present-day circumstances he called upon the Government to invest further in research. There are some pressing questions to which we must find evidence before we can move forward: Why are achievement levels of children from different minority groups widening? Why do proportionally fewer West Indian students gain degree level qualifications? Why do very few parents complain of racial hostility and prejudice at school?

What do we know about the factors which make good schools? What can schools do to reduce the degree of racial prejudice and discrimination on the part of white children in after-school life?

Priorities for action

Fyfe and Figueroa in their separate contributions seek to establish an agenda for the 1990s. It is Fyfe's view that we need a united movement, one which transcends the sectarianism of the past decade. In tracing the recent conceptual and political history of the movement – integrationism to anti-racism – he reveals the schism which has grown from competing ideologies. He proposes that an 'intercultural' approach might achieve the necessary synthesis through a sustained conversation between cultural groups to achieve unity out of diversity. The aim has not changed· equality of opportunity, equality of esteem and opposition to racism. We must become better at managing change and promoting pluralism by harnessing the power of education.

We need to examine every aspect of our educational practice, argues Peter Figueroa, for it is necessary for all educators to seek opportunities to confront ethnocentrism and racism and to be positively multiculturalist. Banks offers a rich analysis of approaches to multicultural education in the United States. While there are many social and economic differences (class, for example, has greater significance within the American black community), we can make use of the conclusions he reaches to help with our own work. We face the same problems in having to cope with reduced financing for social programmes and we share the same demographic trends – an ageing population and a massive decline in the numbers of school leavers entering the workforce. The need to educate all students may be recognised as an economic priority.

But will intercultural education be supported and resourced? The changes to Section 11 funding* will reduce LEAs' and schools' freedom of action. Not only is there a significant reduction in the budget but the money will be granted to support short-life projects not exceeding three years. These projects can only be focused on teaching English as a second language (ESL) or job preparation. Gone are all the oppor-

---

*Section 11 of the 1966 Local Government Act enables the Home Office to allocate Grant Aid to local authorities to tackle disadvantage among ethnic minorites. It is intended to cover housing, leisure, social services, race relations and education. About eighty per cent is currently spent on education.

tunities to support mother tongue teaching, to bring teachers from minority communities into schools, to support awareness programmes and to encourage development in all-white schools. The new rules ignore some of the substantial evidence about educational achievement, for example that children's acquisition of a second language is greatly strengthened by their competence in their first language. Observers believe that this change is the prelude to the termination of Section 11 funding.

Contexts for action

There is cause for optimism when we examine the rhetoric attached to the development of the National Curriculum. The cornerstone of the Education Reform Act, the new curriculum is intended to establish common practice across all schools. It can be argued that the purpose is to create uniformity of approach so that school can be compared with school when results of testing at seven, eleven and fourteen are published. Parents will then have an indicator by which to make choices for their children. In establishing a National Curriculum the Government has also established a statement of entitlement. Our task must be to ensure that this statement is representative of the best possible quality. There were promising starts. The remits of the subject working groups contain an instruction to see that a focus on cultural diversity permeates their work. In addition, the National Curriculum Council's series of curriculum guidance documents identifies multicultural education as a cross-curricular dimension. We have yet to see their detailed thinking; at the time of writing the concept has only appeared as illustration in their statement on the whole curriculum (NCC, 1990).

There is less cause for optimism when looking at the DES Statutory Orders and NCC subject working group final reports. A first glance at the Maths, Science and Technology Orders leads one to conclude that the authors have adopted a novel approach to permeation . . . silence! A multicultural approach is not discouraged, it is just not featured. Nell White and Sue Watts both explore opportunities and contexts for developing anti-racist and multicultural perspectives. They share an approach which underlines the importance of reading Non-statutory Guidance and planning creatively. Technology, maths and science are not limited by national boundaries or languages.

We need to pay special attention to work in the field of English and language across the curriculum. I do not share Michael Marland's optimism concerning government thinking about the English curriculum. The DES has used its word-processor to poor effect in deleting any reference to 'a range of cultures' from the English working group's report. Subsequent assurances from a Minister of State that all children should have access to literature in English from other cultures has not been reinforced in statute to ensure that achievement in such work is rewarded and valued. Once again it will be a voluntary activity. Marland offers us an effective analysis of the potential power of the English curriculum to explore the world in which we live and to value other cultures. He exhorts us to consider the concept of 'englishes' and to investigate the ways in which language development and cultural development intertwine. We need to create a coherent experience for pupils which can only derive from an overarching approach to language – a whole school language curriculum growing out of and supported by specialisms. Understanding language, he argues, is the key to understanding cultures.

It is the plight of ESL speakers that is highlighted by Mitchell and Brumfit. They argue that it is the assessment of the curriculum, in particular Speaking and Listening, which will disadvantage those who are not competent in the single strand of stylistic development proposed by the report. Additionally, there are many unexplored problems associated with objective assessment of spoken language skills. It falls to the modern foreign languages group to explore opportunities for language awareness which may support bilingual pupils. Mitchell and Brumfit argue for the drafting of a language charter to define the language needs of all learners and the commitment of each school or LEA to meeting those needs.

History and geography have, traditionally, made a significant multicultural contribution to the curriculum, but they have both fared badly in the process of drafting National Curriculum subject reports. It is curriculum content which is at stake and the desire to re-establish a greater focus on Britain and its history. The history curriculum is seen as the vehicle to either socialise children and restore national identity; challenge xenophobia and stereotyping; or respect cultural variety. It is choice of content *and* approach to learning which will determine the result. The consultations over history and geography have produced a concentration on the UK and the Western world and a sharp division between European and non-European areas of study. Additionally the primacy of facts over understanding ideology and acquiring skills has become enshrined in the weighting of attainment targets. How does this accord with John Fines' appeal that we make proper use of empathy to look at good will in society? There is a realisation by the DES and more importantly the NCC that the incremental approach to curriculum design is creating a host of inconsistencies and potential problems. In creating a Whole Curriculum committee, the NCC may well provide an important impetus to multicultural education.

Whilst a number of cross-curricular themes are being introduced to supplement curriculum content, there are other essential elements to do with personal social and moral education which will provide a context for development.

Carlton Duncan argues that PSE courses have an important function in challenging the hidden curriculum and ethos of many schools and in educating children about their rights and responsibilities. Including new skills and understanding in a record of achievement may help to address the issue of underachievement in public examinations. Employers will have further positive information about their applicants. It is likely that NCC guidance on citizenship will inform practice in this area but my hope is that they will present a richer model to the 'community service' view encouraged by the Speaker's Commission on Citizenship (1990).

Managing change

We can see that the National Curriculum will provide opportunities and contexts for developing education for cultural diversity, but these will be in the main non-statutory. It will be the responsibility of individuals, schools and LEAs to see that something happens. There will be little national pressure for change and insignificant support in clear financial terms. To be included on an agenda and win appropriate resourcing will require action in each institution. LEAs do have some opportunities for promoting development even after the full delegation of powers and resources to schools. LEA policies should be reflected in institutional development plans.

The case studies of both school-based and LEA-wide management of change support the view that an initial 'top-down' implementation is required in the first instance to convey appropriate status to any development. Reforms need to be holistic if they are to be more than just tinkering. We would be advised to look at research on the management of educational change and plan developments which will be significant and penetrating. Michael Fullan (1990) illustrates the complexity of the process and concludes that successful change is brought about where there is a proper balance between pressure and support, where there is clear leadership, vision and support from senior staff, where priority is given to a project within already overcrowded agendas; where the shift from policy to practice is swift; where thinking about the process of change matches the content of the change; and where all participants feel they are learning from the experience.

It will be interesting to return to this book in ten years' time and to review the progress we have made over that period. Whilst we have very little support from new statutory instruments of government, or from the values enshrined in Local Management of Schools, there is still the wealth of experience and commitment of professionals in education which will make good use of whatever context they work in. Progress will be made – despite the National Curriculum.

References

Commission for Racial Equality. (1990) *Schools of Faith*. CRE, August

Department of Education and Science. (1985) *Education for All* (Swann Report). HMSO

Education Reform Act 1988

Fullan, M. (1990) The management of change: an implementation perspective. In *Facing the Challenge*. Report of the IMTEC 2020 conference, September

National Curriculum Council. (1990) Curriculum Guidance No.3: *The Whole Curriculum*. NCC, March

Speaker's Commission on Citizenship. (1990) *Encouraging Citizenship*. HMSO

PART 1: Context

Chapter 1

Cultural Diversity, Social Reality and Education

Peter Figueroa

History and the National Curriculum

The National Curriculum History Working Group Interim Report (DES, 1989, p. 38) gives 'Invaders, settlers and peoples of the British Isles' as the first British history study unit at Key Stage 2. This unit represents one term's work for pupils aged about seven. Who are these 'invaders, settlers and peoples of the British Isles'? The very next phrase, after a colon, makes this clear. It reads 'a broad treatment of the Roman, Anglo-Saxon, Viking, and Norman invasions and settlements'. The Celts are not mentioned at all, and a line is drawn with the Norman invasion. Do those of us who settled after 1066 not qualify as people of the British Isles?

In the Final Report of the National Curriculum History Working Group (DES, 1990, p. 26) this study unit has been more appropriately renamed 'Invaders and settlers: the Romans, Anglo-Saxons and Vikings in Britain'. Questions remain however. For instance, why not start with the point of view of the inhabitants at the time of the Roman invasion? Or alternatively, if the intention is genuinely to lead to insights into 'the ethnically and culturally diverse nature of British society' (ibid. p. 21), one might start with a much wider view reflecting the rich diversity of the peoples of Britain across the centuries.

In fact, migration, cultural diversity, international links and social change have been common throughout the history of Britain. So have sectional conflicts and inequality.

This chapter draws partly on some of the materials in P. Figueroa (1991) *Education and the Social Construction of 'Race'*. Routledge.

Trading links existed between Europe and India and other parts of the East from ancient times. There were also long-standing links via the Mediterranean with Africa. But with the opening of sea passages in the fifteenth century, trade and contacts increased – as did European, and in particular British, control and domination. European colonisation and empires meant that many Europeans, and in particular British people, from many backgrounds migrated into many parts of the world. Also, the flow of people from many parts of the world into Britain and the rest of Europe grew. In the seventeenth and eighteenth centuries especially, some people were brought into Britain as domestics from India and other parts of the East (GLC Ethnic Minorities Unit, 1986, p. 28). Some came, more or less voluntarily, as seamen or for other reasons such as trade or business.

Black people from Africa came to Britain with the Romans: an African division helped defend Hadrian's Wall in the third century AD. However, it was only with European expansion in the modern era and the growing slave trade that a large black population developed. One estimate is that there were 10,000–15,000 black people in London alone in the latter part of the eighteenth century (ibid. p. 15). By the nineteenth century a substantial black population in Britain 'permeated most ranks of society, through the length and breadth of the country' (Walvin, 1973, p. 72).

Through colonisation and exploitation immense capital was transferred from India, the Caribbean and other places into Britain (see Fryer, 1984, pp. 33–47). The second industrial revolution was largely founded on such capital (Williams, 1944 and Rodney, 1972). J.S. Mill commented that the trade with Africa, India and the West Indies 'is hardly to be considered as external trade, but more resembles the traffic between town and country' (quoted by Rodney, 1972, p. 93).

It was as a consequence of British colonisation and Empire that people from the Indian subcontinent and the Caribbean rallied to the British cause in World Wars I and II, working in the war industry and joining the armed forces. At the end of both wars some of these people stayed on in Britain. After World War II the demand for labour in Britain – and in continental Europe – the depressed economic state in the Caribbean and India, social and political upheavals in India and East Africa, and the virtual closing of the USA to traditional Caribbean out-migration, all led to a growing migration into Britain, first from the Caribbean, then from the Indian subcontinent and finally from East Africa. People also came from other parts of the world. These included Chinese from Hong Kong, Greek and Turkish Cypriots, Italians recruited into the brick industry, refugees from Eastern Europe and large numbers from Ireland – the Irish constituting the largest single group of immigrants from the mid-nineteenth century.

Thus in the post-war era cultural diversity in Britain obtained a new meaning, and this in at least three related senses.

1   The 'mix' is new or, at least, different.
2   Black people in the widest sense and their cultures are unequally located in the society.
3   They tend to be perceived, treated and related to in stereotypical, negative, narrow or distorted ways.

These three, interrelated phenomena have important educational implications. But these implications depend also on our understanding of education and, more widely, on our values and cognitive assumptions.

In referring to cultural diversity I have in mind mainly South Asians and Caribbeans, the response to them and the place they tend to be ascribed within the social structure. It is these groups in particular that have been seen as problematic in Britain. However, many parallels can be found between the situation of these groups and others in Britain, in the rest of Europe and indeed in many other countries.

Post-war cultural diversity

The first point I want to make is that there is a fantastic diversity in Britain today. There is a great deal of variety even among people frequently referred to as 'Asians' and among those often termed 'West Indians'. The inclusive term 'black' has become quite common in Britain. Those who describe themselves in this way use the term not so much as a phenotypical descriptive label but rather as a way of making a political statement. It underlines that one is proud to be the person that one is, thereby rejecting the stereotypes and presuppositions built into the term as used by racists. Secondly, it highlights that all the 'ethnic groups' to which it refers share a common interest in so far as they tend to be disadvantaged by the system, to be unequal, to be exploited. Nevertheless, it is important to realise that there is not just *one* black culture, but many.

'Culture' refers to a system of values and to a conceptual system, to a system of behaviour and to a communication system, which have been socially constructed and are socially transmitted as part of a group's heritage and as the framework and medium of its life. It is easy to see, in terms of languages and religions, that 'Asians' constitute several very different cultural groups. Although it may seem less obvious, so do Caribbean people. The 'British' Caribbean alone consists of a dozen or more island nations or colonies and two continental American nations, one in South America and one in Central America. These territories share many historical and social features, but each has an identity and separate history of its own. They have been variously peopled by many African cultural groups, by Irish, Welsh, Scots and English people from different strata, by other Europeans, and by Chinese, South Asians, Middle Easterners and many others, including Amerindian peoples. Caribbean cultures and languages are closely related to, but significantly different from, the dominant British culture and language. This can actually make the intercultural relationships and educational implications less straightforward in the case of Caribbeans than in that of the South Asians, whose cultures and languages seem so obviously distinctive.

In brief, as the Swann Report (DES, 1985) argues, modern Britain is a 'plural' society. One clear index of this is that over 180 languages other than English are spoken by pupils as their first language in what was the Inner London Education Authority (ILEA Research and Statistics, 1989).

A society can be 'plural' in many different, complex and interacting ways. Apart from cultural and linguistic diversity, articulation by social class and gender is fundamental and interacts with ethnic differentiation.

Inequality

This brings me to the second aspect of culturally diverse post-war Britain: the ethnic minorities, in particular those of Caribbean and South Asian background, tend to be in an unequal position in the society. For instance, the national survey carried out by the Policy Studies Institute in 1982 (Brown, 1984, p. 293) showed that South Asian and Caribbean people in Britain 'are more likely than white people to be unemployed and . . . to have jobs with lower pay and lower status'. Furthermore the rise in the unemployment rate was larger for black people than for white people (ibid. p. 298). In 1982 almost a *half* of Caribbean males aged sixteen to nineteen were unemployed, compared with about a third of South Asians and a third of white men in the same age group (ibid. Table 84).

The same survey (ibid. pp. 305–6) also found that 'overall, the quality of housing of black people is much worse than the quality of housing in general'. Their density of occupation was higher, they more often had to share rooms or amenities with other households and they were substantially over-represented in some of the worst council accommodation.

However, there was a great deal of variation between and among ethnic minorities. For instance, there were 'relatively large proportions of non-manual workers' among African and Asian males; 'a large proportion of skilled manual workers' among Caribbean and Sikh men; but very few Bangladeshi men in 'skilled manual jobs, and very many in semi-skilled work' (ibid. p. 293).

In the field of education there is a good deal of evidence documenting the unequal position overall of Caribbean and South Asians (Taylor, 1981, 1987, 1988 and Taylor with Hegarty, 1985). On the basis of such evidence it is often repeated that some ethnic minorities, in particular Caribbean pupils, 'underachieve', but that 'Asians' 'over-achieve'. This is misleading, and helps to reinforce stereotypes. (See chapter 14 below.)

Racism and ethnicism

The third characteristic of post-war Britain of interest here is the way the majority, both inside and outside the education system, perceive, relate to and treat cultural diversity and more particularly black people and their cultures. This is a central aspect, as well as both cause and effect, of the unequal position of black people. Here we have to do with racism and ethnicism.

The early response – or lack of it – on the part of the education system to the 'immigrants' is illustrative. They tended to be seen as a problem and as creating problems. Afro-Caribbean pupils in particular were disproportionately – and quite wrongly – defined as educationally 'subnormal' or 'remedial'. The cultures and languages of the black minorities were seen, not simply as culturally and linguistically different, but as deficient and so as needing 'compensatory' treatment. Even to the present time the Department of Education and Science has failed to articulate a coherent and explicit policy. Its response to Swann's call for 'Education for All' (DES, 1985) has so far been minimal. The National Curriculum working groups have paid only marginal attention to these issues and the Statutory Orders none at all.

The situation in education is of a piece with that in the wider society. The first survey of black minorities carried out in 1960 by Political and Economic Planning (PEP, 1967), and the second national PEP survey carried out in 1974 (Smith, 1977) provided evidence of the prevalence of prejudice, stereotypes, racism and discrimination. Almost twenty years later Brown (1984, Table 117), reporting on the third national survey in the same series mentioned above, found that most respondents, both black and white, thought some employers in Britain would refuse a job to a person because of their 'race or colour'. Brown and Gay (1985, pp. 30, 31) reporting further on the same survey, concluded that seventeen years after the first Race Relations Act (1965) racist 'discrimination has . . . continued to have a great impact on the employment opportunities of black people'. Besides, there was 'no evidence of a decrease in the extent' of such discrimination during the past decade.

Yet the important issue of racism has remained a sensitive and controversial one, and anti-racist education continues to be widely misunderstood. This, it seems to me, is largely because racism tends to be associated with such phenomena as Nazism, the holocaust, apartheid, the Ku-Klux-Klan and virulent feelings of hatred and rejection – all extreme forms of racism. It is therefore important to clarify here the meaning of racism – as well as that of ethnicism.

The early theories of racism do not provide a great deal of help – in particular, Dollard's (1939) frustration–aggression theory or Adorno's (1950) authoritarian personality theory – for they focus on pathological individual personality phenomena. Racism and ethnicism are more complex than this, and are much more to do with everyday social constructions and structural relations – which mutually support each other. Racism is also more complex than the formula 'racism equals prejudice plus power' suggests.

There are several dimensions or levels to racism and ethnicism: the cultural (a shared image, shared assumptions, beliefs, cognitive systems, values and norms); the individual (attitudes, prejudices and stereotypes); the interpersonal (patterns of relations, including discriminatory behaviour); the institutional (patterns of institutional processes and arrangements); and the structural (systemic differentiations, articulations and relations).

The main difference between racism and ethnicism is that in the case of racism the social defining, the attitudes, the interacting, the processes, the structuring are in terms of phenotypical features (real or supposed) or, in general, of features defined as 'racial'; whereas in the case of ethnicism all this is accomplished in the terms of 'ethnic' features – and that means mainly in terms of cultural features (real or supposed and often distorted). Where the parallel between racism and ethnicism breaks down is in the social significance which is inherent in culture, for there is no social significance inherent in phenotypical features as such.

To simplify matters I will focus on racism – though most of what I say can be transposed to ethnicism (which is discussed further in Figueroa, 1991). Racism, then, at the cultural level can be thought of as the operation of a shared racist frame of reference. By this I mean a socially shared set of assumptions, beliefs, values, attitudes and behavioural norms linked implicitly or explicitly to a concept of 'race'. This racist frame of reference can be thought of as a deep structure, an embedded code, a group myth, ideology or world-view, or a shared paradigm, in which the key differentiating factor is phenotypical (real or supposed) or some other (real or supposed) features taken as inherent defining characteristics. This set of assumptions, this shared code animates and constrains perception, interpretation and action, and structures social relations. The basic assumptions, values, conceptual constructs, beliefs, behavioural norms and symbolic system which constitute the racist frame of reference tend to operate at a tacit or taken-for-granted level. (See also Figueroa, 1974 and 1984.)

Racism cannot be adequately understood without the notion of 'race' as a social construction. As an authoritative publication (Hiernaux, 1965) indicated some years ago, 'race' has no scientific or biological validity. 'Race' is first and foremost a category that people use in defining the situation. Built into this everyday category is typically the notion of inherent features linked in some essential or deterministic way to phenotypical (or other) features defined as 'racial'. This social construction is not just the accomplishment of individual actors, but rather of intragroup and intergroup interaction. The racist social construction, where it takes place, is an important part of the mutual defining and differentiating of groups.

This does not mean, however, that 'racial' groups are just categories, just ideological constructions. First of all, as Cooley said, 'if men define social situations as real, they are real in their consequences'. Each actor's, and more importantly each group's, definition of the situation, and each group's racist frame of reference – which shapes that definition – inform social action and thereby social reality. Secondly, sets of people defined 'racially' do have objective reality depending on the relative power of the definers. Concrete social relations and mechanisms of social ascription mean that certain people end up sharing, or being locked into, an unequal situation, or are incorporated into the society in a subordinated location. The members of such a 'racial' group may thus share or come to define themselves as sharing common interests and a common identity. Although 'race' is not a scientifically objective reality, it may be a socially objective reality.

At the individual level racism may manifest itself as attitudes, stereotypes, prejudice or hostility. However, racism often operates without any virulent feelings of hostility, such as may result from individual psychological factors.

At the interpersonal level are racist discrimination and harassment, and more widely any behaviour and interaction, whether with in-group members or out-group members, within the terms of the racist frame of reference. For instance, a racist joke or remark made entirely among in-group members about some 'racially' defined out-group is a form of racist interpersonal relations. It is largely through such in-group relations and discourse that racist definitions of oneself and of others, of the in-group and the out-group, are accomplished and sustained. It is important to remember this in 'all-white' educational settings.

Racism at the institutional level refers to the way the society, or particular institutions within the society, such as the school, work at least *de facto* to disadvantage certain groups or to advantage others by working within the terms of the racist frame of reference, or by simply failing to take account of the relevant specific needs and rights of those defined as belonging to a different 'race'.

Extreme and formal examples of institutional racism would be racist laws, as in South Africa or Nazi Germany. Indeed, some laws in Britain, such as the Nationality Act (1981), come very close to this sort of institutionalised racism because of the patriality principle. Thus many non-white British subjects in Hong Kong have no right of abode in Britain; but, were there a bloodbath in South Africa, many white 'patrial' South Africans, who are not British subjects or members of the Commonwealth, could gain access to Britain.

There are, however, more subtle and unintentional forms of institutional racism which might operate even where there is no overt prejudice or racism. A good example of this might be the use of intelligence tests or of National Curriculum standardised assessment tasks if they are standardised on a white British population, but are then used unthinkingly on black children from very different cultural and linguistic backgrounds. Lynch (1986, p. 160) has pointed out that when it was found that girls scored higher than boys on the original Binet intelligence test, it was amended in 1937 by Terman and Merrill 'to fit in with their assumption that boys and girls had equal intelligence'. Yet this test has not been amended on the assumption that different 'racial' or ethnic groups, or for that matter social classes, have equal intelligence.

Racism at the structural level refers to the way society is articulated by 'race' so that there is differential distribution of resources, rewards, status and power along racist boundaries. This pattern of relations is, as Giddens (1979, p. 69) has pointed out of social structure generally, 'both the medium and the outcome of the practices' that constitute the racist system and, moreover, shapes those practices. Structural racism intersects in complex ways with other structural realities like social class, ethnicity and gender – but cannot be reduced to any of these.

Anti-racism and anti-ethnicism refer then to such things as the promotion of educational equality and quality for ethnic minorities, and the reconstruction of racist and ethnicist beliefs, assumptions, perceptions, patterns of relations and actions of the majority. Before, however, discussing the implications for education of cultural diversity, ethnic inequality, racism and ethnicism, it may be helpful to consider briefly the key concepts and values of education, pluralism and equality.

Education

It is a little too easy to glide over the issues here by asserting that multicultural education is simply 'good education'. Hargreaves (1982) has, for instance, proposed a new curriculum, about half of which would consist of integrated community studies and the expressive arts. The remaining half would consist of 'options', focusing on special interests or talents, and on 'remedial' work for anyone needing it, even the highly gifted. Public examinations at the age of sixteen would be abolished because of their distorting effect. Assessment would be an integral part of teaching and learning. This is very different from the National Curriculum in conceptualisation, content and the place of testing.

Even if, at a sufficiently high level of abstraction, we can agree on what 'good education' means, in practice this must depend on the specifics of the situation, both within the school and in the wider society. Of particular relevance here would be the existence and form of cultural diversity, the specific rights, needs and inequalities of different pupils and groups, and the extent and forms of ethnicism and racism.

Today we hear a lot about education as preparation for adult life and the world of work, almost as though these two are interchangeable. But as important as the world of work is, there is much more to adult life than that. Although the Education Reform Act 1988 (Part I. s. 1) does state that the curriculum should be 'balanced and broadly based' and that it should promote 'the spiritual, moral, cultural, mental and physical development of pupils at the school and [remarkably] of society', and should prepare 'pupils for the opportunities, responsibilities and experiences of adult life' (all of which is open to very wide interpretation), there is a great hiatus between this and the rest of the Act – which specifies the curriculum in subject terms.

Pring (1989, p. 100) is right in pointing out that the National Curriculum does not address the issue of whether the curriculum might be an integration of a subject-based tradition, a vocationally orientated one and one which stresses personally negotiated learning objectives. However, Pring (ibid. pp. 98, 110) too stresses knowledge, cognitive and discursive skills and the corresponding rationalising values.

All of this is important, and yet it is crucial to recognise that the human person is not a thinking machine. The human person is a complex being: situated, but free; a bodily consciousness; a questioning and reflective being; a being with emotions; a being with commitments and values; and above all an inherently social being, inescapably part of a social network, constantly – if tacitly – 'taking account' of others and being 'taken account' of by them.

Education is concerned with the development of this whole person as an individual *and*, inseparably, as an active *social being* in a specific cultural and socio-historical situation. Education is a process facilitating a growth of consciousness, a growth in critical awareness of self and of the other. It is concerned with initiation into value, symbolic, cognitive, communicative, affective, behavioural and social systems, faculties and skills. This includes the values, knowledge, skills, attitudes and behavioural patterns that a person needs to play an active and rewarding part in their society, and to interact constructively with others however different – to contribute to society's well-being and to 'make a living'.

This is the sort of educational ideal we must have in mind when we consider what the educational implications might be of diversity, inequality and racism. But we must also be clear about the values of pluralism and equality.

Pluralism

It is important not only to acknowledge the *existence* of cultural pluralism but to recognise it as being *valuable*. Pluralism as a value means recognising, and indeed being committed to, the right of others – individuals and groups – to be different. If each person claims to be free then each person must accept the right of others to think differently, to act differently, to have different values. It is necessary to seek commonalities and build bridges but also to accept difference as such. Pluralism also implies that difference is positively desirable and interesting.

Cultures can interact, change and adapt without losing their identities. Interaction between different cultures, as between different personalities, is most rewarding where they are all secure in themselves as well as open to others. One can only be open on the basis of what or who one is.

Furthermore, pluralism does not necessarily imply a radical relativism. That would be self-defeating. All cultures are committed to standards of true and false, and of right and wrong – and so to the very concept of truth and rightness. Cultures must be constructively critical of themselves as well as of others.

Of course, cultures can also come into conflict with each other, and misunderstandings and miscommunications may arise. The conflict may be more or less destructive or it may be creative and productive. Difference and complexity do not automatically imply conflict nor problems of cohesion. The cohesion of a dynamic human society is not one of sameness, but one of mutual stimulus, counterpoint and inter-dependence. Frustration, alienation, conflict and a possible threat to cohesion are more likely to arise not just from difference or pluralism, but from injustice, inequality, exploitation, restricted freedom, dis-crimination, inhumanity and the like.

Contrary to the notion that pluralism inherently tends to the break-up of society, it is the orientation towards the pluralism which is impor-tant. A commitment to pluralism means a commitment to procedures in which all interested parties fully participate. This is crucial for social well-being, for justice and equality.

Equality

The valuing of equality also helps to maintain cohesion across differ-ence. Where the principle of equal rights is not accepted, everyone is potentially under threat. Equality is fundamental in any humane soci-ety and it is fundamental in a plural society.

There are, however, several misunderstandings about the notion of equality. It refers neither to sameness nor to the lowest common denominator. Equality means that irrelevant differences and irrelevant similarities should be disregarded, while relevant similarities *and* relevant differences should be given due regard. Equal treatment means eliminating any unfavourable treatment based on being placed in some category, membership of which is not a justifiable ground for differential treatment. But it also means providing equally favourable treatment where membership of some category *is* a justifiable ground for different treatment. In any case the overall thrust is that of maximising positive potentialities and mutual respect. There is no opposition between equality and quality.

Issues for education

I wish now against this background to focus on five main sets of interrelated issues which have implications for multicultural and anti-racist education. These are:

1   Some possible problems of cross-cultural relations, and especially questions of miscommunication which can result in misunderstanding and negative conflicts.
2   Positive potentialities of intercultural relations.
3   Specific rights and needs relating to cultural differences.
4   Existing educational inequalities and needs arising out of these.
5   Racist and ethnicist orientations towards minorities, minority cultures and cultural diversity.

With all these issues a whole school approach is needed: a whole school policy relating to all aspects of the curriculum and school life; an explicit structure for dealing with these issues; a comprehensive programme of action; adequate resources; strategies for implementation; and arrangements for monitoring, evaluating and modifying. Curriculum, pedagogy, books and other teaching materials, the physical environment, assessment and allocation procedures, pastoral and disciplinary arrangements, school–community links, organisation and management, staffing and staff development: all these and more would have to be analysed and modified as necessary.

Cross-cultural miscommunication

Cross-cultural miscommunication can arise between any culturally different groups. Addressing this matter is important even in monocultural schools, since the wider world in which pupils and teachers live is a diverse one. For example, Scollon and Scollon (1983) argue that difference in communicative styles can lead to ethnic stereotyping and to a negative outcome in gatekeeping encounters where one person has institutional authority to make decisions that affect another. This is so where the parties are not aware of the misinterpretation resulting from differences, for instance in the rules of showing deference or of whose turn it is to speak. It is the person who has less power in such relationships, such as the job-seeker, who will suffer.

A rather different example is provided by Kachru's comparison of standard British English and Indian English as spoken in India. Kachru (1987, p. 98) argues that the influence of the grammatical and discourse patterns of Indic languages on Indian English and 'the socio-cultural and intellectual traditions of India' make it difficult for the standard British English speaker really to understand Indian English.

Similarly, differing language structures, discourse patterns and socio-cultural expectations may result in miscommunication between some Caribbean speakers and standard British English speakers. However, one big difference between the situation of South Asians and Caribbean people in Britain is that it is generally known that South Asians have languages of their own. Besides, these languages belong to a long written tradition. English, it may be thought, is just a second language for them; hence special concessions and provisions must be made. But, since it is not realised that standard Caribbean English does not differ greatly in structure from standard British English, and since the nature of Creole, a fully fledged language mainly within an oral tradition, is not understood, people may often think that Caribbean people speak 'bad English' and that that is their only language – so that they must be linguistically and culturally deficient. Edwards (1979) on the contrary has stressed the linguistic abilities of Caribbean people.

It is essential for teachers to be aware of and informed about such matters. As Holmes (1983, p. 112) points out, the ability of pupils to understand teachers' classroom talk is crucial. But this understanding is a function of language and of culture. Are children from minority linguistic or cultural backgrounds at a disadvantage in school because teacher talk and, in general, school discourse are not sufficiently sensitive to their interpretative schemes, to their definitions of the situation, to their frames of reference? The teacher's sensitivity to, and ability to understand, the pupil's interpretative work and what motivates the pupil is vital.

Especially where the school is essentially mono-ethnic, activities such as links, exchanges and inviting ethnic minority visitors into the school would be desirable. But such activities would have to be fully integrated into the school's practices, and each activity would need proper preparation and follow-up.

In any case the mainstream curriculum and the central processes of the school must be looked at carefully to minimise cross-cultural miscommunication, to avoid the transmission of closed attitudes and to promote cross-cultural understanding and skills. A whole school approach is necessary.

Intercultural benefits

There are important positive aspects too of cultural diversity and of cross-cultural contact. These include: an opening up of a human field of great riches and interest, including a great wealth of new or different ideas and ways of doing things; a gaining of perspective on one's own culture and an ability to be constructively critical about one's taken-for-granteds, as well as those of others; a recognising of the role and contribution in the past and at present of ethnic minorities and of their countries of origin to British history, society and economy; and a better understanding of the place of British society alongside others in the world and in history.

Certainly the history of Europe, and of its achievements, has been a history of the contact, interaction and intermingling of different cultures. De Burgh (1953, p. 498) has argued that the 'civilisations of Israel, Greece and Rome are the basis of Europe's world'. Indeed many other cultures, too, including not least Arab cultures, which largely dominated Spain from the eighth to the fifteenth centuries, have contributed to the making of Europe. Rich cultural diversity in Britain and throughout Europe today offers great potentialities for renewal and further development. The question for us is how this diversity can be recognised, valued and used in a non-trivial way to good advantage in the classroom – and especially in the mono-ethnic classroom.

The rights of different cultures

The third set of educational issues are those to do with specific needs and rights of members of different cultures. These relate to such things as: mother tongue and own culture; high-status heritage languages and cultures; systems of naming; religious, moral and ethical requirements, including requirements of diet, dress and behaviour. Development in mother tongue is important to cognitive development, and a positive orientation to one's cultural heritage is important for identity development. There is also the need for a high level of competence in an acceptable educated English; and for awareness of and competence in the dominant culture – but without the pupil's own cultural heritage being undervalued.

It is crucial for teachers to recognise any differences in learning styles and motivators, and to adopt practice accordingly. In general, the teacher needs to find the child's cultural and experiential wavelength. Ausubel (1968) has stated that the 'most important single factor influencing learning is what the learner already knows. Ascertain this and teach him accordingly'. Donaldson (1978) has found that a child will be better able to solve a given problem where the objects and relationships in which it is expressed are familiar, rather than if the problem is presented in an unfamiliar situation.

Inequality

The fourth set of issues are to do with needs which arise, not from cultural differences, but from educational and social inequality. What can be done, directly and indirectly, in the short term and the long term, where ethnic minority children are not receiving the academic, personal and social education, and the market skills which, like other pupils, they need?

There are no simple answers, but policies and structures are needed, as well as mechanisms for analysing and dealing with specific situations. Necessary measures would include such as the following: intensive tutoring and second-chance arrangements involving ethnic minority staff; support for supplementary schools; full involvement of parents; and special mother tongue and English language work, but not to the neglect of other work (see Figueroa 1974, p. 417).

Longer-term measures would need to address a wide range of issues affecting every aspect of the education system. These measures overlap with those needed to address the issues relating to diversity and racism. The constant concern would be to ensure equitable, humane, appropriate, open-minded and high-quality treatment for all.

Anti-racism

The final set of issues, to do with anti-racism and anti-ethnicism, overlap with the others. Racism and ethnicism block cross-cultural communi-

cation and collaboration, and reinforce, generate and constitute inequality. Measures are needed which address all the interrelated and
interacting levels of racism and ethnicism: the cultural, individual,
interpersonal, institutional and structural. At each level it is necessary
on the one hand to challenge and combat racism and ethnicism and,
on the other, to promote a different, positive state of affairs.

Racist and ethnicist frames of reference – among staff and pupils –
need to be brought to awareness, challenged, deconstructed and trans-
formed. Shared values of openness, solidarity, equality and autonomy
need to be promoted. So too does a constructively critical, questioning
and thoughtful approach to self and others, to issues and arrangements. A commitment to justice needs to be fostered at group and individual levels, and both black people and white people need to be
helped so that they can fight injustice effectively.

Stereotypes and narrow attitudes need challenging. Procedures and
arrangements – such as those of assessment, selection and allocation of
pupils, and appointment and promotion of staff – need to be reviewed
and constantly monitored to try and make sure that they are unbiased.
Authority and power within the classroom, the school, the educational
system, and between the school and the community need to be
founded on a fair, democratic and unbiased basis, and to be used in an
equitable and humane manner.

The Education Reform Act 1988

So often people say that education for a multicultural society is important *but* that in view of the massive changes being introduced with the
Education Reform Act, multicultural education (not to mention anti-
racist education) regrettably has to go on to a 'back-burner' and cede to
more urgent priorities. I sympathise, but disagree. Now is the time,
when far-reaching changes are taking shape, to ensure that multicultural and anti-racist education is fully structured in. Besides, the developments towards the greater integration of the nations of Europe offer
opportunities and make action more imperative. Not only has Europe
historically always been multicultural and multilingual, as well as having been the arena of terrible racism, but multiculturalism and anti-
racism throughout post-war Europe have taken on new urgency and
new importance for the viability of a united Europe and the well-being
of all. If we do not act now, if we do not keep the multicultural and anti-
racist work in the forefront, it will probably be marginalised for another

decade or more – with great injustice and inhumanity to many, with great individual and social loss, and with unhappy social consequences for all.

The Education Reform Act, for all its challenge, and despite the rampant individualism, economism and instrumentalism that sometimes seem to inspire it, likewise offers important opportunities. The Act underlines the rights and the role of parents. This provides an opportunity to work for the full involvement – and for the commitment – of all parents and in particular of black parents. Furthermore there is the increased importance of school governors and the need to get all of the community, including the black community, represented.

Additionally there is the centrality of testing and assessment. The Education Reform Act, combining as it does internal and external assessment, offers the promise of fairer assessment. Furthermore the notion of entitlement which has now been established, and the require ment that all pupils should do GCSE English, mathematics and science, should make it more difficult for minority ethnic pupils to be channelled away from academic endeavours – although the announcement by the Secretary of State for Education and Science in January 1991 (Braid, 1991) that all ten subjects of the National Curriculum would not remain compulsory after age fourteen, does weaken the notion of entitlement. The principles of multiculturalism and of equal opportunities have also been accepted. Some of the relevant issues have been included in the 'theme' of citizenship, a multicultural 'dimension' has been identified and a special working party was established by the NCC in 1989.

This, however, does not go far enough. Multicultural and anti-racist issues cannot be adequately dealt with primarily as a dimension, for they involve important bodies of knowledge, as well as skills, attitudes and values, that need exploring and developing. Besides, the Statutory Orders fight shy of multicultural, let alone anti-racist, issues. Furthermore, will provisions such as LMS and 'opting out' tend to exacerbate the disadvantage of those already disadvantaged? (See chapter 12 below.) And will the provisions for temporary exceptions from the National Curriculum allow the scandalous over representation of some groups in 'special' schools and units to continue?

In any case, none of the opportunities which the National Curriculum and European integration offer will be realised without organisation and action. All aspects of educational provision, including the whole area of the curriculum – the content, the materials, the pedagogy – must be addressed. Every subject provides many educationally legitimate and sound opportunities to confront ethnocentrism, ethnicism and racism, and to be positively multiculturalist, equitable and humane. In addition there must be a specialised slot in the timetable, for instance as part of personal and social education or political education, where such issues as cultural diversity, social equity, democracy, racism and ethnicism are the specific focus, and where awareness is raised, the relevant knowledge is provided and the relevant values, attitudes, behavioural patterns and skills are encouraged.

We need to look carefully at every aspect of our system of schooling with the following questions in mind:

1   What tacit, built-in assumptions does it make about who the peoples of Britain (and of Europe) are and about what is normal?
2   Does it – and how could it better – combat injustice, inhumanity, narrowness, ethnocentrism, ethnicism and racism?
3   Does it – and how could it better – promote pluralism, liberty, openness, solidarity, equality and quality for all, bearing in mind especially the minorities in post-war Britain (and more widely post-war Europe), in particular black people and their situation?

In all of this it is crucial to respect the teacher's professional expertise, experience and knowledge. Given the pivotal importance of the teacher, staffing, staff development and teacher education are crucial. Pre-service and in-service courses need to be multicultural and anti-racist, not only in their aims and contents but also in their practice and organisation. They need to help prepare student-teachers and practising teachers for the range of multicultural and anti-racist tasks and challenges. Similarly, multicultural and anti-racist courses are essential for all other personnel in the education system, including school governors and teacher educators.

There are naturally limits to what the school can do. Nevertheless, the years of schooling provide special and substantial opportunities. The educational implications of cultural diversity and all that that entails may seem daunting. These are large and complex issues and tasks, but they are no more daunting than those of education plain and simple – with which they are in fact co-extensive.

References

Adorno, T.W., Frenkel-Brunswik, E., Levinson, D.J. and Sanford, R.N. (1950) *The Authoritarian Personality*. New York: Harper

Ausubel, D.P. (1968) *Educational Psychology: A Cognitive View*. New York: Holt, Reinhart & Winston

Braid, M. (1991) Clarke retreats on national curriculum. The *Independent*, 5 January, p. 1

Brown, C. (1984) *Black and White Britain: The Third PSI Survey*. Heinemann

Brown C. and Gay, P. (1985) *Racial Discrimination: Seventeen Years after the Act*. Policy Studies Institute

De Burgh, W.G. (1953) *The Legacy of the Ancient World*. Penguin

Department of Education and Science. (1985) *Education for All* (Swann Report). HMSO

(1989) National Curriculum History Working Group: *Interim Report*. HMSO

(1990) National Curriculum History Working Group: *History for Ages 5 to 16: Proposals to the Secretary of State for Education and Science*. HMSO

Dollard, J.L., Doob, L.W., Miller, N.E., Nowrci, O.H. and Sears, R.H. (1939) *Frustration and Aggression*, New Haven: Yale University Press

Donaldson, M. (1978) *Children's Minds*. Fontana

Education Reform Act 1988

Edwards, V. (1979) *The West Indian Language Issue in British Schools: Challenges and Responses*. Routledge

Figueroa, P. (1974) 'West Indian school-leavers in London: A sociological study in ten schools in a London borough 1966–1967.' Unpublished Ph.D. thesis, London School of Economics and Political Science, University of London

(1984) Race relations and cultural differences: Some ideas on a racial frame of reference. In G. Verma and C. Bagley (eds.) *Race Relations and Cultural Differences: Educational and Intercultural Perspectives*. Croom Helm

(1991) *Education and the Social Construction of 'Race'*. Routledge

Fryer, P. (1984) *Staying Power: The History of Black People in Britain*. Pluto Press

Giddens, A. (1979) *Central Problems in Social Theory: Action, Structure and Contradiction in Social Analysis*. Macmillan

Greater London Council Ethnic Minorities Unit. (1986) *A History of the Black Presence in London*. GLC

Hargreaves, D.H. (1982) *The Challenge for the Comprehensive School: Culture, Curriculum and Community*. Routledge

Hiernaux, J. (ed.) (1965) Biological aspects of race. *International Social Science Journal*, xvii (i), pp. 71–161

Holmes, J. (1983) The structure of teachers' directives. In C. Richards and R.W. Schmidt (eds.) *Language and Communication*. Longman

Inner London Education Authority Research and Statistics. (1989) *1989 Language Census*, RS 1361/89 (report written by J. Sinnott). ILEA

Kachru, Y. (1987) Cross-cultural texts, discourse strategies and discourse interpretation. In L.E. Smith (ed.) *Discourse across Cultures: Strategies in World Englishes*. Prentice Hall

Lynch, J. (1986) *Multicultural Education*. Routledge

Political and Economic Planning. (1967) *Racial Discrimination*. PEP

Pring, R. (1989) *The New Curriculum*. Cassell

Rodney, W. (1972) *How Europe Underdeveloped Africa*. Bogle-L'Ouverture

Scollon, R. and Scollon, S.B.K. (1983) Face in interethnic communication. In J.C. Richards and R.W. Schmidt (eds.) *Language and Communication*. Longman

Smith, D.J. (1977) *Racial Disadvantage in Britain* (The PEP Report). Penguin

Taylor, M.J. (1981) *Caught Between: A Review of Research into the Education of Pupils of West Indian Origin*. NFER-Nelson

(1987) *Chinese Pupils in Britain: A Review of Research into the Education of Pupils of Chinese Origin*. NFER-Nelson

(1988) *Worlds Apart? – A Review of Research into the Education of Pupils of Cypriot, Italian, Ukrainian and Vietnamese Origin, Liverpool Blacks and Gypsies*. NFER-Nelson

Taylor, M.J. with Hegarty, S. (1985) *The Best of Both Worlds . . .? – A Review of Research into the Education of Pupils of South Asian Origin*. NFER-Nelson

Walvin, J. (1973) *Black and White: The Negro in English Society 1555–1945*. Allen Lane

Williams, E. (1944) *Capitalism and Slavery*, North Carolina Press

Chapter 2

Multicultural or Anti-racist Education: The Irrelevant Debate

Alec Fyfe

A look back at the 1980s

Both education and race relations are highly contested areas. Not surprisingly, then, any attempt to combine them is bound to produce a heated if not an interminable debate. This has been confused and at times bitter and, as we enter a new decade, it seems an appropriate juncture at which to review the field, take stock and chart a possible future course.

The decade was one of controversies. It began with the Rampton Committee, established in 1979, which emerged as the Swann Report six years later. On the heels of the Rampton Report (1981) came the riots in Bristol, Toxteth and Brixton, followed by the Scarman Report (1981). A headteacher in Bradford, Ray Honeyford, was accused of being a racist and eventually took early retirement, while in London another similarly accused head, Maureen McGoldrick, was eventually reinstated. In the middle of the decade the National Association for Multi-Racial Education (NAME) changed to the National Anti-Racist Movement in Education (also known as NAME). It was the era of 'anti-racism' and RAT (Racism Awareness Training), but in a Manchester secondary school, with an anti-racist policy, a Bengali boy was murdered in the playground by a white pupil. In Dewsbury in 1987 some white parents refused to send their children to an 'Asian' school and had their case accepted in the courts. Finally, it was literally a new ERA (Education Reform Act 1988) with a National Curriculum, which started to be implemented in September 1989. Open enrolment and Local Management of Schools have raised fears that ERA may encourage a trend towards ethnically segregated schools and worsen racial inequalities.

The decade was both the best and worst of times, for it was also the period in which multicultural education gained a significant degree of acceptance as part of the mainstream educational debate.

By the end of the decade, 80 LEAs had policy statements on multicultural education: contrast this with only one at the start of the decade (from the Inner London Education Authority in 1977). Curriculum and organisation in a multi-ethnic society became a national in-service priority within Grant Related In-Service Training (1986) and Educational Support Grants (1985). The GCSE guidelines (1985) required syllabus writers to take a pluralist perspective into account, as did the Council for the Accreditation of Teacher Education criteria.

Multicultural and anti-racist education – the need for unity

The current metaphor for Europe is of a 'common home', but the field that would give educational expression to pluralism enters the new decade 'a house divided'. Throughout the past decade there has been a growing division between the liberal notion of 'multicultural education' and the more radical, harder edged, response to racism and inequality – 'anti-racist education'. Conflict between these supposedly polar opposites has perhaps generated more heat than light, and is a luxury we can ill afford as we face the twin challenges of the National Curriculum and European integration. If we are to really recast our education system to meet the realities of pluralism and inequality we shall, as a minimum condition, require a united national movement. For this to happen, the sectarianism and parochialism of the past will have to be transcended to embrace a more internationalist vision of the field and if, pragmatically, labels matter, perhaps a new one that offers a synthesis of past debates will best serve the cause of progress.

How did we get here?

Britain has always been a culturally diverse society, but it was only after 1945, with immigration from the Caribbean and from the Indian sub-continent, that it became visibly ethnically diverse. The 1950s and 1960s have wryly been characterised as the 'Empire Striking Back'! The initial response to this experience was to emphasise assimilation. Here, Britain followed a pattern elsewhere in Europe, North America and Australia. It is debatable whether the governments of the 1960s were crude assimilationists and whether 'immigrant children' were viewed by governments as 'a problem' or 'the problem'. The education system was, perhaps, bound to view large groups of children with little or no English, from very contrasting social economic and cultural backgrounds, as 'problematic'. There was certainly a partial view of integration, in which the onus lay with the 'immigrants' to do the adjusting. The first official pronouncements in this field, *English for Immigrants* (DES, 1963), and *Second Report of the Commonwealth Immigrants Advisory Council* (1964), and Circular 7/65 (DES, 1965), were largely imbued with the liberal notions of integration, a position classically articulated by Roy Jenkins when Home Secretary in May 1966 as:

> Not a flattening process of assimilation but . . . equal opportunity, accompanied by cultural diversity, in an atmosphere of mutual tolerance. (quoted in Banks and Lynch, 1986)

Nevertheless, the field was defined at the time as 'Immigrant Education' and certainly the emphasis upon special language centres, special funding from Section 11 (Local Government Act 1966) and for a short period after Circular 7/65 of 'dispersal', as well as crude culture bound assessment systems, did contribute to a prevailing, and still enduring, perception of the children and the field of multicultural education as to do with 'the problem'.

As we moved into the 1970s a broader notion of integration became formed. The DES, still using the concept, the 'education of immigrants', began to talk of the education service as helping to:

> promote the acceptance of immigrants as equal members of our society . . . [while also] permitting the expression of differences of attitudes, beliefs and cultures, which may eventually enrich the mainstream of our cultural and social tradition.

At the school level it was recognised that:

> the arrival of immigrant pupils . . . has greatly enriched the lives of other children . . . the new musical, dramatic, dance and visual art forms which they have introduced . . . have given fresh colour and vigour to the life and work of many schools.

This shift towards cultural pluralism and the mainstream was further consolidated in the DES Green Paper, *Education in Schools* (1977), which declared:

> Our society is a multicultural, multiracial one, and the curriculum should reflect a sympathetic understanding of the different cultures and views that now make up our society.

Equally, the document went on to say, the curriculum must reflect the fact the Britain was part of an increasingly interdependent world. This was perhaps the watershed for a pluralist conception of education which has been echoed fairly consistently by the DES and HMI to the point where 'multiculturalism' has become the dominant professional stance in the field of 'race' and education. But it has never been an uncontested position.

Anti-racist education

At the very time that the DES was seeing 'immigrant' children as enrichment for all, Bernard Coard was asserting that West Indian children were being 'made subnormal in the British school system' (1971). Some five years later Gus John was to claim that:

> To wish to integrate with that which alienates and destroys you, rendering you less than a person, is madness. (quoted in BCC, 1976)

It was the beginning of the reversal of the notion of 'the problem' which by the end of the decade was to surface as 'anti-racist education'.

Chris Mullard (born in Hampshire) has been called the father of 'anti-racist' education in Britain. In the early 1980s he began to put together a critique of multicultural education which stressed its restrictive focus on culture, rather than racism, and its failure to connect the domains of race, class, gender or region. For Mullard, multicultural education is 'microscopic' and passive while anti-racist education is 'periscopic' and active/oppositional in approach. While multicultural education seeks quantitative change, anti-racist education relates 'race', class and gender inequalities to underlying economic and political structures. Only qualitative change, both in society and within the education system, will suffice to root out racism. Sivanandan (1982) also exposed the limitation of a cultural approach:

> Just to learn about other people's culture is not to learn about the racism of one's own. To learn about the racism of one's own culture . . . is to approach other cultures objectively.

Hatcher (1987) puts it even more bluntly: 'At the core of anti-racist education is learning about the racism of British culture.' For Mullard and others, who follow a broadly neo-Marxist or 'conflict theory' approach, multicultural education is part of an official conspiracy in social control – a way of containing black resistance to racism thereby keeping schools safe. Additionally, Mullard sees in multicultural education's failure to take root in rural areas further evidence of its inability to make the necessary connections with the whole range of inequalities and injustices because it needs the presence of ethnic minority pupils for its rationale.

Multicultural education is also taken to task for its emphasis on individual ignorance and prejudice rather than on underlying structural factors. Here the concept of institutional racism is central to the anti-racist perspective, transcending as it does individual attitudes and actions, to argue that racial (and class and gender) inequalities are built into the fabric of our society and that the education system both reflects and reproduces them via its organisation, content and practices. The struggle against these 'social crimes' (Mullard, 1984) will therefore require a radical transformation of society and in the thinking and actions of white people to accommodate black definitions and demands. Sivanandan (1985) puts it more extremely when he states that white people cannot escape racism: 'because the system is loaded in their favour, all that whites can be, even when they fight racism, is anti racist racists'.

Critiques of anti-racist education

Jeffcoate (1984) in one of the most penetrating critiques of anti-racist education calls this a 'black vanguardist' view of history. He sees weaknesses in both its theory and practice. To begin with, Jeffcoate points to the general tendency of Marxism to defy refutation by, among other things, its capacity to adjust the facts to suit the theory. There is also the tendency to develop partial/restricted definitions of complex reality. In particular there is the facile definition of racism derived from Katz (1978) that it equals prejudice plus power. This has had a wide take-up and could lead to the contention that in Britain only white people can be racists. On the other hand there has been a tendency noted by Jeffcoate and others (Demaine and Kadadwala, 1989) to stretch the definition of institutional racism to breaking point by associating it with a whole spectrum of phenomena from inadvertent ethnocentricism to violent thuggery.

Central to the whole field and debate is the concept of 'race', and yet as Zec (1989) underscores, there is here a very real dilemma and unease. Given that 'race' has no scientific credence, its constant use runs the risk of legitimising its very misapplication by racists – this appears to be a classic bind. 'Black' is yet another concept that is often a hostage to ideological interpretation. The use of it as a blanket designation for all victims of racism again flies in the face of both common sense and self-depiction, for instance, by many within the Asian communities. The field of race and education still lacks both clear and agreed terminology.

There is, of course, Lenin's classic question: 'What is to be done?' But when one examines the implications of the anti-racist analysis for practice there are considerable practical problems with it. The analysis, dealing as it does with the abstractions of 'system', 'structure' and 'forces', does seem to imply a limited and impotent role for both the individual and for education. The language itself is often inaccessible and by creating anxiety about being labelled ('tokenist', 'racist' etc.) is likely to inhibit any change in the professional practice of ordinary teachers. In fact, as both Parekh (1986) and Tomlinson (1990) point out, when one looks at anti-racist curriculum practice it is largely indistinguishable from multicultural education. Both Jeffcoate and Parekh stress the real danger that overarching concerns with radical social change would turn schools into places of indoctrination that would destroy their educational character. As Parekh rightly reminds us, education has its limits: and the roots of racism lie beyond the control of schools. Here there is general agreement. Parekh warns that to ask schools to do more than play their part in legitimate intellectual and moral development 'is perhaps the surest way to ensure that it will not be able to do even that much'. The real question is how to counter racism and what role schools can and should play; here the neo-Marxists seem to be less clear about the practical steps – things are always evolving, or as Mullard puts it:

> the connections of anti-racist education are within an alternative and largely embryonic educational and social order. (Mullard, 1984)

The practice appears equally flawed when it comes to strategic issues in the management of change (or how to win friends and influence people). In this context Hatcher (1987) has recognised that disunity and fragmentation are the movement's contemporary weakness.

A tendency to be exclusive in the search for ideological purity, to stress what one is against, rather than for, is alienating, and from the mid-1980s has been almost fatally divisive. In fact at the end of the decade, as Tomlinson (1990) reminds us, the real debate is surely not between multiculturalists and anti-racists, but between those who support any sort of change in a multicultural direction and those 'educational nationalists', clinging to a mythological view of the past, who successfully marginalise and vilify the whole issue. Clearly in this polarised debate there has been a tendency to create caricatures of each side. The argument is not then with anti-racism *per se* but about the most effective strategy for its pursuit. Perhaps we need reminding that the alternative to incremental change is often no change at all, and this ought to focus the mind wonderfully.

Bridging the gap

There have been moves to reconcile these supposedly polar opposites and in particular there have been attempts at both bridging and denying the gap between multicultural and anti-racist education. Robin Grinter (1985) has argued strongly for the need to bridge the gap, seeing that:

> Multicultural and anti-racist education are essential to each other. They are logically connected and each alone is inadequate. Each is appropriate to different stages and contexts in education and must be part of a combined strategy if either is to have any real effect.

Bridging the gap will not be easy, claims Grinter, because each perspective is derived from different social and political philosophies resulting in the following dichotomies:

> One is seen as liberal/conservative, the other as radical; one is seen as descriptive, the other analytical; one confirms the established structure, the other questions and seeks to change it; one looks for appreciation of other cultures, the other for criticism of one's own; one appeals primarily to emotion, the other to intellect, one emphasises the social and cultural aspects of life, the other economic and political. (ibid.)

In terms of educational practice, similar distinctions apply:

> One is indirect, the other direct; one persuades, the other challenges; one is an extension of existing practice, the other a challenge to it. (ibid.)

Any synthesis has to be both radical and realistic; able to work in the existing school system, operated by teachers (especially in the 'white highlands') who are not converted to the relevance of the issues for them. Perhaps a more inclusive approach to culture is needed to embrace class, gender and 'race' – as argued by Mullard and others. Education for equality is an essential context for an anti-racist multiculturalism, which is part of a wider political education in citizenship for all pupils. It is an argument for a reconstructed and sharpened multiculturalism.

Grinter goes on then (as indeed does Mal Leicester, 1986) to argue that each implies the other and that any dichotomy is a false one. Any serious multiculturalism must deal with racism as part of its curriculum thrust covering values, respect for others, non-ethnocentrism, bias and critical awareness. Of course you can have soft/tokenistic/celebratory multiculturalism of the 'three Ss' variety (Samosas, Saris and Steelbands), but that is bad education when it is superficial and bolt-on. A multicultural approach *is* tokenistic if cultural celebration, rather than being the starting-point, becomes the end-point. Multicultural education, according to Grinter, starts from where people are, 'a tried and tested route to an anti-racist position'. For Grinter, multicultural education and anti-racism can be viewed as a spectrum: 'We therefore need a variety of strategies to use everyone's concepts'.

Leicester reinforces this call for an anti-racist conception of multicultural education: multiculturalism is necessary because anti-racism demands genuine pluralism in the curriculum, but structural discrimination is also critical and therefore the two must come together. It remains for both Grinter and Leicester an essential liberal notion of working slowly from within the system, with a reminder that we are still talking about education and its limitations. In recent years the debate hardly seems to have moved on, only to the extent of some reversing the concept to multicultural, anti-racist education (Demaine and Kadadwala, 1989).

Moving forward

In order to move forward we need to return to Swann as an important landmark in multicultural education. In a key passage the Report (DES, 1985) suggests that the problem facing the education system is not how to educate children of ethnic minorities, but how to educate all children. And though the Swann Report adopted the vacuous title 'Education for All' (used in the 1944 Act and by the United Nations for the International Year of Literacy, 1990), some of its central concerns still provide critical challenges. Rex (1987) outlines its very thoroughgoing agenda:

1   Education should 'help pupils to understand the world in which they live and the interdependence of individuals, groups and nations'.
2   'The richness of cultural variety in Britain should be appreciated and integrated in educational curricula at all levels.'
3   Education is seen as 'having a major role to play in countering the racism which still persists in Britain today'.
4   *Education for All* therefore seeks 'to identify and to remove those practices and procedures which work, directly and intentionally or indirectly and unintentionally, against pupils from any ethnic group'.
5   The 'syllabus recognising the multi-ethnic character of Britain' should 'be used in all schools'.
6   'It is also essential that the education system caters for any specific needs which [ethnic minority] children may experience in order to offer them the equality of opportunity which [has been] relocated.'
7   The concept of education for all raises immediate and obvious issues in the field of language teaching and religious education but there is a need to re-evaluate the curricula on the basis of the following criteria:
  a   the variety of social, cultural and ethnic groups and a perspective of the world should be evident in visuals, stories, conversation and information;
  b   people from social, cultural and ethnic groups should be presented as individuals with every human attribute;
  c   cultures should be sympathetically described in their own terms and not judged against some notion of 'ethnocentric' or 'Eurocentric' culture;
  d   the curriculum should include accurate information on racial and cultural differences and similarities;
  e   all children should be encouraged to see the cultural diversity of our society in a positive light;
  f   the issue of racism at both institutional and individual levels should be considered openly and efforts made to counter it.
8   Political education should be an essential part of the syllabus. It should 'open pupils' minds to a full appreciation of the role which they as adults can and should play in shaping their futures'.

Swann rejected the two extreme positions of assimilation and separatism for pluralism:

> We consider that a multiracial society such as ours would in fact function most effectively and harmoniously on the basis of pluralism. (DES, 1985)

For Swann, a pluralist society is one where diversity is celebrated within a framework of commonly shared values. But, of course, the defining of those commonly shared values is intensely problematic and Swann did not attempt it. This may be a goal all the more elusive in a society where polarisation seems an increasingly prominent feature.

It is the philosophers of education, like John White (1987), who remind us that the formulation of a shared-value framework is not a discrete, final act, but an ongoing, unending collective activity of the society as a whole. The process is interactive; it is about negotiation or, as White terms it, 'the Great Discussion'. And it is in school where this discussion should begin and where pupils should develop the understanding, attitudes and the skills to engage in this collective quest. It is a process of intercultural dialogue and purposeful conflict – an ongoing conversation between cultural groups to forge unity out of diversity. Education for citizenship has therefore an important role to play, particularly in developing the concept of a pluralistic society.

Intercultural education

Perhaps it is the concept of 'interculturalism' which provides a more appropriate context, not simply for a conversation about shared values, but as one possible mechanism to counter the current polarisation in the field of 'race' and education. Intercultural education is the concept more widely used in other European countries and was first significantly taken up in 1981 by the Council of Europe in its project No. 7 concerned with the education of migrant children. The concept was developed to encompass the mainstream at conferences in 1982 and 1984, the latter held at the London Institute of Education, and the Institute now helps co-ordinate the International Association for Intercultural Education which was established at the 1984 conference. The concept seems to have had an even longer history in the USA, surfacing in the early 1940s as a response to the race riots of 1943, particularly in Detroit (Banks, 1989).

There is an urgent need now to move from 'multicultural' as a factual description of all societies, to 'intercultural' as denoting the active process of intergroup relationships and the educational response to this reality. This emphasis upon interculturalism stresses both the dynamic nature of cultures and the problematic nature of their interpenetration. If intercultural education is to provide that necessary common conceptual ground in the field it must be carefully defined to set it within the broader socio-economic and political context of racism and unequal power relationships.

The more dynamic concept of intercultural education (interculturalism as the active response to multiculturalism) will very importantly help encompass the European dimension in education. The European Commission's *Resolution on the European Dimension in Education* (1988) contains within it important intercultural elements: promoting a sense of European identity; of the Community's common principles of democracy, social justice and respect for human rights; of Europe's links with the world. Such a development should not be viewed as a watering down of the commitment to challenging racism and ethnocentrism, but as a more appropriate concept and response to growing cultural diversity in the 1990s. It is a way of internationalising that response in the most immediate context of Europe. By helping to move the emphasis away from an exclusive (and at times obsessive) focus upon the most contested and polarising issue of 'race', in terms of white versus black, it realistically reflects the full spectrum of cultural diversity in our society. It is a new and more inclusive concept and a practical way for LEAs (as has happened in Hampshire since 1990) to integrate a range of otherwise fragmented issues to do with bilingualism, education for all, travellers' education and the European dimension. It is a new concept for a new era.

References

Banks, J. (1989) Education for cultural diversity: Historical and contemporary developments in the United States. Paper prepared for 'Education for Cultural Diversity' conference, University of Southampton, 25–27 September (see also chapter 3)

Banks, J. and Lynch, J. (1986) *Multicultural Education in Western Societies*. Holt

British Council of Churches. (1976) *The New Black Presence in Britain: A Christian Security*. BCC Publications

Coard, B. (1971) *How the West Indian Child is Made Educationally Subnormal in the British School System*. New Beacon Books

Commonwealth Immigrants Advisory Council. (1964) *Second Report of the Commonwealth Immigrants Advisory Council*. HMSO

Demaine, H. and Kadadwala, D. (1989) Multicultural and anti-racist education: The unnecessary divide. *Multicultural Teaching*, Autumn

Department of Education and Science. (1963) *English for Immigrants*. HMSO

  (1965) *The Education of Immigrants* (Circular 7/65). HMSO

  (1977) Green Paper: *Education in Schools* (Williams and Morris). HMSO

  (1981) *West Indian Children in Our Schools* (Rampton Report). HMSO

  (1985) *Education for All* (Swann Report). HMSO

European Commission. (1988) *Resolution on the European Dimension in Education*. EC, May

Grinter, R. (1985) Bridging the gulf: The need for anti-racist multicultural education. *Multicultural Teaching*, 3, 2, Spring

Hatcher, R. (1987) Race and education: Two perspectives for change. In B. Troyna (ed.) *Racial Inequality in Education*. Tavistock

Jeffcoate, R. (1984) Ideologies and multi-cultural education. In M. Craft (ed.) *Education and Cultural Pluralism*. Falmer Press

Katz, J. (1978) *White Awareness: A Handbook for Antiracism Training*. University of Oklahoma Press

Leicester, M. (1986) Multicultural curriculum or anti-racist education: Denying the gulf. *Multicultural Teaching*, 4, 2, Spring

Mullard, C. (1984) *Anti-Racist Education: The Three O's*. National Anti-Racist Movement in Education

Parekh, B. (1986) The concept of multicultural education. In S. Mogdil *et al. Multicultural Education: The Interminable Debate*. Falmer Press

Rex, J. (1987) Multiculturalism, antiracism and equality of opportunity in the Swann report. In T. Chivers (ed.) *Race and Culture in Education*. NFER-Nelson

Scarman, Lord (1981) *Report of an Inquiry into the Brixton Disorders 10–12 April 1981*. HMSO

Sivanandan, A. (1982) *Patterns of Racism*. Institute of Race Relations

  (1985) RAT and the degradation of the black struggle. *Race and Class*, xxvi (4), pp. 1–33

Tomlinson, S. (1990) *Multicultural Education in White Schools*. Batsford

White, J. (1987) The quest for common values. In G.Haydon *et al. Education for a Pluralist Society*, Bedford Way Papers No. 30. Institute of Education, University of London

Zec, P. (1989) Dealing with racial incidents in schools. Paper prepared for 'Education for Cultural Diversity' conference, University of Southampton, 25–27 September (see also chapter 17)

Chapter 3

Education and Cultural Diversity in the United States

James A. Banks

Ethnic and cultural diversity in early America

When the Europeans arrived in the land that eventually became the United States of America in the fifteenth century, it was inhabited by people who were ethnically and culturally very diverse. The Native Americans consisted of several hundred tribes who spoke more than 2,000 languages and whose physical characteristics varied greatly. Some scholars estimate that there were about 100 million Indians living in America at that time (Dobyns, 1976).

The ethnic and cultural diversity in the Americas was considerably enriched when the Spanish, British and French colonies were established in North America. The arrival of Africans beginning in 1619 further diversified the population both biologically and culturally. This process continued as various racial groups produced children, sometimes through marriage.

Early in America's colonial history, the Anglo-Saxon Protestants from England obtained political, economic and social control of the new nation and set as a major goal of educational policy the assimilation of immigrants from diverse cultures and nations into their own, mainstream culture. Thus, early in the history of the United States, Anglo-conformity, which became known as *Americanization*, became the dominant goal of social, economic, political and educational institutions.

The Anglo-conformity goal had different meanings for European immigrants and people of color such as Native Americans and African Americans. The goal for European immigrants became assimilation and inclusion into the dominant economic, political and social structure. However, the goal for people of color became cultural assimilation but structural exclusion. European Americans who were both willing and able to surrender their primordial or first cultures and acquire the values, behaviors and ethos of Anglo-Saxon Protestants were able to experience structural inclusion and full participation in US society. Because of institutionalized racism in the United States, people of color who became culturally assimilated into the mainstream culture were still denied structural inclusion and full participation within US society.

The establishment of ethnic institutions

Because of the barriers that people of color in the United States face today in becoming structurally assimilated, Gordon (1964) describes the United States as consisting of high levels of cultural assimilation but as structurally pluralistic. Many parallel ethnic institutions exist in the United States today, such as African American churches, publications, fraternities and colleges. These institutions help people of color to satisfy important needs that are not met by predominantly White mainstream institutions.

Education for literacy became one of the major goals of African Americans both during and after slavery. Anderson (1988) describes how African Americans risked their lives to learn to read and write during slavery and how they were the major force for creating schools and colleges for Blacks after the Civil War. African Americans were trying to establish educational institutions in the post-Civil War period at a time when they were experiencing one of the most painful and violent chapters in their history. The Northern White Republicans abandoned the newly freed Blacks after the disputed Hayes-Tilden election of 1876. The Ku Klux Klan was organized during this period and played a pivotal role in the re-establishment and growth of White supremacy in the post-Civil War era.

Apartheid was also institutionalized during this period and sanctioned by the US Supreme Court in the *Plessy vs. Ferguson* decision of 1896. The Court established the constitutionality of the 'separate but equal' principle, which was to remain the law of the land until it was overturned in the *Brown vs. Board of Education of Topeka* decision in 1954. It was in this climate of legal, social, political and economic apartheid that people of color in the United States struggled to attain equal educational opportunities. Their educational goals conflicted with and were inconsistent with the goals of the nation-state and the larger society.

Early African American schools and colleges

In the years following the Civil War, African Americans played an important role in the establishment of Black schools and colleges. Many of these institutions are still playing a significant role in educating African Americans today. These include Fisk University, founded in 1865 and chartered in 1867; Morehouse College (from which Martin Luther King, Jr. graduated), founded in 1867; Atlanta University, founded in 1867, and Spelman College, founded in 1881. Atlanta University, Morehouse College and Spelman College became part of the Atlanta University Center in 1929. Later Clark College, the Interdenominational Theological Center, and Morris Brown College, founded in 1885, became part of the Atlanta University Center. Hampton University, from which Booker T. Washington graduated, was founded in 1868.

Research and scholarship on African Americans

White researchers largely ignored Black life, history and culture during the nineteenth and early twentieth centuries. African Americans did not become a serious subject for American mainstream researchers until the sociological research conducted in the 1940s and 1950s at the University of Chicago. Other people of color, such as Mexican Americans, were also largely ignored by White researchers until contemporary times. The earliest important research on ethnic cultures conducted by American scholars were ethnographies conducted by anthropologists such as Alice C. Fletcher (1838–1923) and Franz Boaz (1858–1942) and his colleagues at Columbia University, one of the most eminent of whom was Ruth F. Benedict.

When people of color appeared in the research of mainstream scholars in the late nineteenth and early twentieth centuries, they were usually described in unsympathetic and stereotypic ways and in ways that justified their oppression and structural exclusion from mainstream society. An important example of this kind of research is Ulrich B. Phillips' highly influential book, *American Negro Slavery*, published in 1918. Ulrich, a professor at the University of Michigan when the book was published, was a respected authority on the antebellum South and on slavery. His book, which became an historical classic, is essentially an apology for Southern slaveholders. An important exception to the dominant genre of White scholarship during this period was the highly partisan popular book by Helen Hunt Jackson, *A Century of Dishonor*, published in 1881. In the book, Jackson stridently decried the treatment of the American Indians. It is important to point out, however, that Jackson was a popular writer and not a member of the academic community.

African American and Mexican American scholars, dismayed by what they found about their people in White mainstream scholarship, created scholarship of their own that documented the experiences of their people and depicted them in more accurate and positive ways. George Washington Williams (1849–1891) was the first African American historian in the United States (Franklin, 1985). A colorful and interesting person, Williams had several careers, including a stint as a legislator in the state of Ohio. His important history of African Americans is an essential source of information for other historians researching Black life and culture. It is significant that the story of Williams' life was almost completely lost until it was resurrected by another African American historian, John Hope Franklin (1985). Franklin is one of America's most eminent and respected historians. He passionately reconstructed the details of Williams' life from thin and scattered evidence.

Other African Americans who made significant contributions to the scholarship on African Americans include W.E.B. DuBois, who received his Ph.D. from Harvard in 1895. DuBois' books, such as *The Suppression of the African Slave Trade* (1896) and *Black Reconstruction in America* (1935), set forth new data and interpretations of the experiences of Blacks in the United States. Carter G. Woodson, another Harvard Ph.D. graduate (1912), made seminal contributions to Black history and education. He founded *The Journal of Negro History* in 1916 (which is still published), inaugurated Negro History Week in 1926 (which is now celebrated during the entire month of February) and wrote and published the seminal book, *The Mis-Education of the Negro* (1933). In this book Woodson argues that White institutions were 'mis-educating' Negroes because they were assimilating them into White mainstream culture, alienating them from their first culture and teaching them contempt for it. Educated Negroes were not being encouraged to return to their communities to contribute to their survival, enhancement and empowerment.

The rise and fall of intergroup education

When the United States entered World War II, a large number of African Americans from the South headed for Northern and Western cities to obtain jobs in war-related industries. Many Southern Whites and Mexicans also settled in US cities during this period. Ethnic and racial conflict developed in these cities over competition for housing and jobs. One of the bloodiest series of race riots and conflicts in US history occurred at this time. Thirty-four people were killed in a Detroit riot in 1943. A serious riot occurred in Los Angeles that same year when Anglos and Mexican Americans clashed.

The series of race riots and conflicts stunned American leaders. They resolved that something had to be done to reduce racial tension in society. Educators responded by creating a movement to improve race relations through school, college and university programs that became known as *intergroup* and *intercultural* education. A major goal of intergroup education was to reduce racial and ethnic prejudice and misunderstanding. Activities designed to achieve this goal included the teaching of isolated units on minority groups, organizing assemblies and cultural get-togethers, disseminating information on racial, ethnic and religious backgrounds, and banning books considered stereotypic and demeaning to ethnic groups (Banks, 1988). A major assumption of the intergroup education movement was that knowledge about ethnic groups would help students to develop more positive racial attitudes towards them.

Some interesting projects, activities and research were created at the school and university levels when intergroup education was at its height in the 1940s and 1950s. However, the movement failed to become institutionalized within the mainstream of American education. It remained on the periphery – something that was done as an add-on, a special unit or project, or for special days and occasions. In their research, Taba, Brady and Robinson (1952) found that educators often perceived intergroup education as something designed only for schools with racial problems. On the eve of the civil rights movement of the 1960s and 1970s, there were few vital signs of the intergroup education movement. It had quietly died; little attention was paid to its demise.

The rise of the multicultural education movement

The current multicultural movement in the United States is a direct product of the civil rights movement of the 1960s and 1970s. However, much of the research, insights and approaches that are incorporated into multicultural education emanated from the historical and sociological research conducted by early African American scholars such as Williams, DuBois, and Woodson, and Mexican American scholars such as George I. Sanchez (1940). Many of the approaches and techniques used in prejudice reduction activities today are closely linked to experiences that were an integral part of intergroup education. The problems of implementing multicultural education today are similar to those that were experienced when intergroup education was implemented in the 1940s and 1950s.

The first educational programs that tackled cultural diversity were outcomes of the civil rights movement of the 1960s and 1970s. The programs related to African Americans because they were the leaders of the protest movements during those decades. They demanded that schools hire more Black teachers and administrators, that they be given more control of schools in their communities, and that the school and university curricula incorporate the experiences of Blacks in the making of world and US history.

Schools, universities and textbooks' publishers implemented a number of reforms in response to demands made by the African American community. Black studies courses became electives in many high schools, a number of universities established courses and programs in Black studies, more Black teachers and university faculty were hired, and publishers put more Black and Brown people in textbooks. However, most of these changes were made primarily to silence ethnic protest rather than to genuinely change institutions so that they would incorporate diverse ethnic and cultural perspectives. Many school and university ethnic studies programs were established without careful planning and implementation. Some critics argued that they were designed to fail. Universities often hired minority faculty to teach ethnic studies courses who had little chance of becoming tenured. Textbooks' publishers usually integrated textbooks by coloring White people brown.

Because of the hurried and superficial ways in which many of the reforms were implemented during the 1960s and 1970s, they often failed to become institutionalized within schools, colleges, and in the textbook industry. Consequently, many of them were easily eradicated when schools and universities faced tight budgets and a conservative political atmosphere during the 1980s. With the waning of ethnic pressure on them, textbook publishers are publishing textbook series that are dominated by mainstream perspectives and with textbook writing teams that have no or few writers of color.

Despite these setbacks, some of the reforms of the sixties and seventies related to cultural diversity are becoming institutionalized in US schools, colleges and universities. A number of leading universities, including Stanford, the University of Minnesota and the University of California at Berkeley, have recently established an ethnic studies course requirement for all of their undergraduate students. Universities such as the University of California at Berkeley, Stanford, Harvard, the University of Massachusetts and the University of Washington at Seattle have well-regarded courses and programs in ethnic studies. Berkeley offers a Ph.D. degree in ethnic studies. Women studies courses and departments have also been established at a number of leading American colleges and universities.

The main accreditation agency for teacher education in the United States is the National Council for Accreditation of Teacher Education (NCATE). It requires its member institutions, which include about eighty per cent of the teacher education institutions in the United States, to have a multicultural component in their teacher education programs. The implementation of this requirement varies tremendously within schools and colleges of education.

The scope of the civil rights movement expands

Viewing what they perceived as the successes of the Black civil rights movement, other ethnic groups, such as Mexican Americans, American Indians and Asian Americans, made similar demands on the educational establishment that had been made by Blacks. Later, White ethnic groups, primarily those of Southern, Central and Eastern European origin, also demanded that ethnic studies courses and programs that reflected their experiences be established. During the 1970s, as the women rights movement gained momentum, feminists also demanded more rights for women and women studies courses and programs.

As a result of the expanding quest for rights in the United States and the increasing recognition that victimized and marginalized groups share many concerns and goals, multicultural education is increasingly becoming education that focuses on the concerns of a range of victimized groups and the interrelationship of variables related to these groups (Banks and Banks, 1989). However, a number of theorists, such as Banks (1988) and Gay (1983), believe that while it is necessary to focus on a range of groups in multicultural education, it is also important to keep a strong focus on the unique needs of specific groups, and especially on issues related to institutionalized racism and discrimination.

Multicultural education in the United States – a typology of approaches

Multicultural education in the United States consists of a wide variety of approaches, paradigms (Banks, 1986, 1988), concepts and strategies (Banks, 1991a) that differ in some substantial ways. Sleeter and Grant (1987) concluded that the only common meaning of multicultural education is that it refers to changes in education that are supposed to benefit people of color.

I will describe three major approaches to multicultural education as well as some of the important differences that exist within each approach. The three major approaches – *Curriculum Content*, *Achievement* and *Intergroup Education*, are described in Table 1. As with any typology, the three approaches to multicultural education are not mutually exclusive. For example, some of the content changes (Curriculum Content Approaches) might help students of color, women, and students who are handicapped, to increase their academic achievement (Achievement Approaches). The typology focuses on the primary aims of the approaches rather than on their ancillary outcomes and effects.

Curriculum Content Approaches. These approaches conceptualize multicultural education as an educational process that involves some kind of additions or changes in the content of the school curriculum. The goal of this approach is to incorporate content about cultural and gender groups into the curriculum.

Achievement Approaches. These approaches conceptualize multicultural education as a set of goals, theories and strategies designed to increase the academic achievement of lower-class students, students of color, women, and students who are handicapped.

Intergroup Education Approaches. The primary goal of these approaches is to help all students to develop more positive attitudes towards people from various racial, gender and cultural groups. Another goal is to help members of victimized groups to develop more positive self-concepts and attitudes toward their own groups. Several of the approaches

Approach	Description	Major goals	Examples of pratices
Curriculum Content	A process that involves additions to or changes in the content of the curriculum.	To incorporate content about cultural groups into the curriculum. To enable students to look at curriculum content from new and different perspectives. To transform the canon and paradigms on which the curriculum is based.	Celebration of cultural heroes and holidays. Multicultural curriculum guides. Multicultural content workshops for teachers and administrators. Textbooks that incorporate multicultural content.
Achievement	A set of theories, practices, and strategies designed to increase the academic achievement of lower-class students, students of color, women, or students who are handicapped.	To increase the academic achievement of students from different ethnic, cultural and gender groups.	Programs that match teaching styles with the learning styles of students. Bilingual-bicultural education programs. Language programs that incorporate the language and culture of African American students. Special math and science programs for female students.
Intergroup Education	Knowledge, content, and processes designed to help students to develop democratic intergroup attitudes and values.	To help all students to develop positive attitudes toward diverse racial, ethnic and cultural groups. To help members of victimized and marginalized groups to develop more positive attitudes towards their own cultural group.	Prejudice reduction projects, such as the World of Difference Project, sponsored by the Anti-Defamation League of B'nai B'rith. Desegregated schools, classrooms, and programs. Cooperative learning strategies and techniques.

Table 1   Approaches to multicultural education. (Copyright © 1990 by James A. Banks. All rights reserved.)

within the intergroup education paradigm also have as an important but secondary goal increasing the academic achievement of students of victimized groups. Interventions such as school desegregation and co-operative learning are designed to help students to develop more positive intergroup attitudes as well as to increase academic achievement.

Curriculum content approaches

CONTRIBUTIONS APPROACH

Several identifiable approaches to the integration of multicultural content into the curriculum have evolved in the United States since the 1960s. The contributions approach to integration is one of the most frequently used. It is characterized by the addition of cultural heroes to the curriculum, selected using criteria similar to those used to select mainstream male heroes. The mainstream curriculum remains basically unchanged.

The heroes and holidays approach is a variant of the contributions approach. Ethnic content or content about women is limited primarily to special days, weeks and months. Martin Luther King's Birthday, Black History Month and Women's History Week are examples. During these celebrations, teachers involve students in lessons, experiences and pageants related to the cultural groups being commemorated. When this approach is used, the class studies little or nothing about the group before or after the special event or occasion.

The contributions approach is easy to use but has several serious limitations. Students see ethnic and women issues and events primarily as an addition to the curriculum, and consequently as an appendage to it. This approach also tends to gloss over important concepts and issues related to the victimization and oppression of ethnic groups and women and their struggles against racism and sexism and for power. Issues such as racism, sexism, poverty and oppression tend to be evaded. The focus, rather, tends to be on success and the validation of the myth that every American who is willing to work hard can go from rags to riches and pull himself or herself up by the bootstrap.

The contributions approach often results in the trivialization of ethnic cultures and the reinforcement of stereotypes and misconceptions. When the focus is on the contributions and unique aspects of cultures, students are not helped to understand them as complete and dynamic wholes.

When teachers use the contributions approach to integrate cultural content, students view the experiences of cultural groups within the context of mainstream paradigms and the mainstream canon. This canon, rarely explicitly defined or discussed, is European-centric and male-dominated. It often marginalizes the experiences of people of color, Third World nations and cultures, and the perspectives and histories of women.

THE CULTURAL ADDITIVE APPROACH

Another important approach to the integration of multicultural content to the curriculum is the addition of content, concepts, themes and perspectives to the curriculum without changing its basic structure, purposes and characteristics. The additive approach is often accomplished by the addition of a book, a unit, or a course to the curriculum within the existing framework. This approach, unlike the contributions approach, involves the addition of curriculum elements other than contributions and heroes. It might involve the addition of concepts, problems, issues and other aspects of the experiences of ethnic, cultural and gender groups.

This approach can be the first phase in an effort designed to transform the curriculum and to restructure it with multicultural content, perspectives and paradigms. However, this approach shares several disadvantages with the contributions approach. It usually results in the viewing of multicultural content from the perspectives of mainstream male historians, writers, artists and scientists. The events, concepts, issues and problems selected for study are selected using the mainstream-centric and Eurocentric canon. This canon results in the Americas being called the 'New World', in the notion that Columbus 'discovered' America, and in the description of the Anglo immigrants' rush to the West as the 'Westward Movement'. Calling the Americas 'The New World' subtly denies the nearly 45,000 years that Native Americans have lived in the Americas.

THE TRANSFORMATION APPROACH

The transformation approach differs fundamentally from the contributions and additive approaches. It changes the canon, paradigms and basic assumptions of the curriculum and enables students to view concepts, issues, themes and problems from different perspectives and points of view. The goals of this approach are to extend students' understanding of the nature, development and complexity of US society and to enable them to participate in the formulation of new canons and paradigms, from which they will view concepts, issues and events.

An example of curriculum transformation is the reconceptualization of traditional chapters in a United States history textbook for junior high school students (Banks with Sebesta, 1982). Instead of calling Chapter 4 'Columbus Discovers America', I conceptualized it as 'Christopher Columbus and the Arawak Indians'. This involved more than a change in title, which was important in itself. The students were able to view this important cultural contact from the perspectives of both Columbus and the Arawaks, the native people of the Caribbean. Finally, they were asked to formulate their own views and perspectives on the meeting of Columbus and the Arawak Indians. In the transformation approach, the students hear and listen to multiple voices, including the voices of the victims and the vanquished, those of the teacher and other students, as well as their own.

THE DECISION-MAKING AND SOCIAL ACTION APPROACH

This approach includes all the elements of the transformation approach but adds components that require and help students to make reflective decisions and to take actions related to the concept, issue or problem they have studied in the unit. An important goal of this approach is to help students to make reflective moral commitments and to take personal, social and civic action that will help to create a more just society. For example, the students might raise this question: 'What actions should we take to reduce prejudice and discrimination in our personal life, our school and our community?' They gather pertinent data, analyze their values and beliefs, identify alternative courses of action and finally decide what, if any, actions they will take. Major goals of the decision-making and social action approach are to teach students thinking and decision-making skills, to empower them for action, and to help them acquire a sense of personal, social and political efficacy (Banks with Clegg, 1990).

MIXING AND BLENDING THE APPROACHES

The four approaches that I have described are often mixed and blended in actual teaching situations. One approach, such as the contributions approach, can also be used as a vehicle to move to other and more intellectually challenging approaches, such as the transformation and the decision-making and social action approaches. It is not realistic to expect a teacher to move directly from a highly mainstream-centric curriculum to one that focuses on decision-making and social action.

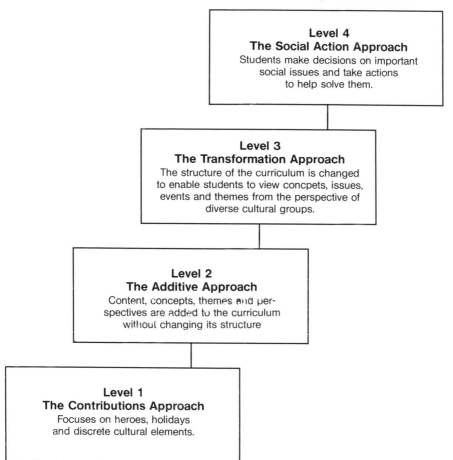

Fig.1   Levels of integration of multicultural content. (Copyright © 1989 by James A. Banks. All rights reserved.)

Rather, the move from the first to the higher levels of multicultural content integration is likely to be gradual and cumulative (see Fig. 1).

Achievement approaches

A variety of educational approaches are designed to help lower-class students and students of color to increase their academic achievement. These approaches include early childhood intervention programs, interventions that focus on the learning styles of minority group children, bilingual-bicultural education programs, effective schools interventions (Edmonds, 1986) and school-based family involvement programs (Comer, 1988). These diverse approaches are undergirded by two major paradigms and philosophical positions: the *cultural deprivation* paradigm and the *cultural difference* paradigm. I will discuss the assumptions and goals that underlie each of these paradigms.

THE CULTURAL DEPRIVATION PARADIGM

Cultural deprivation was one of the first theories that emerged in the 1960s concerned with the education of lower-class students (Reissman, 1962). Cultural deprivation theorists believe that characteristics such as poverty, disorganized families and fatherless homes cause students from poor families to experience 'cultural deprivation' and 'irreversible cognitive deficits'.

They believe that lower-class students will achieve academically if the school is able to compensate for their deprived cultural environment and alienate them from it. They see the major problem as the culture of the students rather than the culture of the school. Many early childhood intervention programs, such as Head Start and Follow-Through, are based on the cultural deprivation paradigm. This paradigm has attained renewed popularity in the 1980s. Lower-class students and students of color are now referred to as 'students at risk'. By trying to alienate poor students from their cultures, blaming their cultures for their academic failures rather than the school and by evaluating their cultures negatively, cultural deprivation theorists violate what Ramirez and Castaneda (1974) call 'cultural democracy'.

THE CULTURAL DIFFERENCE PARADIGM

Cultural difference theorists reject the idea that lower-class students and students of color have cultural deficits. They believe that ethnic groups such as African Americans, Mexican Americans and Native Americans have strong, rich and diverse cultures (Shade, 1982; Hale-Benson, 1986). These cultures, argue the cultural difference theorists, consist of languages, values, behavioral styles and perspectives that can enrich the lives of other Americans. They contend that many students of color fail to achieve in school not because they have deprived cultures but because their cultures are different from the school's. The school fails to help students of color achieve because they ignore or try to alienate them from their cultures. The school must change in ways that will allow it to respect and reflect the cultures of its students and at the same time use teaching strategies that are consistent with their cultural characteristics and that will draw upon their cultural strengths and life-styles.

Cultural difference theorists frequently cite research that shows how the cultures of the school and of students of color differ in values, norms and behaviors (Shade, 1982; Hale-Benson, 1986). However, few studies have been done to determine the extent to which teachers can successfully adapt their teaching in ways that will make it more consistent with the cultural and learning styles of students of color. This gap in theory and practice has caused some researchers to question the attention being focused on cultural differences, particularly learning and cognitive style differences (Kleinfeld and Nelson, 1988).

Intergroup education approaches

Intergroup education approaches have as one of their major goals helping students to develop more positive intergroup attitudes and helping students from various cultural and gender groups to develop more positive attitudes toward themselves and their cultures.

The *Brown vs. Board of Education of Topeka* decision of 1954 had as one of its major goals preventing Black students from developing a sense of racial inferiority. The Supreme Court ruled that school segregation was 'inherently unequal'. Chief Justice Warren, writing the majority opinion, stated:

> To separate them from others of similar age and qualifications solely because of their race generates a feeling of inferiority as to their status in the community that may affect their hearts and minds in a way unlikely ever to be undone.

The plaintiffs who brought the cases that collectively became known as *Brown* in the Supreme Court were concerned primarily about equity and equal educational opportunity for African American students. However, perhaps in part because of the way in which the Supreme Court ruled on the *Brown* case, helping students to develop positive racial attitudes became one of the primary justifications for school desegregation. Another important justification that developed in time was the achievement argument. Advocates of desegregation argued that it not only helped students to develop more positive racial attitudes but that it increased equity for Black students because they attained higher levels of academic achievement in desegregated than in segregated schools (US Commission on Civil Rights, 1967). School desegregation remains highly controversial in the United States and increasingly impractical in the nation's largest cities where there are few Whites left in the school districts to desegregate with African Americans and other students of color.

Prejudice reduction techniques have as their major goal helping students to develop more positive racial attitudes. Banks (1991b) has conducted a comprehensive review of curriculum intervention research designed to reduce racial and gender prejudice. Several major types of racial attitude modification studies exist: (a) studies that examine the effects of courses, curriculum content and units (e.g. Litcher and Johnson, 1969), (b) studies that examine reinforcement techniques (e.g. Parish, Shirazi and Lambert, 1976), (c) perceptual differentiation studies (e.g. Katz and Zalk, 1978) and (d) studies that examine the effects of co-operative classroom and school environments (e.g. Slavin, 1985).

The richest and most productive work has been done on reinforcement techniques, perceptual approaches, and the effects of co-operative learning environments. This research has also resulted in rather consistent positive findings. The least work and the most inconsistent findings have resulted from curriculum and course intervention studies.

Research using reinforcement, perceptual approaches and co-operative learning techniques are encouraging to educators because these techniques have resulted in positive attitude changes in a number of studies. In one such study, Katz and Zalk (1978) compared the effects of four short-term intervention techniques on the racial attitudes of high-prejudice White students in the second and fifth grades. They assessed attitudes after two weeks and again four to six months later. The four techniques were: (a) increased positive racial contact, (b) vicarious interracial contact, (c) reinforcement of the color black and (d) perceptual differentiation of minority group faces. All of the experimental groups experienced a short-term reduction in mean prejudice scores on combined measures. However, the reductions were greater for the vicarious contact and perceptual groups than for the racial contact and reinforcement groups. The effects were less pronounced in the long-term assessment. However, some experimental gains were maintained by the vicarious contact and perceptual differentiation groups. This study is encouraging because each treatment lasted only fifteen minutes.

Cooperative learning is now a popular teaching strategy in American education at all levels. Studies have rather consistently indicated that students from different ethnic groups develop more positive racial attitudes when they participate in cooperative learning activities (Slavin, 1985; Aronson and Gonzalez, 1988). Students of color also tend to experience academic achievement gains. The achievement of White students tends to be about the same in both cooperative and competitive learning environments.

The future of multicultural education in the United States

Multicultural education faces a rough road ahead in the 1990s because of the huge budget cuts in social programs and the gigantic deficit inherited from the Reagan administration. The acute individualism that is pervasive among the 'haves' in the United States will also make it difficult to gain public support for social and educational programs. During the Reagan years the gap between the rich and poor widened in the United States, many social and educational programs were severely cut or eliminated, and the nation's commitment to improve the status of its poor and unfortunate citizens, strong during the Johnson years, plummeted during the Reagan era.

Recent economic and political developments give us little reason to be hopeful about the future of multicultural education in the United States. The Bush administration is not departing substantially from the Reagan education and social policies. However, emerging demographic trends indicate that the United States must act quickly to educate its underclass, a disproportionate share of whom are students of color, or face the future as a second-rate and declining nation. This is because the White population is ageing and declining as a percentage of the population, while the population of people of color, especially Hispanics, is growing by leaps and bounds. In the future, people of color will make up a disproportionate share of US workers. Whites will make up a disproportionate share of the retirees, who will be heavily dependent on workers of color to support them through the social security benefit system. During the 1950s, seventeen US workers supported every retiree. By 1992 the number will be down to three, one of whom will be a person of color. By 2030 the ratio will have narrowed to 2.2 workers to one retiree (*Education Week*, 1986).

The White proportion of the population is declining because of its comparatively low birthrate, the small percentage of immigrants entering the United States from Europe, and the rush of immigrants from Latin America and Asia. Between 1971 and 1980, about 82 per cent of the legal immigrants to the United States came from Latin America and Asia; 18 per cent came from Europe and other nations. A large but unknown number of illegal or undocumented immigrants also enter the United States each year. By the turn of the century one of every three Americans will be a person of color (The Commission, 1988). The magazine, *American Demographics*, predicts that African American, Hispanic and Asian youth under eighteen will make up 31 per cent of the total US youth population in 1990 and 38 per cent by 2000 (*Business Week*, 1989).

The tremendous increase in the population of people of color in the United States is having and will continue to have a major influence on the nation's workforce. Eighty per cent of the new entrants to the labor force between now and 2000 will be women, immigrants, or people of color. One-third of these new entrants will be people of color. By the year 2000, 21.8 million of the 140.5 million people in the US labor force will be people of color (Johnston and Packer, 1987).

America's poor children and children of color are its future. America's ultimate test as a nation will be not how it treats its citizens who are successful but how it responds to the desperate plight of its citizens who are poor and undereducated. These citizens have the potential to help it enter the twenty-first century with strength and compassion. There are some hopeful signs that an increasing number of Americans are beginning to realize that bold steps must be taken to educate its citizens of color and to educate all of its citizens to live in a multicultural society, not out of kindness for the downtrodden, but for national survival.

References

Anderson, J.D. (1988) *The Education of Blacks in the South 1860–1935*. Chapel Hill: The University of North Carolina Press

Aronson, E. and Gonzalez, A. (1988) Desegregation, jigsaw, and the Mexican-American experience. In P.A. Katz and D.A. Taylor (eds.) *Eliminating Racism: Profiles in Controversy*. NY: Plenum Press

Banks, J.A. (1986) Multicultural education: Development, paradigms, and goals. In J.A. Banks and J. Lynch (eds.) *Multicultural Education in Western Societies*. Holt

(1988) *Multiethnic Education: Theory and Practice*, 2nd edn. Boston: Allyn & Bacon

(1991a) *Teaching Strategies for Ethnic Studies*, 5th edn. Boston: Allyn & Bacon

(1991b) Multicultural education: Its effects on students' racial and gender role attitudes. In J.P. Shaver (ed.) *Handbook of Research on Social Studies Teaching and Learning*. NY: Macmillan

Banks, J.A. with Sebesta, S.L. (1982) *We Americans: Our History and People*. Boston: Allyn & Bacon

Banks, J.A. and Banks, C.A.M. (eds.) (1989) *Multicultural Education: Issues and Perspectives*. Boston: Allyn & Bacon

Banks, J.A. with Clegg, A.A. Jr. (1990) *Teaching Strategies for the Social Studies: Inquiry, Valuing and Decision-Making*, 4th edn. White Plains, NY: Longman, Inc.

Benedict, R. (1934) *Patterns of Culture*. Boston: Houghton Mifflin

Boaz, F. (1948) *Race, Language and Culture*. NY: Macmillan

Business Week. (1989) US population may swell most at the bottom rungs. July 10

Comer, J.P. (1988) Educating poor minority children. *Scientific American*. 259, November, pp.42–8

The Commission of Minority Participation in Education and American Life. (1988) *One-Third of a Nation*. Washington, DC: The American Council on Education, May

Dobyns, H.F. (1976) *Native American Demography: A Critical Bibliography*. Bloomington, Ind: Indiana University Press

DuBois, W.E.B. (1896; 1965 reprint edn) *The Suppression of the African Slave Trade to the United States (1638–1870)*. Baton Rouge: Louisiana State University Press

  (1935; 1953 reprint edn) *Black Reconstruction in America*. NY: Russell & Russell

Edmonds, R. (1986) Characteristics of effective schools. In U. Neisser (ed.) *The School Achievement of Minority Children: New Perspectives*. Hillside, NJ: Lawrence Erlbaum Associates Publishers

Education Week (1986) Here they come ready or not (Special Report), May 14

Fletcher, A.C. (1910) War and discipline. In F.W. Hodge (ed.) *Handbook of American Indians North of Mexico*, vol. 2. *Bureau of American Ethnology Bulletin*, 30. Washington, DC

Franklin, J.H. (1985) *George Washington Williams: A Biography*. Chicago: The University of Chicago Press

Gay, G. (1983) Multiethnic education: Historical developments and future prospects. *Phi Delta Kappan*, 64, pp. 560–3

Gordon, M.M. (1964) *Assimilation in American Life*. NY: Oxford University Press

Hale-Benson, J. (1986) *Black Children: Their Roots, Culture, and Learning Styles*, rev. edn Baltimore: The Johns Hopkins University Press

Jackson, H. Hunt (1881) *A Century of Dishonor: A Sketch of the United States Government's Dealings with Some of the Indian Tribes*. NY: Harper &

Brothers

Johnston, W.E. and Packer, A.E. (1987) *Workforce 2000: Work and Workers for the 21st Century*. Indianapolis: Hudson Institute

Katz, P.A. and Zalk, S.R. (1978) Modification of children's racial attitudes. *Developmental Psychology*, 14, pp. 447–61

Kleinfeld, J.S. and Nelson, P. (1988) Adapting instruction to Native Americans learning style: An iconoclastic view. In W.J. Lonner and V.O. Taylor Jr. (eds.) *Cultural and Ethnic Factors in Learning and Motivation: Implications for Education*. Bellingham: Western Washington University

Litcher, J.H. and Johnson, D.W. (1969) Changes in attitudes toward Negroes of White elementary school students after use of multiethnic readers. *Journal of Educational Psychology*, 60, pp. 148–52

National Council for the Accreditation of Teacher Education. (1977) *Standards for the Accreditation of Teacher Education*. Washington, DC: NCATE

Parish, T.S., Shirazi, A. and Lambert, F. (1976) Conditioning away prejudicial attitudes in children. *Perceptual and Motor Skills*, 43, pp. 907–12

Phillips, U.B. (1918) *American Negro Slavery*. NY: D. Appleton & Company

Ramirez, M. and Castaneda, A. (1974) *Cultural Democracy, Bicognitive Development and Education*. NY: Academic Press

Reissman, F. (1962) *The Culturally Deprived Child*. NY: Harper

Sanchez, G.I. (1940) *Forgotten People*. Albuquerque: The University of New Mexico Press

Shade, B.J. (1982) Afro-American cognitive style: A variable in school success? *Review of Educational Research*, 52, pp. 219–44

Slavin, R.E. (1985) Cooperative learning: Applying contact theory in desegregated schools. *Journal of Social Issues*, 41, pp. 45–62

Sleeter, C.E. and Grant, C.A. (1987) An analysis of multicultural education in the United States. *Harvard Educational Review*, 57, pp. 421–44

Taba, H., Brady, E.H. and Robinson, J.T. (1952) *Intergroup Education in Public Schools*. Washington, DC: American Council on Education

US Commission on Civil Rights. (1967) *Racial Isolation in the Public Schools*. Washington, DC: US Government Printing Office

Woodson, C.G. (1933) *The Mis-Education of the Negro*. Washington, DC: Associated Publishers

PART 2: The Whole Curriculum

Introduction

Alec Fyfe

It was only in October 1989, with the issuing of Circular No. 6 (on curriculum guidance) by the National Curriculum Council, that there appeared any systematic treatment, post-Education Reform Act, of the whole curriculum. Curriculum Guidance No. 3 (CG3) on the whole curriculum followed in March 1990. Given the history of the National Curriculum, which was conceived in subject terms (indeed in hierarchical terms with core and foundation subjects, plus religious education), there was, and is, an inevitable sense of a breathless catching up and resultant shallow conceptual thinking.

Education for a multicultural society features in NCC documents as a cross-curricular dimension along with personal and social education (PSE) and equal opportunities. In addition, the five identified cross-curricular themes also help to promote multicultural concerns. Given the notion of entitlement established by Section 1 of ERA, there is throughout CG3 a strong commitment to equal opportunities.

Institutions have not traditionally thought and acted on a whole curriculum basis and therefore have viewed concerns like multicultural education as additional elements that had to be fitted into an already overloaded timetable. CG3 is helpful in providing a sensible framework within which the cross-curricular elements can be viewed as integral, integrative and enriching – literally part of the tapestry of the whole curriculum. Multicultural education enriches subject areas and provides a context for developing knowledge, attitudes and skills.

That having been said, there are problems with the NCC framework. Dimensions and themes overlap and in practice are difficult to distinguish, as all seem to have across-the-curriculum implications; while multicultural education has important content elements which make it theme-like. The European dimension remains problematic with initial attempts to make it part of 'citizenship'. But the greatest flaw is in ERA itself. If we had wanted to get to the notion of the whole curriculum we should hardly have started down a linear and hierarchical subject road. Here the Irish and the Scots have been more enlightened. The reforms in Northern Ireland are particularly instructive, for they have started with overarching themes such as 'education for mutual understanding' and looked to subjects to service them, not the other way round.

In this section of the book we have deliberately started at the other end and have taken a whole curriculum view before moving on to the National Curriculum subjects.

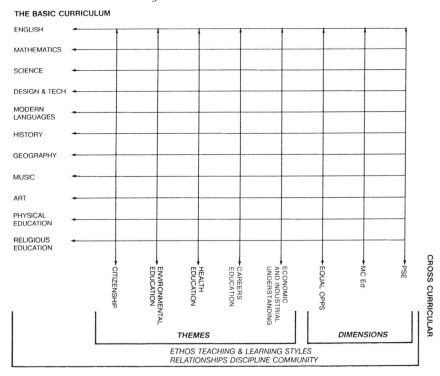

Fig.1   The whole curriculum

References

National Curriculum Council. (1989) Circular No. 6: *Curriculum Guidance*. NCC, October
    (1990) Curriculum Guidance No. 3: *The Whole Curriculum*. NCC, March

Chapter 4

Personal and Social Education: Cultural Diversity Considered

Carlton Duncan

The role of PSE

I have some difficulty in attempting to distinguish between personal and social education (PSE) and what is termed 'the pastoral curriculum'. It may well be that I have been wasting time in the pursuit of a non-existent distinction. But if PSE and 'the pastoral curriculum' are the same thing, further difficulties with what lies behind the terms are presented.

The term 'pastoral curriculum' implies a division between the pastoral work and the curriculum efforts of a school. In my view there can be no such sensible division, as I have argued elsewhere (Duncan, 1988). Even if this unwholesome division is not contemplated, it is unwise to leave open an opportunity for this division to be pondered at all.

Further, the delivery arrangements for PSE, or the pastoral curriculum, in many schools tend to suggest that it is separate from the rest of the curriculum. But this idea is really quite astonishing. The practice of separateness for PSE creates a difficulty which bedevilled the old-style general studies diet which was largely used as a filler for sixth-form students' timetables. PSE is generally viewed as being non-academic and without examination orientation. Problems of credibility, currency, motivation and commitment are thus introduced, particularly on the parts of pupils and teachers. These last two problems might diminish in importance as a result of constraints placed upon curriculum time by the National Curriculum and the particular emphasis which it places on certain subject areas.

It may be that schools will find it impossible to treat PSE as a separate curriculum entity deserving of its own timetable sector, given that the National Curriculum Council Circular No. 6 and Curriculum Guidance No. 3 have defined PSE as a cross-curricular dimension and part of the whole curriculum, while careers, health and citizenship education are seen as themes.

In my view, this very worthwhile and essential area of a child's learning and development has now been accorded its rightful role in the National Curriculum arrangements:

> The foundation subjects are certainly not a complete curriculum . . . The whole curriculum for all pupils will certainly need to include at appropriate (and in some cases all) stages:
>
> - careers education and guidance
> - health education
> - other aspects of personal and social education, and
> - coverage across the curriculum of gender and multicultural issues.
>
> . . . they are clearly required in the curriculum which all pupils are entitled to by virtue of Section 1 of the Act.
> (DES, 1989, para 3, 8. See also NCC, 1989)

Next, while there is consensus about some of the contents or subject matter of PSE, the reverse is true on other matters. For example, not all PSE syllabuses take on board important areas such as political, racial and cultural issues. Notwithstanding these reservations, however, it has to be recognised that because of the rapid growth and changes in the social, moral and economic life of this and other western countries, schools are being challenged as never before to justify their purpose and methods. They are having to answer questions in relation to their preparation of young people to face up to the challenges, contradictions and uncertainties of life after school as citizens.

Comprehensivisation has meant the demise of the small secondary school as the norm. Personal examples and relationships which worked well in the small-school environment are not as productive in the larger schools which we have come to know. There is room for concern about relationships in these larger schools.

Size, however, is not the only problem:

> There is a growing depersonalisation in our society, and there has been a world-wide challenge to authority that has inevitably influenced attitudes and relationships in school. (Button, 1983)

It is for this reason, and more, that we have witnessed so much development in the field of PSE, both in terms of practice and literature. Schools must take far more seriously their duty to enable the total and complete development of the individual pupil far beyond the purely academic.

It is important that due attention is given to four other important areas of a child's development. These may be broadly classified as:

1   Health education
    a   diets
    b   sex education
    c   physical education
2   Relationship building
    a   love and marriage
    b   careers choice, practice and development
    c   race and cultural issues
    d   equal opportunities – gender matters
3   Political education
    a   the citizens' rights and duties as good national, European and world citizens
    b   records of achievement and profiling
4   Religious multiplicity
    a   the Education Act 1944
    b   the Education Reform Act 1988
    c   working practice

In our planning and delivery of the subject matters of PSE, we should not forget that we have a responsibility to prepare all children equitably. This means two things at once. Firstly, we need to prepare all pupils for a multicultural and multiracial world. Secondly, we need to cater for black pupils who are in the minority but, nevertheless, have equal claim on the education system. (I use the term 'black' here to include all who are not 'white'.)

Health education

Diets

White Europeans do not have the monopoly of superior dietary practices. Politicians and education practitioners alike must be careful not to give this impression to any of our pupils. Practitioners in schools do, however, give this impression when they omit other peoples' cuisines from the home economics curriculum. It is all too easy to imply to pupils that good practices and healthy habits are possible only via English cuisine. No negative statement needs to be made about other cuisines. The mere omission will suffice to belittle them and encourage related stereotypes.

Yet only a little imagination in terms of planning and methods would soon indicate how we might make good use of the community, in-service training and, in some cases, parents and pupils in avoiding this pitfall.

Sex education

At present there is considerable interest in how schools impart knowledge regarding sexual issues, so much so that Parliament has turned its attention to the subject:

> The local education authority by whom any county, voluntary or special school is maintained, and the governing body and headteacher of the school, shall take such steps as are reasonably practicable to secure that where sex education is given to any registered pupils at the school it is given in such a manner as to encourage those pupils to have due regard to moral considerations and the value of family life. (The Education (No.2) Act 1986 s.5 (46))

Irrespective of such parliamentary intervention, the assumption should never be made that it is safe to teach about sexual activities to black children without further planning, consultation and arrangements, even where there are national guidelines. It is not enough to rely on guidelines whether given nationally, locally or by school governors and headteachers. The only safe and proper thing to do is to seek substantial and meaningful consultation with all parents and communities, particularly those parents and communities for whom culture and religion will have a bearing in this context. Here, as elsewhere, cultural pluralism is desirable and must be pursued.

Some of the issues which schools should agree with their parents in this area of education must include questions about both content and delivery. How much should pupils be taught and at what ages? Should classes be single sex in composition? Is it acceptable that male teachers should teach sex education to girls? Parents and community guidance on all these issues are vital and must be sought.

Meeting all tastes and wishes under these circumstances will present enormous challenges, but the challenges should be met and vanquished in preference to taking easier but discriminatory routes.

Physical education

There can be no doubt that the health argument for teaching physical education is a compelling one. Yet some children are discriminated against because their needs and wishes extend beyond the pure health concerns. These are usually black children. Ironically, or paradoxically, this area of the curriculum is arguably one where blacks get most attention. However, it is often the kind of attention which leads either to the formation or the reinforcement of stereotypes: the kind of stereotypes which imply that blacks are good at sports and, with the exception of certain types of music, nothing else.

In the interests of equity and health, it should be the policy of a school to require all pupils to participate in its physical education programme – except, of course, those excused on medical grounds. Cultural considerations may mean detailed attention to such things as changing and showering facilities. Some parents may wish their boys and girls to cover themselves during showers and to be alone at changing times. The practical answer is to separate changing and showering cubicles.

For health and safety reasons children should, at all times, be appropriately and safely dressed. Where some parents do not wish their daughters to wear conventional PE clothing, the wearing of either tracksuits or *churidar pyjama* (narrow, lightweight trousers) with tee-shirt or blouse should be allowed.

Another important cultural consideration is that of single sex lessons. Generally Asian, and more particularly Muslim, parents will insist for quite sound cultural reasons on single sex lessons, as opposed to the quite common practice of mixed PE lessons.

It is of considerable importance, whatever the school's arrangements are, that the school should consult with parents about their children's involvement in physical education. If schools are unable to make suitable arrangements, particularly in the areas of changing, showering, dance, swimming and so on, parents should be told this and given the right to withdraw their children from physical education.

Relationship building

Love and marriage

A loving courtship leading eventually to marriage bonds is seen as the ideal first step to family life, Western-style. This practice has its advantages but is certainly not free from drawbacks – divorce is very common.

A number of cultural groups in Britain, however, place more value on the 'arranged' or 'assisted' marriage system as the road to an ideal family life. This system, too, has its pros and cons and it is, therefore, a matter of cultural tastes and values.

Arranged marriages appear to be associated with greater stability than love marriages. It can also be shown that Western-style marriages are not entirely free of arrangements. The further up the social stratification ladder one goes in the West, the greater is the tendency towards arranged marriages, although never to the same extent as in the East, and not really comparable with those of the East. Yet there is a tendency among British teachers and others to, at least, indirectly belittle 'arranged' marriages. For example, I have often heard colleagues say how sorry they are for Asian girls who, it is said, are crying out for freedom from this kind of system. This is, with respect, an evaluation based upon British values and can be totally misleading with disastrous effects.

I do not argue that there is no evidence of black pupils, and in particular girls, being caught up between two cultures. There are stories of girls leaving their homes for a variety of reasons, but boys leave their homes too, and so do white children. It is a dangerous assumption to make that in such cases the motivation is to seek British-style freedom. For every apparent rejection of cultural dictates, there are hundreds who are quite happy to follow in the line of their cultural traditions. It is, therefore, unsafe to generalise.

The whole area of love and marriage is bedevilled with pitfalls. The teacher must be sensitive, cautious, caring and informed enough to take measures which will avoid such dangers. All pupils need to learn to appreciate and value their cultural backgrounds and those of others with equal respect.

Careers choice, practice and development

Careers guidance is seen:

> as comprising planned sequences of experiences designed to facilitate the development respectively of (a) opportunity-awareness, (b) self-awareness, (c) decision learning and (d) transition learning. (Watts and Fawcett, 1984)

This is an excellent definition of what careers education should be about. If all schools were to deliver the entire package involved in this definition, they would be offering pupils the best chance of complete development towards a career. However, such a model should also include the different cultural needs and experiences of its pupils if all pupils are to benefit from the model equitably.

Careers teachers/personnel managers and institutions are often affected by racist thinking and practices. Here too, as elsewhere in education, the black child is negatively stereotyped and consequently often discouraged from making ambitious strides.

Vocational guidance is but one aspect of education which black Afro-Caribbean communities feel has contributed to black children's failure. But what of the successful black children? They are so few, and at what cost to the children and communities are they successful? (See more on this in Annex 'A' to Chapter 3 of *Education for All*, the Swann Report, DES, 1985.) The following comments will illustrate the problems.

From an Afro-Caribbean girl:

> Our careers teacher might as well stay in bed all day. A girl in my class wants to be an engineer. She was told, 'You don't want to do that; why not reception or clerical work?'

Another Afro-Caribbean girl reported:

> They said catering. It's just because my mum's a dinner lady. I wanted to do youth work and she said, 'What do your parents do?' I said, 'My mum's a canteen manageress', and she said, 'Why not do catering?' I got no information at all on how to do youth work.

But black youngsters have to survive much more than the demotivation and discouragement of the careers guidance system. Employment opportunities in the job market largely depend upon how employers view colour and race.

A recent survey on the employment of school leavers stated:

> A significant shift in the ethnic make-up of the population of school leavers is taking place . . . Black school leavers continue to be significantly under-represented in quality jobs and on employer-led YTS schemes . . . This may result in the creation of a pool of unskilled and untrained black labour force . . . The minority ethnic school leavers, and girls especially, are entering a narrow band of occupations more likely to be lower level in terms of training, skills and, ultimately, pay and prospects. Providers of opportunities in employment, training and education need to adopt positive policies and practices to open up access to all. (Birmingham City Council, 1988)

The answer to many of these difficulties lies in measures designed to alter attitudes and expectations held by teachers about black pupils. Adequate training is needed – both at initial and at in-service levels.

Black role-models in positions of authority would help considerably. Schools urgently need to rethink their staffing and promotion policies if we are to make inroads on this problem before losing yet another generation of black youngsters.

The advice given to young people must never be demotivating, must never be stereotypical. Young people need to be guided in making sensible career choices but, in doing so, their own aspirations and enthusiasms must be encouraged and supported. Careers teachers and advisers must be aware of the debilitating dangers of low expectations, negative preconceptions and stereotypes when they advise black children.

Race and cultural issues

PSE must take on board part of the responsibility for eradicating ignorance and preconceived stereotypes held by white children about other races and cultures. The 'no problem here' attitude of some education practitioners and others in the 'white highlands' remains a very dangerous one in terms of the life chances of black children.

That blacks are still seen in terms of 'problems' is itself indicative of the scale of the problem in such areas. For a start, practitioners should realise that they have a responsibility for educating children to take their places in a multiracial world – not just in their own little corner of it. Secondly, such white children go on to become employers and others in positions of responsibility. In these positions they affect the life chances of others, including black people. It is, therefore, most important that their early education prepares them for this exercise from a position of fairness and equity.

There is evidence that white children hold very negative and stereotypical views of black people, even where they have no first-hand experience:

> When the immigrants come into Britain and complain, the government should throw them out of Britain for good. Also white people should have first choices about jobs.

> I have learnt that they are pulling this country down because they all depend on social security. (DES, 1981, p. 28)

These are just two examples of the negative views recorded in the

Rampton Report. Consider, too, the antics of the National Front. Many of the insults, physical attacks to and upon black people are actually carried out by white youngsters who, by law, are still schoolchildren.

No responsible teacher can allow such views to go unchallenged, not if we subscribe to the principles of fairness and justice. David Wright made this same point with much force when, following his examination of two commonly used geography textbooks, he concluded:

> If teachers with sufficient expertise to be authors of standard textbooks write this insensitive material, what hope is there that other books – and other lessons – are less biased? At a conservative estimate 100,000 pupils have studied *Man and his World*. Some of them are now policemen, teachers, social workers. Others will soon qualify in these fields. What will their attitudes to race be? (Wright, 1983)

A possible effect of these negatives on black children is illustrated well in an article which appeared in the *Education Guardian* some time ago. In a first-year art class at a south London secondary school the topic was a local street scene. Studying the work of an Afro-Caribbean pupil, the teacher asked:

> 'Why don't you draw any black people in the picture?'
> 'Miss, are we allowed to?' was the reply. (The *Guardian*, 1973)

PSE syllabuses must include these issues quite purposefully. There is room, too, for spontaneous discussions around matters of this kind.

Equal opportunities – gender matters

PSE must forcefully challenge the hidden curriculum and ethos of many schools. It must contradict many of the assumptions of the homes and external societies of our pupils.

When tackling gender issues, schools which also challenge racism may encounter a policy conflict. The intercultural roles of women can be quite different. The teacher who believes in encouraging all pupils towards further education may encounter the occasional difficulty in that some black parents might be culturally opposed to such encouragement. Open discussions about the intentions of the school and about the cultural aspirations of the resisting family usually prove useful one way or the other. It is the author's view that if all else fails, the parents' views should prevail. This, after all, is consistent with section 7 of the 1944 Education Act:

so far as is compatible with the provison of efficient instruction and training, and the avoidance of unreasonable public expenditure, pupils are to be educated in accordance with the wishes of their parents.

Political education

The citizens' rights and duties as good national, European and world citizens

Judy Katz's is one of the more popular definitions of racism: 'prejudice plus power' (Katz, 1978). It is not always a formula readily agreed to by those who see racial prejudice operating not only between white and black but also among blacks themselves. It might help us to accept this definition of racism if we look at the issue from a political point of view. It is important to understand the processes which lead to power in society generally.

There need to be lessons in civics and the processes of democracy. In this way pupils will learn how it is possible for some people to legally affect the lives of others, adversely or otherwise. They will see how all of us usually have the same duties in relation to the payment of state dues, such as the Rates, Community Charge, council income and income taxes; how the state then provides benefits from such dues. If these relationships are fully understood it is then easy to see how racism enters the picture: whites hold the power cards and, therefore, are in a position to make their racial prejudices meaningful.

Section 44 of The Education (No.2) Act 1986 provides against political indoctrination, but a sound knowledge of political matters might be gained without a biased indoctrination of any kind. A good education about our political system including human rights education is absolutely essential to an effective understanding of the relationship between the citizen's rights and duties.

Records of achievement and profiling

Since the Government first announced its intention, in November 1985, that all pupils should leave school with a record detailing their positive achievements throughout their school-life, various schools, local authorities and the Department of Education and Science have begun to make progress in this direction, even if somewhat slowly. These records are to consist of:

1   details of all public examination results
2   other evidence of academic achievements, and
3   information about each pupil's personal characteristics and achievements.

Area 2 will enable schools to complete a profile of each pupil's total positive academic experiences throughout their school days, while area 3 will provide the opportunity to record the pupil's achievements beyond the classroom or the school vicinity. In this way, too, the opportunity is provided to benefit from the judgement of others about the pupils, judgements from those not formally associated with the school. These others could legitimately include parents, religious leaders, community leaders and, indeed, the pupils themselves.

Profiling and records of achievement might well provide us with a means of countering some of the difficulties the black child faces in school. These will have the effect of getting pupils more involved in their work and thereby becoming more motivated.

To the potential employer, more positive information is provided. This could help employers to overcome some, at least, of their unfounded prejudices against black candidates.

Most importantly, black children can be viewed in their community settings; their work might be judged and valued by others besides their teachers. In short, they have a far better chance of being considered a success, at least in some things.

Some caution, however, must be advised. We must not allow the non-realisation of our low expectations to prejudice in any way what we record about black children. For example, remarks, such as 'Baljit has done surprisingly well in . . .' are unhelpful and likely to negate the purpose of the record of achievement.

Further, activities and their valuation must not be culturally loaded. Excellence in Creole should be rated as highly as excellence in English, Urdu and so on. It will not do to reject or omit an activity simply because it does not accord with the teacher's own value system. It is for this reason that it is extremely important to draw upon the judgement, skills and expertise of the different communities.

Religious multiplicity

The Education Act 1944

This Act provided for schools to start the day with an act of collective worship and made the teaching of religious education (RE) compulsory. The Act, however, stayed silent on the nature of the religion and the worship which was to be practised.

In a multicultural society it was to be expected that there would be many faiths. In many schools – mainly inner city schools – it became difficult to put the Act into effect because of the multiplicity of faiths practised by the school population. In many such schools sensible arrangements to accommodate all pupils and their religions were reached. By and large the system worked well in that religions were equally valued, even if it could be shown that some of these schools were in breach of the Act.

The Education Reform Act 1988

This Act has now upset the apple cart, in that the provisions of the 1944 Act are now more vigorously re-enacted. There must now be a collective act of worship as before – with three essential differences:

1 This need not be at the start of the day, but must be held.
2 This must be monitored.
3 This must be broadly Christian in nature.

The teaching of RE remains compulsory. As with the 1944 Act, there are arrangements for pupils to be withdrawn from collective worship on the grounds of conscience. Schools may also seek the permission of their local Standing Advisory Council on Religious Education (SACRE) to practise other arrangements.

The composition of the local SACREs makes it difficult to see that many permissions will be granted to practise other than the Christian faith. There is a clear membership bias in favour of Christianity.

Working practice

The whole principle of anti-racist/multicultural education for equality and justice is called into question by the 1988 Act. Can there by any justification for schools to advocate the principles of one religion as opposed to another in a multifaith society? What are the real implications of this? Why should it be necessary for some of our pupils to seek permission to have their religion represented (or get nothing) whilst others get theirs as a matter of law? Is this equality? Herein lie some real and demanding challenges for PSE!

The old and familiar saying, characteristic of colleagues teaching in all-white schools, 'there is no problem here', does not have a place in sound and just educational thought. Colleagues, everywhere, must be interested in educating for equality, humanity and justice.

PSE, then, is not solely concerned with making children more knowledgeable; it has central to its aims the business of fair play and the development of the individual on all levels. It is about the processes of learning to be human and learning through the appropriate medium of 'learning by doing', co-operating, tolerating and participating. An education which does not do this is at best useless and at worst dangerous – a fact which is echoed in the lines of the letter which follows:

> Dear Teacher,
> I am a survivor of a concentration camp. My eyes saw what no man should witness:
>
> Gas chambers built by learned engineers.
> Children poisoned by educated physicians.
> Infants killed by trained nurses.
> Women and babies shot and burned by high school and college graduates.
>
> So, I am suspicious of education.
>
> My request is: Help your students become human. Your efforts must never produce learned monsters, skilled psychopaths, educated Eichmanns.
>
> Reading, writing, arithmetic are important only if they serve to make our children more human. (Taken from a lecture given by Professor Richard Pring, May 1989)

References

Birmingham City Council Careers Service. (1988) *Survey of the Destinations of Fifth-Year Pupils from Birmingham Schools in 1988*. Birmingham City Council Careers Service

Button, L. (1983) The pastoral curriculum. *Pastoral Care in Education: National Association for Pastoral Care in Education (NAPCE) Journal*, 1, 2. Basil Blackwell

Department of Education and Science. (1981) *West Indian Children in Our Schools* (Rampton Report). HMSO

(1985) *Education for All* (Swann Report). HMSO

(1989) *National Curriculum: From Policy to Practice.* HMSO

Duncan, C. (1988) *Pastoral Care: An Antiracist/Multicultural Perspective.* Basil Blackwell

Education Act 1944

Education (No. 2) Act 1986

The *Guardian* (1973) In search of heroes, 2 May

Katz, J. (1978) *White Awareness: A Handbook for Antiracist Training.* University of Oklahoma Press

National Curriculum Council.(1989) Circular No. 6: *Curriculum Guidance.* NCC, October

(1990) Curriculum Guidance No. 3: *The Whole Curriculum.* NCC, March

Watts, A.G. and Fawcett, B. (1984) Pastoral care and careers education. In R. Best, C. Jarvis and P. Ribbins (eds.) *Perspectives on Pastoral Care.* Heinemann Educational

Wright, D. (1983) The geography of race. *The Times Educational Supplement*, 15 July

Chapter 5

Arts Education and Cultural Diversity

Maggie Semple

A wise griot summing up his message for an audience reminded them of the saying: 'One hand cannot clap.' A young boy laughed out loud at this, shouting, 'Of course one hand can clap but it needs the assistance of another.' The griot turned slowly and smiled. He surveyed the hushed audience and paused on the two shining eyes of the impetuous speaker. 'You are right my young friend, when a hand of one and the hand of another meet they signify respect and harmony. It is when only one hand is portrayed and only part of a message told that we see a limited view of reality.'

The aim of this chapter is to portray another view of arts educaton, one which differs from most arts writing through its concern with arts education and cultural diversity; the one hand meeting another in sustained applause.

Like the griot, I often find myself in the position of storyteller, relating the experiences of artists in schools and colleges to teachers and educationalists: stories are a way to make personal and communal meaning out of human experience.

Arts Education for a Multicultural Society

AEMS is the national Arts Education for a Multicultural Society project, jointly initiated and funded by the Arts Council, the Calouste Gulbenkian Foundation and the Commission for Racial Equality, with additional funding from the Further Education Unit. It is located within the Commonwealth Institute, London. The aim of the project is to implement multicultural/anti-racist policies in and through the arts curriculum.

The project seeks to broaden and deepen approaches to the arts, to extend knowledge of the diversity of cultures and assert their relevance to education and contemporary society. AEMS has located and trained a pool of black professional artists whose practice reflects different perspectives from those prevalent in most educational establishments. During 1988/89 over 400 visits by artists took place in schools and colleges, with the aim of effecting curriculum change. AEMS is currently working with eighty educational establishments in partnership with eight local education authorities and regional arts associations throughout England and Wales. It works, through advocacy, co-ordination, resourcing and documentation to achieve a new paradigm for arts education. This arts education model comprises the performing, verbal, written and visual arts (including craft), as well as design, film, video and photography.

The AEMS project argues that black artists are not paradigm bound. The duality of their cultural experience provides the unique image of an agent of change, happily functioning within two paradigm structures. The artists bring specific and unique qualities as role models for both black and white students; they challenge assumptions and stereotypes; work through new skills in a cross-curricular way; establish artistic excellence through a democratic approach stressing collaboration and co-operation, testing in a positive way some established didactic methods.

By twinning this contribution from the artist with the AEMS anti-racist initiative we are in a position to bring to any school or college the framework for a negotiable project – negotiated by students, artists and teachers.

Arts in society – at odds with the political agenda?

The arts have always led a precarious existence in society. They can subvert, persuade, seduce, startle and reflect attitudes and behaviour, and have the ability to challenge or maintain the status quo. The arts can act as powerful agents and often live a dual existence, conforming to or opposing the dominant aesthetic.

Currently the arts in society and arts education have a unique relationship, in that both have been subjected to intense scrutiny by a political ideology which has redefined their function. Arts in society has attempted to legitimise its role by proving that the arts are a viable economic industry. We read (Myerscough, 1988) of how the arts earn more annually than the motor industry, or of initiatives for local authorities to use the talents of artists to improve the environment. The 1988 education legislation reveals almost no influence of decades of work and debate by arts educators or policy makers. The arts as a generic area of the curriculum seems to be at odds with the political agenda and it could be argued that by naming some of the arts, the National Curriculum has established a hierarchy between them.

Another aspect which unites arts in society and arts education is the range of responses to the arts from outside the European tradition. The dichotomy is between divided interests and the subsequent provision; between what is worthy of funding and teaching and by whose criteria this is judged. I would argue that the arts are created and interpreted within a social context and are expressions of creativity in time, place, culture and technology.

There are also examples of well-established 'intercultural' ideas. These are adopted widely, without the need to refer to their cultural origin. R.C. Kwant, addressing the International Association for Intercultural Education in Bergen, 1987, suggests the example of Arabic numbers:

> counting is a basic activity of people who observe that there are individuals of the same kind and get interested in their number. Initially we counted with the help of words, but at a certain level words become insufficient: we invented other symbols which we call numbers, we learned to 'operate' with numbers. There are many different systems of numbers. The Hebrew, Greek and Latin systems made use of some letters of their alphabet. The Arabs invented a new, simple and effective system using numbers 1 to 9 with 0. Operations which were difficult in preceding systems, like multiplying using Roman numbers – DCXXXVII × DCCCXXIX – became easy: 637 × 829. All arithmetic operations could be accomplished just as well above and below 1, creating a system of fractions. This system has been invented within a particular culture, but it is so clear, so rational that it has been adopted by other cultures and now is accepted all over the world. It can be called an intercultural reality.

This example of 'intercultural reality' is adopted by cultures without having to enter into Arabic culture to understand it. It maintains its own identity and is not weakened if we forget its origin. However, Kwant then points out that artistic expression is not intercultural in this sense, because it is *thoroughly* rooted in a particular culture:

> There is an immense difference between an intercultural object as the Arabic system of numbers and an artistic expression. Both are

cultural creations. But the first is completely loosened from its individual and cultural roots. It has become a formal system that completely speaks for itself. The artistic expression however remains connected with its personal and cultural roots. The maker remains recognisable in it and it bears the stamp of the culture in which it came into existence.

Artistic expression does not present a world of final solutions. It rather stresses problems and unmasks solutions. But in this way it brings cultures nearer to each other, not as finally united but as scenarios of the same ambivalence and struggle. (Kwant, 1987).

A perceived cultural hierarchy

Responses to the arts reflect values, ideas, and beliefs and in Britain there is a perceived hierarchy rooted in the critical values and aesthetic understanding of Western European art forms. This is the dominant aesthetic, held to be the pinnacle of artistic achievement, consequently placing non-European art in opposition to it. This perceived hierarchy is also perpetuated in arts education, despite the effective work of some practitioners. It can be found in initial teacher training courses, specialist colleges of dance, music, drama, and A-level courses and, inevitably, in the curriculum of schools.

'Being creative', in the Western-European tradition, is too often thought to be a personal talent, not arising from a creator's circumstance; a private ownership of ideas viewed as property, on sale to the highest bidder.

The perceived hierarchy and these inflexible notions of creativity have led to some dominant discourse presenting the Eurocentric 'grand narrative', as though it were universal. Michael McMillan (1990) mentions a recent example:

> 'The Other Story', an exhibition of artists of African, Caribbean and Asian descent celebrated the contribution made by black artists to the post-war period of British art. It is a major achievement for Rasheed Araeen, the exhibition's curator, who succeeded not only in assembling the work but doing so in the Hayward Gallery, one of the key shrines of the art establishment.
>
> Yet the national press reacted towards the exhibition with indifferent, patronising, and in some cases blatantly racist attitudes. It seems that the presence of black art within the mainstream touches

a raw nerve of the art establishment diseased with fears and fantasies of the 'otherness' of the other story.

Our attention is drawn to the 'world music' statements of rock musician Paul Simon, described by Mark Cooper writing in the *Independent on Sunday* as a 'backpacking muse':

> Simon may be searching for excitement . . . but his records manage to domesticate and control the alien pulse of his discoveries. 'World Music' is an invention of the West that inevitably taints the cultures it appropriates with Western pop music's own sense of exhaustion. (Cooper, 1990)

We must address ourselves to cultural diversity as philosophy and practice, not just policy, as Gavin Jantjes made clear in his address to the Arts Council:

> What would the arts in Britain be like if the nation's black arts were free of their history of neglect? Properly funded? Correctly managed? And, most importantly, allowed to contribute to the mainstream of culture? . . . Our first task for integration lies in the realm of culture: to move from a monocultural to a multicultural perception of the arts and thereby arrive at a conception of the artistic culture which is broad and heterogeneous, its make-up reflecting the diversity of cultural achievements we need to place alongside one another to construct through their diverse autonomies a new non-hierarchical superstructure of cultural practice. (Jantjes, 1989)

Rewriting history

Eighteenth- and nineteenth-century Romantics and scholars in Europe could not accept that Ancient Greece, the fount of all Western civilisations, was a result of African and Phoenician influence. They wanted to preserve the image of Greece as the basis of Europe's artistic and scientific cultural achievement: this necessitated a reconstruction of history to eliminate Afro-Asian influence on Greek society. As Martin Bernal puts it:

> After the rise of black slavery and racism, European thinkers were concerned to keep black Africans as far as possible from European civilisation. (Bernal, 1987)

Here and elsewhere was born the insidious notion that the colour of a person's skin and their physical attributes determined an ability to be civilised and be part of a creative culture. Even now our access to the work of these civilisations is deliberately limited: the new £2 million Nehru Gallery at the Victoria and Albert Museum in London will display five per cent of the museum's Indian collection. For this we can blame the prejudices of directors, a series of governments underfunding the museum, but principally a hierarchy of the arts that above all gives priority to European painting.

The residue of these received values can still be found in some quirky educational structures, content and pedagogy today. *Little Black Sambo* (1895) is still being reprinted and used in the early school years' curriculum; graduate students of English do not analyse Aphra Behn's work of 1688 to provide a context for their understanding of the twentieth-century novel; music students continue to work only in staff notation and rarely learn of an aural tradition. Mark Dery, writing in *Keyboard* magazine, summarises for us:

> It wasn't long ago, however, that the European musical establishment deemed worthless the music made by those with skin a shade or two darker, eyes a bit more oblique than theirs. In an example of misplaced Darwinism, scholars put forth the notion that the artistic achievements of ancient or primitive traditions, many of them oral, constituted lower rungs on the evolutionary ladder of cultural development. The trailblazing ethnomusicologist, Curt Sachs, recalls in *Wellsprings of Music*, 'the days when ancient Egyptian art was disdainfully judged as a not yet matured precursor of Greek and Roman classicism, and Romanesque architecture a somewhat lowly preparatory step towards dizzying Gothic cathedrals, which in due time led to the noble perfection of Renaissance building'. As our horizons widened he notes, we came to realise that 'there cannot be a steady, straight evolution from childish beginnings to an ever more perfect art, as evolutionists once dreamed. There is rather a bewildering sequence of sudden changes by leaps and bounds, indeed, a constant reversal to older, new and foreign ideals.' (Dery, 1990)

Clearly, an educational ideology based on omission by colour is deficient and offers a limited reality to all those engaged in it.

Multicultural/anti-racist education

While multicultural/anti-racist education has a history of documentation, there has been little recording and debate of an arts philosophy which reflects an understanding of cultural diversity. Some teachers have responded to the challenge of the National Curriculum by conducting their own internal arts audit, which has enabled them to re-examine their curricular content and practice. It is simple enough to understand that drawing from a fixed point of observation produces one kind of a picture with one perspective and therefore one way of depicting reality. A multicultural/anti-racist arts curriculum rejects this singular view and begins by acknowledging that Britain has always been a culturally diverse society.

B.R. Singh wrote a checklist for the aims of art education in a 'multiracial, multicultural education context':

   a familiarise pupils with the 'art forms' of many cultures;
   b convey to pupils the notion that an 'art form' is a product of the culture in which it has developed and show what the 'arts' of other cultures mean to those cultures;
   c make known to pupils the different criteria which need to be employed in responding, comparing and contrasting the 'art forms' of different cultures and to show and illustrate how different 'art forms' have influenced each other and how they are now beginning to manifest themselves in our contemporary pluralist society;
   d provide pupils with meaningful encounter in order that through familiarisation pupils will develop deeper understanding of arts and life. . .

Underlying all these aims, is the basic notion that the pupils' education must assist him/her in his/her task of knowing, understanding and appreciating the diversity of 'art forms' within a pluralist multicultural, multiracial democratic society. The educational process should help the pupil to understand the 'artistic' heritage of society and, at a later stage, to assess the significance and value of this heritage for the well-being of everyone. (Singh, 1988)

Arts and culture

For some educators the arts are seen as forceful purveyors of culture and therefore an obvious curriculum area in which to begin examining multicultural/anti-racist issues. Errol Lloyd states:

that to be effective multicultural education should permeate society at large, and there can be no better starting-point than through the arts which transcend national and cultural barriers. (Lloyd, 1985)

There are two points worth exploring here. The first is that the way the arts work, for example through metaphor or direct engagement, may enable the participants to grasp an understanding of different cultures. This, however, needs positive reinforcement and continuous debate to begin to identify what is actually being learned. Placing a Ghanaian dancer in a school for a workshop, without the experience being placed in a context, is arts practice believing in the unstated, hopeful of an accidental cultural exchange. For some schools the arts are seen as the main and only channel of transmitting culturally diverse values.

The second point is more contentious: the arts 'transcend national and cultural barriers'. David Best outlines the dialogue between the two opposed positions of Realism and Relativism in analysing statements like the above:

> Thus it is through one's own cultural tradition that one is able to grasp what art *really* is. There is no sense in the notion of adopting a logically 'free' position, detached from *all* artistic preconceptions, in order to appraise the merits of other supposed artistic traditions. Such a notion is as unintelligible as the suggestion of seeing through someone else's eyes.
>
> . . .The case for realism is impressive. But the relativist points out that there are unquestionably other cultures with their different artistic concepts. The realist dismisses these as at best inferior, primitive attempts at art . . . the relativist acknowledges that understanding of the nature of reality is given with the conceptions of a culture, but since there are different cultures, there are, he(she) insists, different conceptions of reality, and therefore of art. The art of each culture can be recognised and evaluated only in its own terms; it cannot be externally criticised; it is as worthy of respect as any other; the ascription of primitiveness reveals simply the prejudice of the ascriber. (Best, 1986)

I take a relativist stance here as I find the notion of the universality of the arts, uniting all humankind, to be ephemeral. Universal themes of love, death, hate, for example, do unite all people but how the arts convey this meaning is culturally determined. I would prefer to adopt the 'stranger' concept (Schutz, 1971) which suggests that you can only understand yourself when you have been a stranger elsewhere.

If education could be seen as initiation into worthwhile 'forms of life', then an educated person could be seen as one who understands his/her culture, history, past-literature, 'art forms' – music, dance, folk-songs etc. Whatever education is, it must at least be concerned with the development of desirable states of mind, and in the context of the 'arts' for a multicultural, multiracial social environment, it must be concerned with artistic understanding and an appreciation across cultures and ethnicity. (Singh, 1988)

The arts process is at its most potent and sophisticated when it enables translation of one set of criteria to another, enabling cross-cultural understanding.

Educational ideology and multicultural arts

Over the last forty years there have been three broad phases of educational ideology created in response to people of colour: assimilation, integration and multiculturalism. These phases, not locked in time, have seen the following practices:

PHASE	ARTS PRACTICE
Assimilation	The notion of 'primitive'. Cultures were viewed as deviant from the dominant aesthetic, and work was seen within a European folk context. Forms such as opera and ballet were seen as only having significance within the Western tradition.
Integration	The notion of 'tokenism'. Arts focused on 'black arts' which were outside the dominant aesthetic. Aspects such as language were appropriated.
Multiculturalism	The notion of 'difference'. Artists were encouraged to work in education to share their artistic culture. The acceptance of different cultures, customs and life-styles.
Anti-racist	Seeking to redress the balance by perceiving racism as having to do with power structures in society first and then with attitudes in, and organisation of, education. By dismantling and restructuring unjust structures, racism and cultural hegemony may be removed.

Marie-Françoise Chavanne stresses three aspects of 'Many cultures; many arts':

1   The *plural*: it guarantees multiplicity and diversity, and assures us of a broad view without hierarchical ordering of cultures or arts.

2   *Interactions* between arts and cultures – the phenomena of osmosis and cultural contacts have for centuries accompanied the life of civilisations.

3   Permanent *evolution* of culture and arts, which bear witness to the past but which remain perpetually active and in constant development. (Chavanne, 1986)

AEMS has developed multicultural ideology by fusing it with an anti-racist stance. Multiculturalism and anti-racism can be two sides of the same coin and work simultaneously. AEMS acknowledges that arts teaching has a European derivation and that a balanced arts curriculum means including the arts from outside the European tradition. AEMS is concerned with placing black artists who practise outside the European tradition into educational establishments. AEMS does not rely on the occasional workshop with a black artist to improve race relations but on a systematic approach of working through the arts to ensure effective practice. AEMS therefore is not directly concerned with challenging attitudes but with changing and improving teachers' educational prac-tice which can then be monitored and evaluated. From the practical work between artists, teachers and students a new aesthetic framework and understanding should emerge.

Whose arts?

While many teachers are willing to reappraise their content and deliv-ery to ensure a culturally balanced arts curriculum, the dilemma for them is often, *whose* arts should be presented? It is important that we answer that question with regard to establishing cultural pluralism, rather than with reference only to the pupils and students of a particu-lar school or college. As Baroness Young believed:

It is just as important in schools where there are no ethnic minor-ity pupils for the teaching there to refer to the different cultures now present in Britain, as it is for the teaching in inner areas of cities like Birmingham and London. (quoted in Peacock, 1987)

Our definition of activity as arts activity also needs careful consideration, given that outside the European tradition arts are not homogeneous subject areas, that important structural relationships exist between separate modes of creativity. David Best returns to his 'realist', 'relativist' conflict:

> The realist correctly contends that it is senseless to suppose that we can simply *choose* to understand *anything* as art, since what determines our calling it 'art' is what kind of thing it really is. The relativist correctly insists that what can count as art depends upon human conceptions given with a culture, and assumes that therefore these conceptions can be adopted at will. (Best, 1986)

The arts play an important role in establishing and maintaining an individual's sense of cultural identity. However, all cultures are dynamic and organic, evolving and changing in response to outside influences. There is a need to be sensitive to the competing and sometimes conflicting tensions between cultural conservation and cultural development and synthesis. These two notions, however, need not be mutually exclusive. At its most crude, a culturally balanced curriculum would not consist of a lesson on Africa one week followed by India the next, but would present a broad and heterogeneous curriculum which draws positive advantage from different cultural traditions. We need also to guard against the 'exegetical multiculturalist' identified by Ralph Smith (1983) and referred to by David Best:

> the 'exegetical multiculturalist', who never has a profound encounter with *any* art form, and merely indulges in a shallow recirculation of preconceived notions. Such people, by insulating themselves against ideological shock, are rather like travellers who stay at the Hilton wherever they go. These exegetical multiculturalists proliferate at international conferences, where they pontificate from an apparently impressive, but actually superficial, acquaintance with many cultures, and consequent genuine appreciation of none . . . Understanding requires a far more sensitive and objective interaction with a whole culture. (quoted in Best, 1986)

Understanding also requires us to place cultural achievements alongside one another to construct a new non-hierarchical structure for cultural practice rather than replace one set of practices and content with another. The arts are expressions of a particular reality, set in the framework of specific cultural and historical forces and it is the proximity of cultures and their reciprocity which is essential to cultural growth and development. In the AEMS project it is black artists who are the impetus for teachers beginning the synthesis of new knowledge.

Black artists in education

AEMS black artists who work in education do so for very particular reasons. All of them are committed to multicultural/anti-racist education and believe that through the arts, teachers and students are given the opportunity to ask questions and seek solutions. Artists, aware of the cultures of schools and colleges, often view their work as being in opposition to the dominant educational ideology. For many artists their work deals with and produces ideas which may or may not be in sympathy with the dominant ideology and an inevitable and fundamental question is, 'How political can an artist be when exploring issues?' The artists need to understand that the dominant culture of an educational establishment is not a monolith into which nothing can permeate without permission granted from the top. Within the hierarchy there are spaces which can be occupied by oppositional views, without necessarily disturbing the basic framework. The artist's responsibility is seen within a broader syndrome.

When work is created in opposition it does not mean that the stance adopted need be confrontational, but that it can celebrate a symbiotic relationship between the different modes of expression inherent in the arts. The artists struggle to create their own logic and excellence through political, social and psychological issues and subvert the dominant aesthetic as an inspiration for creative activity.

Conrad MacNeil proposes that education:

> must be perceived as a liberating investment in a struggle not only to eradicate debilitating economic conditions and thereby social oppression, but also more importantly to enlarge the human capacity by allowing people to share in establishing social systems that foster the sensibilities of citizenship, develop the spirit and establish attitudes of mind that will redirect thinking away from a siege mentality. (MacNeil, 1988)

Arts in daily life – orature

Many artists from outside the European tradition view the arts as insep-

arable from daily life. The physical, cultural, psychological, economic
and political dimensions of society are all bound up with the arts. Consequently when non-European artefacts are placed within a European
context they are often seen as exotic. Arts which are inseparable from
daily life produce artefacts that are not only functional but also symbolic of complex relationships within the society. This understanding is
called *orature*, in which the main thrust resists and challenges the trend
towards art as purely decorative. Orature includes the structures, aesthetics, process of creativity, values and traditions of a society; the most
important 'actors', 'poets', 'directors', 'painters' are the people, living
out their life dramas and expressing themselves through cultural media
and institutions. It is with this view of arts production that black artists
legitimise their role within education. Artists are aware that not only do
they bring a different perspective into most educational establishments
but also that they present an alternative methodology. Most artists
move easily between a theme (e.g. journeys, legends), an issue (e.g.
representation, slavery) and a subject (e.g. batik, storytelling). Artists
believe that orature is at its best when it operates within a democratic
structure of creativity. This means that the approach is not didactic,
with a marked distinction between expert and non-expert; nor is it
learner-centred where the student may be locked into racist views and
behaviour: it stresses collaborative group-centred learning. The production of the work is as important as the work itself in that the origin
of materials and how they are used are essential issues for motivating
debate.

Many black artists come from societies which have been culturally
diverse for centuries and are well placed to enhance education in Britain.
For many teachers, the artists' ability to work comfortably in a cross-
curricular way is seen as unusual, but for artists their work is multi-
faceted because it reflects cultural diversity.

Teachers working with artists

Many teachers have asked how they are to acquire the skills and understanding presented by the artists. Teachers have been discouraged from
imitating artists' work, but by working alongside them they are now
finding ways of synthesising some of the values, techniques and information with their own cultural understanding. One way to ensure curriculum development is for the artists to present work which raises
issues and stimulates further questions once they have left. In all of the
AEMS workshops, the artist leaves a 'legacy' which manifests itself in a

variety of ways. It may be an artefact such as a thirty-metre batik wall-hanging exhibited in a county hall, or Benin heads made from papier mâché; or a process which can be applied across the arts and integrated into the existing provision. Whatever form it takes, the legacy is active and provokes revision of current arts pedagogy.

AEMS has established a twelve-point plan for an effective collaboration with artists, teachers and students. It summarises the anticipated relationships:

1   Teachers identify broad areas for work.
2   A meeting is arranged for teachers to consult with a co-ordinator.
3   The co-ordinator consults with the AEMS central team and researches lists of artists to match needs and expertise.
4   Teachers visit the artists at work, in performance, at exhibitions, readings, museums.
5   A meeting is arranged for teachers and artists. Artists usually give an insight into their approaches and content. There is no obligation on either side, but artists are paid for their time.
6   The co-ordinator administrates the project: fee, time-scale, materials needed, general co-ordination.
7   Teachers communicate with the artists, usually at another meeting to consolidate plans and prepare students.
8   The artist visits the teaching venue to observe students at work, meet other teachers and see what resources are available.
9   The co-ordinator prepares for the unexpected and plans for review sessions throughout the project.
10 Teachers and pupils document the work as it takes place.
11 The co-ordinator leads the debriefing for all involved as part of the evaluation.
12 The co-ordinator oversees a follow-up plan designed and undertaken by the teachers. (AEMS, 1990b)

Assessment and evaluation

AEMS work poses many questions concerning assessment in the arts. If the arts curriculum is reviewed and its content changed, it would follow that the process and the criteria of assessment should also be re-examined. AEMS is currently undertaking this research and has found that a real tension exists amongst educators about how they perceive the arts. Some are locked in their own cultural prisons and seem unable to view non-Western arts within a contemporary framework. Non-Western arts are seen as time-bound, trapped in the past. There is difficulty in understanding that these arts deal with a contemporary world. Implicit in the notion of 'primitive' and 'high arts' is the belief that not only is there a hierarchy of values but also that the former easily describe non-Western European arts and the latter, Western European arts.

Keith Swanwick in *Music, Mind and Education* examines prejudice and valuing in music:

> musical signals serve either to invite immediate acceptance or rejection. All that is needed is one phrase, sometimes a single bar or chord . . . Music alienates people when they perceive:
>
> *a*   its sound materials are strange, or threatening;
> *b*   its expressive character to be strongly identified with another culture;
> *c*   its structure as either repetitive or confusing or aimless.

Swanwick answers all three 'impediments' by proposing that students:

> handle the materials of music for themselves, experimenting with various types of instruments, working with different scale and tuning systems;
> by trying to understand why and under what conditions the music comes to be made;
> by familiarising students with different structural conventions through active engagement. (Swanwick, 1988)

Another tension amongst educators is the sometimes confusing terminology and the challenge of finding a language to which all of the arts can belong. Artists are stripped semantically when they are seen as or called 'African' or 'Asian' without qualification. This is like a group of Morris dancers resident in Gambia being viewed as the sole representatives of British culture and arts practice. All educators must take time to learn and use the language of how other people would like themselves described.

All of the work completed with AEMS artists shows evidence of deep commitment and support from heads, principals, advisors and members of LEA administration. This support at all levels has served to enrich and enhance the outcomes of the project, just as artists working in the classroom with teachers has enriched the process of learning for everyone.

Many of the AEMS educators are documenting their work and it will be these people who will contribute to the changes of perceptions and practice. In the next few years AEMS will attempt to provide the much needed conceptual framework of arts education within a culturally diverse society. This responsibility is shared with the artists, who have substantial collective experience of working within education.

Conclusion

AEMS teachers and artists ensure a context in which non-Western art does not appear quaint, primitive, confused or unworthy of serious critical attention. They are storytellers in the time-honoured tradition, who remind us of our responsibilities, our special gifts, our right place in the interplay of ideas. We are embarked on a journey through different aesthetics, where 'races' and genders, spiritual beliefs, levels of phrasing, are mixed – boundaries are broken. I believe this produces a new, strong aesthetic and creativity informed by relationship, harmony, balance and dignity.

I am reminded of Grace Nichols' poem, from the Commonwealth Poetry Prize anthology, *Under Another Sky*:

> I have crossed an ocean
> I have lost my tongue
> from the root of the old one
> a new one has sprung.

References and bibliography

Aboud, F. (1988) *Children and Prejudice*. Basil Blackwell

Araeen, R. (1989) *The Other Story*. South Bank Centre

Arora, R. and Duncan, C. (eds.) *Multicultural Education: Towards Good Practice*. Routledge

Arts Education for a Multicultural Society. (1990a) *Duniya Ki Ankhe* (Eyes of the World). AEMS Publications

(1990b) *National Exhibition Catalogue*. AEMS Publications

Arts Education for a Multicultural Society Music Working Party. (1989) *Breaking the Sound Barrier*. AEMS Publications

Banks, J.A. (1981) *Multiethnic Education: Theory and Practice*. Boston: Allyn & Bacon

Further details of AEMS work and publications can be obtained from: AEMS, The Commonwealth Institute, Kensington High Street, London W8 6NQ, telephone 071-603 4535 ext. 242.

Bannerman, H. (1895) *Little Black Sambo*. Reinhardt Books

Bernal, M. (1987) *Black Athena*. Free Association Books

Best, D. (1985) *Feeling and Reason in the Arts*. George Allen & Unwin (1986) Culture-consciousness: Understanding the arts of other cultures. *Journal of Art and Design Education*, 5, 1

Blacking, J. (1987) *A Commonsense View of All Music*. Cambridge University Press

Burtonwood, N. (1986) *The Culture Concept in Educational Studies*. NFER-Nelson

Chavanne, M-F. (1986) Many cultures; many arts. *Journal of Art and Design Education*, 5, 1

Cohen, L. and Manion, L. (1983) *Multicultural Classrooms*. Croom Helm

Cooper, M. (1990) Melancholy beat of a backpacking magpie. The *Independent on Sunday*, 28 October

Craft, M. (1984) *Education and Cultural Pluralism*. Falmer Press

Dery, M. (1990) The world pulse. *Keyboard* magazine, Miller Freeman Publications, San Francisco

Gundara, J.S. (1987) Art history in a multicultural society. Paper prepared for International Association for Intercultural Education conference, Bergen, Netherlands

James, A. and Jeffcoate, R. (eds.) (1981) *The School in the Multicultural Society*. Harper & Row Jones

Jantjes, G. (1989) An integrated approach. In *The Arts and Cultural Diversity*. Arts Council of Great Britain

Kwant, R.C. (1987) Arts education in a multicultural society. Paper prepared for International Association for Intercultural Education conference, Bergen, Netherlands

Lloyd, E. (1985) Black perspectives in arts education. *World Studies Journal*, 5, 1

Lynch, J. (1983) *The Multicultural Curriculum*. Batsford

McMillan, M. (1990) Cultural grounding. Paper prepared for the Visual Arts Department, Arts Council of Great Britain

MacNeil, C. (1988) The National Curriculum: A black perspective. *Multicultural Teaching*, 6, 2, Spring

Mullard, C. (1980) *Racism in Society and Schools: History, Policy and Practice*. Centre for Multicultural Education, University of London

Myerscough, J. (1988) *The Economic Importance of the Arts in Britain*. Policy Studies Unit

Nichols, G. (1987) 'Epilogue'. In A. Niven (ed.) *Under Another Sky*. Carcanet Press

Owusu, K. (1986) *The Struggle for Black Arts in Britain*. Comedia Publishing

Owusu, K. (ed.) (1988) *Storms of the Heart*. Camden Press

Peacock, D. (1987) Multicultural education: Background, benefits and problems. *Music Teacher*, 66, 2, February

Schutz, A. (1971) The Stranger. In B. R. Cosin *et al.* (eds) *School and Society*. Routledge

Singh, B.R. (1988) Ensuring a good education in the arts: Guide to teachers. *Education Today*, 38, 4

Small, C. (1987) *Music of the Common Tongue*. John Calder

Swanwick, K. (1988) *Music, Mind and Education*. Routledge

Chapter 6

The Place of Drama in Intercultural Education

Alistair Black

The Arts in Schools, published by the Calouste Gulbenkian Foundation in 1982, gives an excellent justification for the inclusion of all the arts in the curriculum, and in Chapter 3, 'Arts education and the cultural heritage', it develops the relationship of the arts to intercultural education. The whole book is certainly worth reading but this paragraph from Chapter 3 merits quoting in full:

> The arts are only one aspect – albeit an important one – of the life of any community. To talk of its culture is to connote the whole network of habits, beliefs, customs, attitudes and forms of behaviour which hold it together as a community. Even to talk of the culture of a society is misleading in so far as each section, group or class within a society has varying cultural forms and values. This larger view of culture suggests three features of the cultures of industrial societies which need to be taken into account in education: those of diversity, relativity and change. (Robinson, 1982)

Drama and the human condition

Drama is, by and large, concerned with the human condition and it works by allowing participants (and audience) to explore their reality through a fiction. In other words, pretending. For example, it may be that a class of six-year-olds have been hearing the story of *Snow White and the Seven Dwarfs* followed by acting out aspects of the story, or possible alternative scenes. The children will be using the story as a starting-point to create their own imagined world with its own rules and conventions. By creating a world that matches their sense of right and wrong it will help illuminate some of the injustices in the real world.

Prejudice, bigotry and racial hatred are engaged within intercultural education and are also the kinds of human failings which are regularly explored in the drama studios and classrooms in our schools. It is therefore not surprising that many drama teachers find themselves in the 'frontline' of supporting the progress and development of intercultural education. Daring to teach where angels fear to tread.

A balanced drama experience

Drama is not named as a foundation subject in the National Curriculum but is currently a very popular subject in our secondary schools and is increasingly finding a more explicit role in primary education. Drama in schools can be expressed in two ways and both are needed to provide a balanced drama experience:

1   Learning *through* drama, where drama is used as a tool or vehicle or method to explore and express ideas, concepts etc., and
2   Learning *in* drama, where knowledge, skills etc. are developed and which is associated with theatre activities.

In simplistic terms it's the old process–product debate.

In Key Stages 1 and 2 it tends to be the process-strand which we most often find. This is usually to do with using drama strategies, techniques and conventions to learn about other things, for example history or science. At this stage we often hear teachers extol the virtues of drama in terms of a child's social and personal development and, indeed, in the seventies and early eighties it seemed that this was the *only* function for drama and that as an art form in its own right it had little status. The phrase most often used by teachers at this time was that drama was different from other experiences as it 'allowed you to stand in other people's shoes'.

This quality is at the heart of drama as a mode of learning and must not be underestimated, and is why it is so powerful an approach to learning; it involves not only learning about other cultures but also experiencing what it might feel like to be part of another culture. However, it is important to remember that although it certainly does help give us some insights as to what it might be like to be in a similar situation, in terms of intercultural education it will not get you inside other people's skins.

In drama we constantly ask the pupils to pretend to be other people. To ask a white child to pretend to be black will not necessarily change that child's understanding or, more importantly, his or her attitude, especially if the pretending to be black takes place against a 'white background', that is, in an all-white area. Just as in an all-boys' school where we may find boys representing girls there is no guarantee that their gender awareness will be improved. It is this act of representing which is the key to learning when using drama as a tool.

If we ask the pupil to pretend to be someone who lives in a society where they are treated as outcasts because they don't conform to the majority, a parallel understanding of sorts might begin to occur. In this example we are tackling the issue of prejudice in an oblique way and allowing the opportunity for the pupil to make connections and come to a more fundamental understanding concerning power.

It is possible to identify two major camps in intercultural education: those who wish to concentrate on celebrating difference, encouraging a valuing of other cultures and their contribution to society; and those who want to start by exploring the racism in our country. I believe it is not possible to separate these two emphases and both must be addressed, just as both learning *in* and learning *through* drama need to be balanced.

Having spent six years as Drama Adviser/Inspector in Hampshire where, in many of our schools, black children are hardly seen, and before that as the Drama Adviser for an outer London borough where some schools had eighty per cent black children, I am fully convinced that the need for cultural understanding is equally crucial in *both*. Drama in these two very different authorities makes a significant contribution to education both in *and* for a multicultural society.

The temptation to perceive culture only in terms of colour is a trap many of us fall into. It is no use our pupils engaging in work which gives them some understanding of the black population, while they hate the Jews or the Gypsies or the Scots. If that is the case then the educational experience has been worthless, as it has clearly not addressed the fundamental issues of bigotry, prejudice and abuse of power, but has simply touched on the obvious external badge of difference.

Drama has always, from earliest times and in all parts of the world, been concerned with the human condition and the dilemmas we face which are universal. While in recent years drama has tended to focus on the emotional, feeling aspect of the individual, there has been a danger of failing to take note of the political and cultural dimensions in learning which have to be understood before considering the personal development of the individual, as no individual develops in isolation.

In Curriculum Matters No. 17: *Drama from 5 to 16*, HMI attempt to describe how drama operates.

In drama three things must be done at the same time. First, we must re-create other people's behaviour from evidence, observation, memory or imagination. Second, we must articulate a personal response based upon real or imagined experiences, which give the action conviction and meaning. Third, we must distance ourselves from both the created behaviour and the personal response in a way that is often difficult to manage in real life, when our own reactions and feelings may be spontaneous. (DES, 1989, para 3)

In dealing with some of the potentially 'hot' issues associated with intercultural education as well as the joyous celebratory events, it is the protection afforded by this 'distancing' which makes drama the ideal vehicle. Not only does it allow us to explore feelings from a distance (in that it is 'not me who said that but the person I'm pretending to be'), it also allows us to examine closely human behaviour. We can replay the scene; we can cross-examine the characters; we can move time to see what might have happened to cause the reaction or what might happen as a result of the reaction.

Geoff Readman, Drama Inspector for Nottinghamshire, used as a context for some drama work the factual account of how Dr Barnardo's children were shipped to Australia in the 1950s, virtually as cheap labour. This proved to be an excellent means of enabling all-white classes to find a point of entry and some empathy with wider issues of immigration. It was distanced but had connection points. To have asked white children to pretend to be black slaves in the eighteenth century would probably have led to romantic or melodramatic scenes owing more to poor films and books than any reality.

Many drama lessons encourage the children to take on the role of people from other cultures, but teachers should beware lest the drama presents a rather idealised notion of that culture (such as the idea of 'the noble savage'). If the teacher only allows the pupils to remain at that level of thought, then crucial learning opportunities will have been lost. Real intercultural learning will take place when we introduce the uncomfortable notion of the power relationship between the various cultures in a community. This is when it starts to get messy and when, in the average classroom, anecdotes are shared which can lead to reinforcement of prejudices. In drama we can ask the most difficult of questions 'from the inside', which challenge accepted ideas.

For example:

1   Is it possible that some of the early British missionaries abused their power to achieve their deeply held convictions? or

2   Do you think the British in India were brave adventurers in a strange land? or

3   Are the rituals of other cultures acceptable regardless of their nature because they are from another culture and therefore not to be questioned?

By engaging in dramas, where we pretend to be missionaries or adventurers or people from another culture, we can ask the questions not in isolation but from within an imagined context, and we don't answer them as ourselves but as the person we are pretending to be. We are protected. By acting out situations in an imagined world we are able to safely question and explore; to safely teach where angels fear to tread.

This mode of learning is not purely the province of the drama teacher but should be used whenever a safety net would be helpful. Nearly every aspect of the curriculum can and ought to reflect, in some degree, cultural diversity. All of us, regardless of race, are aware of the chauvinism which can exist even between streets in small towns, and this can provide a very worthwhile context for drama dealing with the universal issue of the irrational fear and suspicion of anything and anyone 'different'.

Learning through drama

Drama can be used to help learn about a variety of subject areas, as the following examples show:

1   The Native American is a popular topic in many of our schools. Their way of life on the plains of America provides a wonderful context for delivering much of the National Curriculum in Key Stages 1 and 2. It also provides opportunities to help children appreciate the complexity of factors which create cultures and this encourages them to question the stereotypes which abound in films and other forms of fiction and which, in turn, allows them to consider stereotypes in their own time.

2   In a secondary school in Southampton, the history, modern languages and drama teachers collaborated in a project which not only satisfied the requirements of each subject area's 'programmes of study', but was also an example of good intercultural education.

The starting-point was the arrival in Southampton of Spanish children in the 1930s, fleeing the Spanish Civil War. By pretending to be the Spanish children, as well as the local Southampton children of the time, the pupils created dramas, talked in Spanish and learnt both local and European history. Increasingly teachers of modern languages are using drama as a way of providing a context for talk which also may deal with human issues.

3   In a primary school the pupils were studying the Norman 'invasion' and were pretending to be the Normans and seeing the events from their viewpoint. The drama allowed the teacher and pupils to explore the whole issue of how we tend to perceive Britain as 'invaded' by others while we in turn merely 'discover' and 'civilise' other countries.

The above examples indicate how drama can be used to learn about other subject areas as well as creating opportunities for intercultural education as a cross-curricular dimension; in other words, drama was used to serve the curriculum, both overt and hidden.

In-service activities

In-service training activities also provide opportunities for using drama and theatre to create learning opportunities. In Hampshire I, and another colleague who felt confident in using theatre skills, attended a number of professional training days for headteachers as well as individual whole school closures, and used our performing skills to provide focus and stimulus for intercultural training. This was achieved by the two of us acting out a variety of situations which could be found in many schools throughout the county. For example, two teachers complaining that they have too many things to do without this 'new thing' called intercultural education; or two governors concerned that the new head is seemingly eroding our heritage by her insistence on positive action on intercultural education; or two teachers having a violent argument where one accuses the other of racism and creates a huge divide in the staffroom. Having seen the situations acted out, the teachers were asked to put themselves in the shoes of the members of staff in the imagined school and, in groups, to discuss how the situation might be resolved. They were not asked to act merely to solve a 'fictional' human problem. This was designed as part of a structured day which was concerned with the implementation of the county policy for intercultural education so enabling schools to establish their own whole school policy. The result of the activity was that anxiety levels were reduced and a safe and effective atmosphere was created which allowed fears, and indeed prejudices, to be expressed without risk. Teachers were allowed to 'come out of the closet', to give an honest (but protected) response, admit to uncertainties and so begin to move forward.

Theatre in Education

The above is an example of theatre being used to support education. It reaches a high level of sophistication with the establishment of Theatre in Education companies (TIE). In Hampshire we are fortunate to support such a company which currently performs free in our schools and which creates pieces of theatre which reflect the needs of children and teachers.

The company has a policy of integrated casting which means, as far as possible, it employs a mixed-race cast with sometimes cross-casting within that (when black actors take white roles and vice versa). The company toured a piece for fifteen-year-olds on Mary Seacole, who lived in Hampshire before she went out to the Crimea as a nurse at the same time as Florence Nightingale (another Hampshire person). Mary was black, and for some of our schools the black woman who played her may have been the first professional black woman the white, and indeed black, pupils may have come across. Regardless of the content of the play, this in itself was an important experience. The company also provided an extensive teachers' pack which was to be used by the teacher both before and after the visit. It is crucial that the children are prepared for any visit such as this so that the experience does not happen in isolation.

Any professional artist, actor, dancer, musician, writer or visual artist must establish some form of discussion with the school prior to the visit, to ensure each is aware of the other's 'hidden agenda' as well as the stated aims. Many wonderful artists are not at their best when working with young people and what might have been a rich intercultural experience could end up confirming prejudices through lack of a shared sense of responsibility and understanding.

The same company also performed a piece on travellers which was particularly relevant in Hampshire in intercultural terms, just as an Asian piece would be in Hounslow.

Learning in drama

The English Statutory Order (DES, 1990) stresses the need for pupils to have access to a wide range of reading material which should include plays. It is important that our pupils are encouraged to read texts from other cultures and equally important that they have the opportunity to decode a wide range of texts, and not just literary ones. The reading must be placed in a wider cultural context so that the pupils are able to make cultural connections as they read, and not perceive it as an exotic tale. (Media education has a central role in this respect in that television and the tabloid press have an enormous influence on young people, and we, as teachers, have a responsibility in ensuring that they appreciate how they are constructed. The links with drama and media are, as yet, undeveloped but both are concerned with representation and are structured in order to create meaning.)

The theatre experienced in the 1980s indicated the breaking down of a narrow Eurocentric theatre diet of the past and that theatre influences from many cultures will find their way into British productions. There is much to be done, and it is still possible to find lists of recommended play texts provided by examination groups which seem to ignore any play text either written after 1960 or written by an author who was neither British nor American. I was delighted to note that the Schools Curriculum Development Committee (SCDC) 'Arts in Schools Project' (now absorbed by the NCC) included in the seven learning objectives for all the arts that pupils should 'demonstrate a relevant knowledge and understanding of different cultural practices and traditions of the arts'.

The Royal National Theatre has, in this respect, provided us with some good examples. In 1990 they toured Britain with a very unusual production of Moliere's play *Tartuffe*. It was produced by the Education Department at the National and had been adapted and directed by Jatinder Verma, the director of Tara Arts, Britain's leading Asian Theatre Company, and was performed by British Asian actors. The production was set in India and was able to find many cultural connections and was appreciated by audiences from all cultural backgrounds.

At a more humble level, but certainly no less important, was a production of that wonderful epic Indian tale, *The Mahabharata*, which I saw performed by students at a further education college in Hampshire. The performers, between the ages of sixteen and nineteen, all came from a part of Hampshire where almost everyone is white. However, in this small market town there is a tiny Asian community, who in fact provided much valuable guidance for the production. Quite apart from the non-European content, it was performed in a completely non-European style and was probably one of the best pieces of youth theatre I have ever seen. The students (all white) took part in a theatre activity which was not only worthwhile in its own terms, but which also gave them insights into another culture and most certainly gave enormous status to the Asian community in the town, doing more for intercultural understanding and tolerance than years of polite tokenism.

I was also interested to hear of a production of Shakespeare's *Twelfth Night* performed in Ethiopia where the black audience were able to identify with the play as they felt that the character types and human problems presented were to be found in any country. The Ethiopian audience and the Hampshire audience both had shared in a theatre experience which brought new personal and cultural understanding.

At a more prosaic level, the assembly in an infant school can provide exactly the same opportunity. The celebration of Diwali or Christmas or Eid or Jewish New Year or St David's Day provides both participants and audience with an opportunity to take part in a shared cultural event when *public* statements can be made and values made explicit. It doesn't have to be the celebration of a particular date; in fact any story acted out will provide a public opportunity to express values and attitudes. The stereotypes portrayed and challenged can provide the starting-point for future discussion. In Hampshire our TIE company developed this ability in their production of *The Practical Princess*, performed to five, six and seven-year-olds, which challenged many of the images presented to young people that influence their perceptions and understandings. In this play the princess (who was black) saved the prince and made friends with the dragon. The dragon was, of course, a possible metaphor for any monster which causes fear, in this case a misguided fear born out of ignorance. The children, reflecting on the play with the help of the teacher, will no doubt identify their own 'monsters'. The experience of theatre, which has been carefully planned to be relevant to a particular age range and which is accompanied by teaching materials for the schools, can be a powerful learning experience.

For those LEAs without the benefit of a TIE company it is worth contacting your nearest theatre to find out about their attitude to education. Increasingly theatres are employing education officers and may be able to help. I'd also recommend contacting the theatre officer of your regional arts association who should be able to put you in touch with theatre companies which tour your area.

If you work in the primary phase why not contact the drama department in your nearest secondary school or further education college? They may well be delighted to devise a piece of theatre to bring to your classroom as part of their GCSE or A-level work in drama. Very often students at this level use theatre to explore issues which are concerned with intercultural education and may be pleased to work with a specific audience in mind. It is good liaison and a good opportunity to let your children meet the culture of the frightening big school and a readily available way of gaining access to theatre.

The arts have a duty to disturb. In order to do this they need to confront us with the monsters within ourselves and within our society; to make us face difficult questions at both an intellectual and emotional level. Drama and theatre allow us to do this in a detached way which also protects our individual feelings. The black princess who saves the prince without resorting to violence against the monster can exist in a drama fiction and so inform our reality and help effect change in an interdependent world.

References

Department of Education and Science. (1989) Curriculum Matters No. 17: *Drama from 5 to 16*. HMSO

(1990) *English in the National Curriculum*. HMSO

National Curriculum Council. (1990) *The Arts 5–16: A Curriculum Framework*. Oliver & Boyd

Robinson, K. (ed.) (1982) *The Arts in Schools: Principles, Practice and Provision*, reprinted with new introduction 1989. Calouste Gulbenkian Foundation

Chapter 7

Mathematics with a Multicultural Perspective

Nell White

This chapter is a product of mathematics work which has taken place in an Education Support Grant (ESG) project, one of those which flew into LEAs on the wings of a white 'Swann'. Our purpose was to implement the recommendations of that same report as it applies to schools with few ethnic minorities. Many other projects throughout the country were working with the same objectives and meeting common barriers. In retrospect this was hardly surprising but it provoked many energetic and experienced people to seek ways, methods or strategies to make an impact.

A universal language

The strategy we used had as its essence the following philosophy: 'Multicultural mathematics' needs very little justification in the sense that we know already that mathematics is the product of cultures from around the world throughout human history. Mathematics is also a universal language, used by everyone in their daily lives, for their work, and/or their leisure.

Not all the mathematics that has been generated by every culture throughout history, however, is going to be useful in the teaching of maths in schools today. To be included in the school curriculum, a teacher must ask if a piece of knowledge satisfies one of these sound educational objectives:

1 Will people learn what I hope they will learn from this?
2 Will it include the use of skills which need to be learned or practised?
3 Will it highlight the conceptual structures which are needed for mental agility?

4   Will it provide the opportunity to employ strategies for problem solving or investigational work?

5   Will it encourage personal qualities such as a positive attitude to maths?

These objectives were to assist staff when making decisions in schools about which mathematics they would include in the curriculum, and the objectives apply equally to mathematics which has been generated or used by any culture.

Presenting facts about the origins of a specific piece of mathematical knowledge, along with the other facts which can be learned, for example about the 3 × 3 magic square (Lo Shu), has a purpose. That purpose is to enable children to understand the origins of mathematics, since not to do this may leave an impression that it has either appeared out of thin air or has been made up by teachers just to make life difficult for everyone! More seriously one may assume, unless one is told otherwise, that all the pieces of mathematical knowledge that one learns are a product of one's culture. Such a distorted impression will not assist in creating positive images of cultures other than one's own and could reinforce a belief that they are necessarily inferior.

The difficulties of teaching mathematics

At the time the project was taking place, in 1986, good practice – problem solving and investigation – was making children's mathematics exciting and enjoyable. There was success in many ways apart from the objectives outlined. Parents were involved and informed. Classroom organisation was highlighted and many pupils were given a context to explore and achieve in mathematics.

However, this masks the difficulties associated with few well-qualified staff in mathematics, or teachers who lack the confidence to teach mathematics, and the primary school without a framework for teaching this subject. Consequently the likelihood of a National Curriculum was welcomed, in that it could be a means of improving mathematical teaching in schools, and primary schools in particular. With reference to *Mathematics from 5 to 16* (DES, 1985a), many colleagues applauded its principles of progression and continuity which in effect emphasise a child's individual progress rather than competitiveness. The report itself will be very useful for teachers who require guidance.

But the multicultural/anti-racist dimensions were not quite so reassuring. At an HMI invitation conference held to collate responses to this element in the maths and science documents, some relevant sections were revised, rewritten and fed into the consultation process. The mathematics and science advisers present were not at all happy with the section on 'Cultural Diversity'.

There were many irregularities in the report which suggested that the working party members were not clear about the term 'equal opportunity' nor had a clear definition of their own. For instance, they separated gender, special needs and 'race' (with its new name of 'cultural diversity'). Are 'race' and 'anti-racism' words one doesn't mention now? In the mathematics report one cannot find the term 'multicultural' apart from 10.20: 'We have not therefore included any 'multicultural' aspects in any of our attainment targets.' 'Multicultural mathematics' – in inverted commas – suggests that the subject had only a confusing ideological quality and was without educational value. Contrast this with the value placed on a cross-cultural perspective and the countering of racial stereotypes found in the science and technology reports.

The multicultural dimension

Teachers are now expected to teach the new mathematics curriculum and heed the Non-statutory Guidance (NCC, 1989) issued just before the end of the summer term 1989. The first concern is the recommendation that the NCC consultation document be referred to (NCC, 1988). This is especially worrying since it explains and outlines multicultural maths in a derogatory fashion. Teachers who use this document as a ready reference will acquire some powerful negative misinformation. The section on cultural diversity gives little insight into what multicultural maths is, and how it could be used in a classroom which has few ethnic minority pupils. It is implied that only pupils of non-European parents would benefit from knowing that the number system is of Hindu–Arabic origin (10.21). The overall impression given is that cultural diversity in maths is only about children with English as a second language. This is a very narrow perspective.

Furthermore, ethnic minority children are defined as a problem (deficit model) rather than an asset. However, in the Introduction there is an indication of future willingness to take these issues up. It states:

> 1.4 It is planned to issue further guidance materials in due course, and to supplement and up-date existing materials when

appropriate. In particular, special educational needs and matters relating to multicultural issues and equal opportunities, which have implications across the curriculum, will be the subject of specific guidance at a later date. (NCC, 1989)

So the intention is to consider multicultural aspects, but as an afterthought rather than as a fundamental approach for all children, as recommended by the Swann Report (DES, 1985b).

Despite the worrying political framework, the Non-statutory Guidance can provide a powerful case for anti-racist/multicultural mathematics, especially when one realises that teaching methods are not prescribed and that it will be individual teachers who will deliver the curriculum. In the Introduction, for instance, it states:

> 2.1 Mathematics provides a way of viewing and making sense of the world. It is used to analyse and communicate information and ideas to tackle a range of practical tasks and real-life problems.
> 2.2 Mathematics also provides the material and means for creating new imaginative worlds to explore. Through exploration within mathematics itself, new mathematics is created and current ideas are modified and extended. (NCC, 1989)

Case study – Islamic and Rangoli patterns

A realisation of these objectives can be fully achieved by work on Islamic and Rangoli patterns. Table 1 identifies how pupils' work can match the attainment targets of the National Curriculum through much better examples than those in the consultation document, which seem to be nothing more than an endless analysis of cars, traffic and travel.

Rangoli patterns

Rangoli patterns are used by Hindu and Sikh families to decorate their homes during festivals like Diwali. Some are pictorial, while others are geometrical and abstract. By studying Rangoli patterns, children are provided with a way of making sense of the world. In this case they will understand their use in Hindu and Sikh homes. Rangoli patterns are often made on doorsteps from foodstuffs such as rice, lentils, split peas and seeds so that anyone coming into the house would pass over the

Attainment Target: Level: Part	Statement of Attainment
9:3:1, 2, 3	Select materials and the maths to use for a task. Explain work being done. Make and test predictions.
10:4:1, 2	Understand and use language associated with angle. Construct simple 2-D shapes from given information and know associated language.
10:5:1, 2	Understand congruence of simple shapes. Explain and use angle properties associated with intersecting and parallel lines and triangles, and know associated language.
10:6:1, 2, 3, 4	Know and use angle symmetry, properties of polygons. Recognise 2-D representations of 3-D objects. Use computers to generate and transform 2-D shapes. Classify and define types of quadrilaterals.
11:1:1	State a position using prepositions.
11:2:3	Recognise different types of movement: translation, rotation, reflection.
11:3;1	Recognise reflective symmetry in a variety of shapes.
11:4:1, 2	Specify location by means of co-ordinates. Recognise rotational symmetry.
11:5:1	Identify the symmetries of various shapes.
11:6:2, 4	Reflect simple shapes in a mirror line. Devise instructions for a computer to produce desired shapes and paths.

Table 1   Rangoli and Islamic patterns match some of the attainment targets of the National Curriculum

design and have good luck. Another type of Rangoli pattern is that which is used by women to decorate their hands and feet during weddings. They are drawn with 'mendi' – a mixture of powdered henna, lemon juice and water – and applied with a sharp stick. (See figs. 1 and 2.)

This work communicates information and ideas and provides the context for a range of practical tasks and real-life problems. For example, when a design has been drawn on dotted paper it can be used as a basis for collage work, block printing, embroidery, batik work, and so on. It certainly provides material and means for creating new imaginative worlds for children to explore. These new worlds provide for white

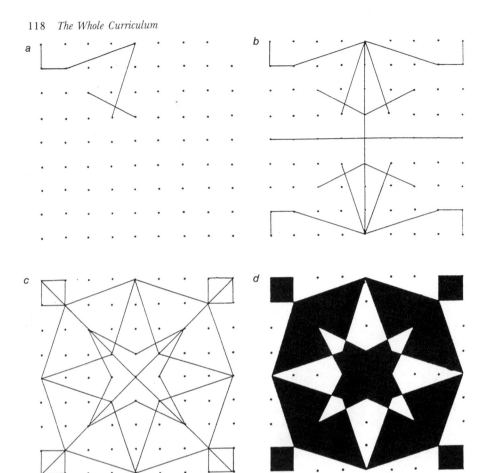

a   Select a square grid and draw a few lines by joining pairs of dots.

b and *c*   Reflect these lines in each of the four axes of symmetry of the square.

d   Shade in the regions to accentuate some of the shapes.

The finished pattern can then be repeated.

Fig.1   Creating Rangoli patterns (© Wiltshire County Council)

children a preparation for adult life in a multicultural society; for ethnic minority children it goes some way to countering the myth that their culture has not contributed to the development of mathematics. Such work will be essential in providing various contexts for all children to use mathematics.

Islamic patterns

Islamic patterns are more elaborate than Rangoli patterns. They are geometrical and abstract and can be found decorating many Islamic

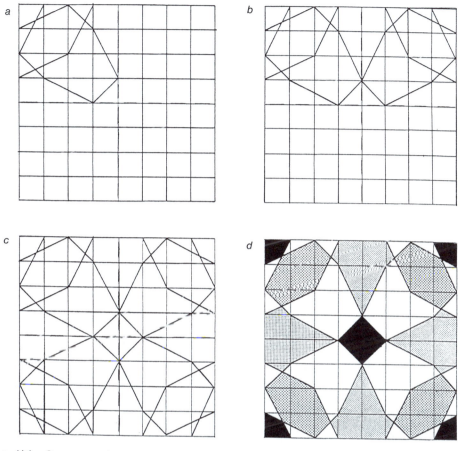

a   Using 2 cm squared paper, draw a square 8 × 8. Divide this square into quarters by outlining the axes of symmetry – thus creating four small squares within the large one. Select one of the squares and draw a pattern within it.

b   With the help of a mirror, reflect this pattern into the adjacent square.

c   Next, draw the reflections of the mirrored pattern into the remaining two squares.

d   Finally, rub out the axes of symmetry and shade in the regions.

Fig.2   Adapting Rangoli patterns for infants (© Wilsthire County Council)

buildings now appearing in Britain, such as the Aga Khan's Ismaili Institute in Kensington. Tessellations manually or using the computer extends this work to many levels. (See fig. 3.)

The work on Rangoli and Islamic patterns easily fits the specifications:

> 2:4 Learning skills, such as adding two numbers, calculating the area of a triangle . . . form a large part of pupils' work in

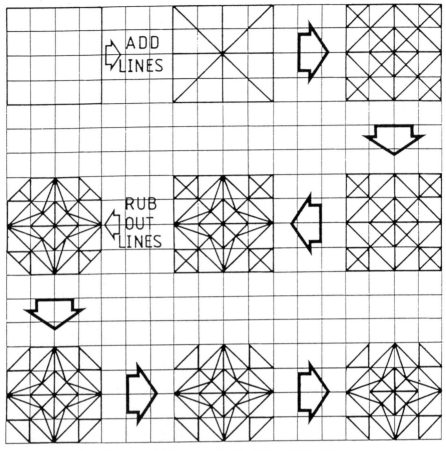

(Pattern by Matthew Fryer (aged 12) of Avon Middle School, Salisbury)

The pattern is initiated within the square by drawing in lines such as diagonals, joining midpoints of lines, and so on – making sure that symmetry is maintained in the four axes of the square. Parts of these lines are then rubbed out – again keeping to the symmetry – until a satisfactory pattern has been produced. The completed pattern is then tessellated to produce a large design.

Fig.3 Creating Islamic patterns (© Wiltshire County Council)

school. Important though they are, such skills are only a means to an end, and should be taught and learned in a context that provides purpose and meaning.

2:5 It [mathematics] should be a source of delight and wonder, offering pupils intellectual excitement and an appreciation of its essential creativity.

2:6 Mathematics is a structure composed of a whole network of concepts and relationships, and when being used mathematics becomes a living process of creativity.

2:7 Both the broad nature of mathematics itself and the individual
nature of learning need to be recognised in the flexibility and
variety of teaching and learning styles employed in the classroom. (ibid.)

If one uses Islamic patterns as an example, what could be more purposeful than designing a decoration for a religious building, and
explaining an art form? In all the classroom work in this project, children have been excited by the outcome of their individual mathematical activity.

Intellectual excitement has always been a very marked response
when Vedic squares are introduced and investigated. Again this piece
of work readily fits the prescribed attainment targets. (See Table 2.) (For
further information on Islamic and Rangoli patterns and Vedic squares
see Wiltshire Education Authority, 1987.)

Cross-curricular approaches

A further area of agreement is found in 2.12 and 3.0 regarding cross-
curricular approaches and activities:

Programmes of study and attainment targets in mathematics
should not be viewed in isolation from those in other foundation

Attainment Target: Level: Part	Statement of Attainment
2:4:2	Understand the effect of multiplying by 10 or 100.
3:3:3	Know and use multiplication facts up to 5 × 5.
3:4:1, 2	Know and use multiplication facts up to 10 × 10. Add mentally several single-digit numbers.
5:3:1, 2	Explain number patterns and predict subsequent numbers where appropriate. Find number patterns and use these to perform mental calculations.
10:4:2	Construct 2-D shapes from given information
10:5:1	Understand congruence of simple shapes.
11:4:2	Recognise rotational symmetry.
11:I:1, 2	State a position using prepositions. Give instructions for moving along a line.

Table 2 Vedic squares and attainment targets

subjects . . . detailed planning of topics, themes and activities which draw together elements within mathematics can also provide contexts for work to be linked. (ibid.)

It is a pleasure to read that any mathematical topic can be pursued across the curriculum.

The potential contribution of mathematics to promoting cultural diversity and countering racism has not been realised in the Non-statutory Guidance. This stance is not mirrored by the Design and Technology Report, nor to such an extent in the Science Report. Yet good multicultural mathematics activities meet all the criteria required for quality mathematical learning, and can be freely incorporated into the attainment target structure. However, this will be implemented in a fragmentary way, reliant upon the initiative of individual teachers, INSET course providers, and the awareness of inspectors/advisers and advisory teachers. But this need not be a lost cause for there is much evidence that far from 'multicultural mathematics' being an inferior sub-mathematics, it is simply good educational practice, and it is on educational grounds that the battle has to be fought and won, particularly in all-white areas. It is a prize worth winning for once one has made the case in relation to the subject most widely viewed as culture-free, an important strategic breakthrough will have been made for the whole multicultural/anti-racist movement in education.

References

Department of Education and Science. (1985a) Curriculum Matters No. 3: *Mathematics from 5 to 16*. HMSO

(1985b) *Education for All* (Swann Report). HMSO

National Curriculum Council. (1988) *Mathematics for Ages 5–16: Proposals of the Secretary of State for Education and Science and the Secretary of State for Wales*. NCC, August

(1989) Non-statutory Guidance: *Mathematics*. NCC, July

Wiltshire Education Authority. (1987) *Maths For All*. Wiltshire County Council

Chapter 8

Science in the National Curriculum: Developing an Anti-racist and Multicultural Perspective

Sue Watts

In this chapter I attempt to explore how the requirements of the National Curriculum for science can be implemented with an anti-racist and multicultural perspective. The issues relating to science education in a culturally diverse society have been discussed for a number of years and have been the subject of a number of articles and publications (see the references for examples). This is a very important time for all science teachers but those of us who have been involved in this debate need to ensure that the understandings, ideas and strategies we have developed are fully incorporated in the implementation of the National Curriculum. The examples which I will use will be from the point of view of a secondary school teacher (Key Stages 3 and 4) although the principles apply equally across the whole age range.

Broad perspectives in the teaching of science

In 1985 the Swann Report quoted from guidelines for reviewing the curriculum which had been submitted to them by one LEA which suggested 'broader perspectives' for the teaching of the sciences:

- the development of themes related to conservation and pollution, disease, food and health and population growth needs to be considered in relation to humankind as a whole and the issues of regional and group differences need to be worked out and developed in the context of interdependence and unequal resources;
- the issue of 'race' and the origins of humankind need to be considered carefully in relation to the myths surrounding theories of race;

- the question of difference of pigment and physical features and the assumptions made about identities on the basis of pigment need to be explored more fully;
- the history of science, particularly the early history of chemistry and medicine, needs to be developed comparatively;
- the selection of examples for classroom use needs to take account of the contribution and participation in scientific endeavours of people from a range of backgrounds and cultures;
- the question of science as being only a European phenomenon needs to be raised and discussed. (DES, 1985, p. 332)

In my article in an SSCR publication (Watts, 1987) I quoted a list of general principles for a science education that promotes equal opportunities. These had been developed by a group of teachers and teacher educators at a workshop held in Birmingham by the Commission for Racial Equality in 1986. They were as follows:

1 Incorporating a global perspective.
2 Understanding issues relating to justice and equality.
3 Elaborating science in its social, political and economic context.
4 Making apparent the distribution of and access to power.
5 Making all people involved in science overt and not hidden.
6 Incorporating a historical perspective.
7 Starting from and valuing the experience and knowledge of children.
8 Using flexible teaching and learning strategies and giving emphasis to the learning of science.
9 Integrating practical approaches with the work as a whole. (Watts, 1987, p. 19)

The group of teachers felt that the first six of these principles were those which uniquely distinguished this approach and that the other three were considered to be good practice in science education by most teachers.

We are now, several years later, in the position where we have to make the requirements of the National Curriculum a reality in science classrooms and departments within our schools. Does the National Curriculum give us scope to develop science education which is appropriate for our culturally diverse society? Will it be possible for teachers to bear in mind the principles quoted above in the development of their schemes of work and practice in the science classroom? Will it be possible to maintain the developments already made in anti-racist science education with a multicultural perspective?

I hope that the rest of this chapter will go some way to addressing these questions. I will consider four main interrelated areas, which are:

1   The view of the nature of science portrayed by science education.
2   The knowledge content of the curriculum and the contexts in which that knowledge is presented.
3   The teaching and learning strategies employed.
4   Specific issues concerning ethnic minority children including those related to language, culture and religion.

The nature of science

This is the title given to Attainment Target 17 and it is an area about which many science teachers feel very wary. The Non-statutory Guidance points out that:

> Through work for AT17: The Nature of Science, pupils will be encouraged to reflect upon the nature of science and how scientific ideas have developed in other times and in other cultures . . . Science is a human construction. We define its boundaries and decide what shall count as science . . . School science is a reflection of science in the 'real' world, where scientists learn from each other and extend the boundaries of knowledge by research. (NCC, 1989)

In the programmes of study and the attainment targets themselves, we are given the basis we need to incorporate many of the points made in the quotation from *Education for All* and by the Commission for Racial Equality (CRE) group.

The programme of study for Key Stage 3 states:

> Through their own investigations and the use of text, film, other secondary sources, and case studies, for example, focused on the life and work of famous scientists and/or the development of an important idea in science, pupils should be given opportunities to:
> •   study the ideas and theories used in other times to explain natural phenomena;

- relate such ideas and theories to present scientific and technological understanding and knowledge;
- compare such ideas and theories with their own emerging
  understanding and relate them to available evidence.

In Key Stage 4 it is stated that pupils should continue the programme
of study outlined for Key Stage 3 but in addition they should also:

- distinguish between claims and arguments based on scientific
  considerations and those which are not;
- consider how the development of a particular scientific idea
  or theory relates to its historical, and cultural – including the
  spiritual and moral – context;
- study examples of scientific controversies and the ways in
  which scientific ideas have changed.

It is possible to develop a module of work on people which considers
the concept of 'race', amongst other issues. This would look at stereotyping and would be ideal for developing a distinction between arguments based on scientific considerations and those which are not. The
content of this work would cover elements of Attainment Target 4:
Genetics and Evolution, and would satisfy one of the suggestions from
the list quoted by Swann. Indeed the Non-statutory Guidance issued in
1989 suggests that 'Pupils should come to realise the international
nature of science and the potential it has for helping to overcome racial
prejudice' (NCC, 1989, p. A10). (For discussion relating to teaching
about race see Hoyle and Watts, 1986.)

The Non-statutory Guidance contains a considerable amount of discussion relating to the use of Attainment Target 17. It is suggested that:

> Pupils' knowledge and understanding of the nature of science will
> originate from their own science activities. Therefore if these
> activities are exploratory and explanatory the pupils will associate
> this with science itself, and may also be well-motivated towards
> learning it. (NCC, 1989)

This, of course relates to the learning experiences planned by the
teacher and will be discussed further, later in this chapter.

Science Travels, a booklet developed at Sydenham School (Moy and
Watts, 1985), attempts to show pupils in year 7 (the beginning of Key
Stage 3) that people from many cultures have contributed to the knowledge that we call 'science'. We hoped to be able to begin to counteract
the prevailing view held by many pupils (and teachers) that science is

the preserve of white people with a Western background. It is intended that use of such materials will contribute to conveying to pupils the notion that:

> People from all cultures are involved in scientific enterprise. The curriculum should reflect the contributions from different cultures, for example the origins and growth of chemistry from ancient Egypt, Greece and Arabia to the later Byzantine and European cultures, and parallel developments in China and India. (NCC, 1989)

We began by asking, 'Where has science come from?':

> The knowledge that we call science has been discovered by people from all parts of the world. In this booklet you will be able to read about some of the knowledge that people have discovered at different times and in many different places. These ideas have been used by people and have often travelled with people as they have moved from one place to another. The science that you will learn in school has widespread origins. This booklet tells you about some of these. (Moy and Watts, 1985)

After some discussion about people from many places finding things out and using these discoveries (for example, paper, metals), we describe the trade routes which also served to facilitate the exchange of ideas. We then introduce other trade routes:

> Also, hundreds of years ago in Europe, ships were built to travel to the rich vast lands of the Americas, Africa and India. These ships brought back wealth in the form of gold, cotton and other raw materials. Many people who studied and used scientific ideas grew rich because they were able to exploit the wealth that came from trade. Many of the scientific ideas developed at this time were to improve the ships and navigation techniques used for trading. (ibid.)

We describe how some ideas and information spread slowly around the world from India, China, Arabia, Egypt and Greece, hundreds of years ago, until they reached Europe.

A number of pupil activities are suggested. These include tracing on maps the routes that ideas and inventions might have taken, and making time-lines for the inventions and discoveries described in the booklet. We also suggest activities such as the following:

> Imagine that it is 1005 AD and you have just travelled to China. Make up a story or play in which you tell people about gunpowder when you get back home. You may like to present your play or story to the class, write it down or make a tape. (ibid.)

(For further details about *Science Travels* see Hoyle and Watts, 1986 and Watts, 1987.)

It is a pity that the way in which some of the attainment target statements are expressed will almost automatically lead to examples being chosen from 'Western' science. However, with careful thought, there are a number of examples which could be chosen as case studies in an anti-racist science curriculum.

> Pupils should be able to give an account of some scientific advance, for example, in the context of medicine, agriculture, industry or engineering, describing the new ideas and investigation or invention and the life and times of the principal scientist involved. (AT17.4)

A useful case study would be an account of the life and work of the Black American scientist, Charles Drew (1904–50). His main research was in the field of blood preservation. It was through his work that blood banks were first set up and blood transfusions were made possible during the Second World War. Ironically he died because, after having been involved in a road accident, the nearest hospital was for whites only. He was refused admission and died before he could receive a blood transfusion from a black hospital. (For further details see Hoyle and Watts, 1986 and the references given there.)

There are a number of resources that give a global view of the history of science (see ibid.), which could be used by science teachers to provide materials for teaching Attainment Target 17. Teachers will need imagination and time if they wish to produce their own materials and teaching schemes to reflect this world-view of science, its nature and its history, rather than a narrow European view.

The knowledge content of the science curriculum

There are very many opportunities to introduce a perspective which reflects the culturally diverse nature of our society in the stated content of the attainment targets and programmes of study of the National Curriculum. There is only space here to develop a few ideas.

Attainment Target 7, Making New Materials:

Level 4:   Pupils should know that an important feature of manufacture is the conversion of raw materials, by chemical
reactions, into useful products.

Level 5:   Pupils should understand the application of biochemical
processes in manufacture, for example, fermentation.

There have been a number of published accounts of curriculum
work which exemplify these areas. The work of the CRE group mentioned earlier included a plan for teaching about metals using copper
as an exemplar. This was published in *Science Teaching,* 2 (see Hoyle
and Watts, 1986) and includes an appreciation of copper as a material
and its uses, studies of copper in history, its discovery, the geographical
distribution of the ores and their detection. The article then suggests
that pupils go on to consider the extraction of copper from its ores,
including traditional methods. Pupils can try a number of these methods for themselves and can also carry out a demonstration of the
electrolytical purification of copper. The use of sulphur-containing
ores and the possible implications for the production of acid rain are
discussed. There are considerations of the economic and political
grounds for the locations where copper is purified and discussion of
the wider social implications of the production of copper – for example
the effects on the standard of living of people in areas where copper is
mined, the effects on the land and possibilities for reclamation. Finally
the section of work ends with a discussion of recycling, including both
the straightforward scientific aspects and the economic aspects like the
cost of scrap copper.

There is always a temptation to discuss fermentation only with
respect to the production of alcoholic drinks. A number of the cultural
groups which are represented in our schools do not allow the use of
alcohol as a stimulant. There are other very good reasons for the industrial production of alcohol – these include its use as a fuel and as a sol-
vent. Science teachers should always give emphasis to these alternative
reasons for the industrial production of alcohol when teaching about
the application of the biochemical process of fermentation.

Attainment Target 9, Earth and Atmosphere:

Level 4:   Pupils should be able to measure temperature, rainfall,
wind speed and direction; be able to explain that wind is
air in motion.

Pupils should know that climate determines the success

of agriculture and understand the impact of occasional catastrophic events.

We all gain through having access, through pupils with a range of experiences, to a wide variety of examples. Many pupils at inner city schools have first-hand experience of the strong winds around very tall buildings. In fact at my present school we have our own tower block and we have no trouble in getting over the concept that wind is air in motion! Additionally we are able to considerably extend discussions of the nature of climate and its effects on agriculture by recourse to pupils with experiences from other parts of the world. It is pointed out in the Non-statutory Guidance that 'a pupil's own experience should be used as a context for learning so that it can be an agent for that learning'. I would add that this sort of use of a pupil's own experiences can give a pupil status as an 'expert' within the class and with other pupils, so enhancing their view of themselves and thereby further facilitating learning.

There are many examples of content which can both reflect the culturally diverse nature of our society and give a global perspective to our work as science teachers. Again, we require science teachers with imagination and the time, energy and resources to develop the schemes of work and the teaching and learning materials in order to carry this perspective forward.

Teaching and learning strategies

It is pointed out in the Non-statutory Guidance that:

> It is well established that the choice of learning context has a strong effect on the pupil's performance and this applies particularly to ethnic minority pupils. It is important that a pupil's own experience should be used as a context for learning so that it can be an agent for that learning. In setting up learning and assessment tasks, it is vital that ethnic or cultural bias is excluded from any activity. Science readily lends itself to the use of different social contexts, for example diet, nutrition, energy, health, the ecosystem. Cultural diversity can be a positive influence on the richness of the curriculum, provided that the teacher does not take a narrow view of 'correctness', for example in a discussion on diet or alternative energy. (NCC, 1989)

Activities which encourage all pupils to participate and take an active role in their own learning as they develop and become independent learners are, in general, the sort of activities which we should be encouraging in our science lessons. In *Talking Science*, Pauline Hoyle and Chris Laine put forward the following ideas:

> The activities . . . involve pupils in a range of roles and skills – working co-operatively on a task and sharing ideas as well as reading, observing, debating, justifying conclusions and relating personal experience to a scientific activity. Pupils are therefore able to display interests and expertise in ways often unrecognised in more conventional learning situations. (Hoyle and Laine, 1989)

Where teachers generate the conditions for active learning to take place, the pupils will gain because they have particular kinds of expertise and experience to contribute and they feel that they and their cultural background are valued. The Non-statutory Guidance points out that the adoption of teaching and learning strategies which emphasise co-operative and tentative approaches to the subject will reinforce these approaches in the children's view of science and of how it operates.

There are a range of teaching strategies which can and should be adopted. Creating contexts for meaningful discussion and for children to work collaboratively should ensure maximum participation from all pupils and also that all pupils have the opportunity to achieve high standards in science.

Increased use of reading, listening and watching in science lessons will facilitate the development of ideas about the nature of science and how scientists work. This not only complements work on Attainment Target 17 but also increases the participation of all pupils, including those from ethnic minorities.

Some issues related to language, culture and religion

> Teachers must take account of ethnic and cultural diversity within their school and within society at large. Different ethnic groups will have different interpretations of the view of science presented in the science Order and the sections of Non-statutory Guidance. It is at the school and teacher level that such interpretations need to be taken into account, in order to deliver the most effective curriculum. A pupil who has difficulties with the language of instruction will find access to many scientific activities blocked. The language

of science can be complex and the science teacher will naturally seek to be sensitive to the pupil's understanding of language and terminology. The science teacher, perhaps in consultation with a language specialist, may be able to provide a range of tangible examples which will help such pupils to widen their vocabulary and powers of communication, for example through carefully structured group discussion during science lessons linked to planning and reporting activities. (NCC, 1989)

There are many activities which can be used by science teachers to extend the development of the English of bilingual pupils. Most of these involve the children working collaboratively in groups. The publication, *Talking Science* (Hoyle and Laine, 1989), contains a range of exemplars of collaborative work developed for use with children in science lessons, together with suggestions of other topics which are suited to the use of these kinds of strategies. I have worked with another teacher in my present school to develop materials that pupils can use collaboratively and have found that their success is well worth the time and effort involved in their construction.

In a culturally diverse classroom, teachers have to ensure that they do not include any examples which could be offensive to pupils because of their culture or religious beliefs. If science is presented interestingly as one of a range of ways of understanding, explaining and finding out more about the world, it should not provide any conflict with religious beliefs. There is much scope here for collaboration between science and religious studies teachers.

Conclusion

To conclude, I would like to quote the checklist given in the Non-statutory Guidance for the evaluation of learning experiences:

Will the experience give pupils the opportunity to:
• develop scientific strategies and skills;
• develop attitudes appropriate to working scientifically;
• develop basic scientific concepts;
• reach a satisfactory outcome;
• apply scientific ideas to real-life problems, including those which require a design and technological solution;
• work co-operatively and communicate scientific ideas to others;

- develop an understanding of the relationship of scientific ideas to spiritual, ethical and moral dilemmas;
- discuss the ways in which scientists work?

Will the experience:

- stimulate curiosity;
- relate to the interests and everyday experiences of the pupils;
- appeal to both boys and girls and those of all cultural backgrounds;
- help pupils to understand the world about them through their own mental and physical interaction with it;
- involve the use of simple and safe equipment and materials;
- involve resources and strategies available to teachers;
- contribute to a broad and balanced science curriculum, bearing in mind experiences already selected? (NCC, 1989)

If we can manage to meet the requirements of this checklist then I believe we will be closer to providing a science education which is appropriate for our culturally diverse society by taking an anti-racist stance and adopting a multicultural perspective. In my view, the National Curriculum presents us, as science teachers, with a range of opportunities to develop and implement a science curriculum that has wider perspectives and begins to meet many of the requirements outlined at the beginning of this chapter. There are a number of questions which remain: Do teachers have the time, expertise and resources to carry out this work? Most of the mentions of education for a culturally diverse society are contained in the Non-statutory Guidance, does this mean that all science teachers will ensure that this perspective is included in their work?

The next few years will tell whether the science educators of this country are able to meet the challenge of the National Curriculum and incorporate an anti-racist and multicultural perspective to the ultimate benefit of all the children in their care.

References and bibliography

Bentley, D. and Watts, M. (eds.) (1989) *Learning and Teaching in School Science*. Open University Press

Department of Education and Science. (1985) *Education for All* (Swann Report). HMSO

(1989) *Science in the National Curriculum*. HMSO

Hoyle, P. and Laine, C. (1989) *Talking Science*. ILEA Learning Resources Branch

Hoyle, P. and Watts, S. (1986) Race in science teaching. In M. Hollins (ed.) *Science Teaching in a Multi-Ethnic Society*, 2. North London Science Centre

Moy, S. and Watts, S. (1985) *Science Travels*, school-based curriculum materials. Sydenham School, ILEA

National Curriculum Council. (1989) Non-statutory Guidance: *Science*. NCC, July

Newnham, H. and Watts, S. (1984) Developing a multicultural science curriculum. In M. Straker-Welds (ed.) *Education for a Multicultural Society*. Bell & Hyman

Watts, S. (1986) Science education for a multicultural society. In R. Arora and C. Duncan (eds.) *Multicultural Education: Towards Good Practice*. Routledge

(1987) Working for a multicultural society. In C. Ditchfield (ed.) *Better Science: Working for a Multicultural Society*. Heinemann/Secondary Science Curriculum Review

Wright, S. (1985) 'Secondary education for a multi-cultural society: An investigation into the implications for science education.' Unpublished M.A. dissertation. King's College, University of London

Chapter 9

Cultures, Literatures and English

Michael Marland

The cultural range of English courses

'English' as the very title of a subject, discipline or course would suggest a national approach which is singly focused – concentrating on a single culture, its literature and its language. Paradoxically, though, teachers of school English courses have in many ways been in the forefront of opening up the cultural range of the curriculum, often as a response to the cultural range of their students. For instance, Caribbean literature was read in English courses before a multicultural curriculum was much explored elsewhere (see Marland, 1978). However, it could not be said that cultural diversity has been used as a *principle* of the curriculum planning of secondary English courses. When, for instance, David Holbrook recommended reading Chinese poetry (Holbrook, 1961), it was *English for Maturity* (the title and theme of his best-known book on the teaching of English), certainly not 'English for cultural understanding'. The writing of poetry in the form of Japanese Haiku was recommended in the 1960s but only for its value in the use of English. As Ranjana Ash says in the introduction to her pioneering collection *Short Stories from India, Pakistan and Bangladesh* as late as 1980: 'The use of literature to understand a foreign culture has only recently been appreciated' (Ash, 1980, p. 7).

Teachers of the school subject 'English' have been among the most open-minded and flexible in opening up the Anglocentric curriculum by their choice of texts but they have lacked a curriculum rationale for this.

Some sections of this chapter originally appeared in 'Arts, cultures and the curriculum', published in *The Journal of Multicultural Teaching*, 8, 1, Autumn 1989.

English and legislation

Now, perhaps to the surprise of many English specialists, we have a specific statutory demand for cultural diversity in the curriculum, 'Cultural . . . development of pupils' is now a statutory requirement. As the Education Reform Act 1988 legislates:

> The curriculum satisfies the requirements of this section if it is a balanced and broadly based curriculum which promotes the . . . cultural . . . development of pupils at the school and of society. (Section 1)

The DES explanatory circular stresses that:

> The curriculum should reflect the culturally diverse society to which pupils belong and of which they will become adult members. (DES, 1989a, p. 7)

These are demands on the *planning* of a school curriculum which are new, fundamental and important; the pupil is to be seen as requiring cultural understanding, and the world in which and for which the pupil is being educated is to be recognised as 'culturally diverse'. This cultural range is the right of *all*, not only of those of minority background.

This underlying curriculum planning requirement is respecified in the programmes of study for English. I see it in the point made about teaching about language, which 'should focus on: regional and social variations in accents and dialects of the English language and attitudes to such variations' (DES, 1990, p. 25). This needs expansion in a school's language curriculum for 'knowledge about language'. However, for school English courses the clearest application of the general requirements of cultural diversity are in reading. The programme of study for Key Stage 2 requires (my italics):

> The reading materials provided should include a range of fiction, non-fiction and poetry, as well as periodicals suitable for children of this age. *These should include works written in English from other cultures*. (DES, 1990)

And for Key Stages 3 and 4 there is a similar demand (again my italics):

> Teachers should encourage pupils to read a variety of genres, e.g. autobiographies, letters, diaries or travel books as well as short stories, novels, poetry and plays. *These should include literature from different countries written in English*. (ibid. p. 31)

It has to be said that a few months after the publication of the Order, there were accusations that the Government had toned down the requirements. I believe they were clarified and strengthened, and the Minister of State wrote publicly:

> There is no question about our objective that all pupils should study literature written in English from other countries and cultures. The Order we have made will achieve that. (*TES*, 1990)

Finally, the GCSE criteria in English include the crucial demand that pupils must 'show an informed engagement with the work of a wide range of authors from a variety of cultures and times' (SEAC, 1990, p. 2).

One could say that the cultural range to which many teachers of English courses aspired has now been given statutory weight, and a new impetus given to the concept of 'cultures' in the curriculum as well as a new demand that it must be planned.

English as subject and course

The profligate British use of the term 'subject' needs clarifying. It is used interchangeably between 'discipline', 'course' and 'planning epistemology'. English in British universities has come to mean literature, mainly in English by British, Irish or US Americans. In schools it has been seen as a unified literature and language course, and Bullock's attempts at 'language across the curriculum' (DES, 1975) sadly did little to break the synonymity of English as a 'subject' and English as a time-tabled separate 'course'.

English as defined by the Education Reform Act and the National Curriculum Council is a *planning* division of the curriculum not one of the *delivery*. Indeed this is made absolutely clear by the terms of the relevant DES circular: 5.89. Every school has the freedom and the responsibility to plan both its own overall curriculum offer and within that its division into delivery courses.

In this chapter cultural diversity is considered in terms of both the NCC *planning* subject 'English' for *all* the school's courses (including the tutorial programme) and the course 'English' itself. (However, this chapter does not include media or drama.) Cultural diversity is a cross-curricular demand, to which *every* course must respond. Cross-cultural approaches are integral by current legislation, and cultural exchange should therefore be a key planning mode.

English and literature

Every English department in a British secondary school shares the world-wide agonies that were epitomised in the University of Nairobi in 1968. Ngugi Wa Thiongo and his colleagues argued that 'English' was limiting the literary traditions being studied. As one commentator put it:

> To circumvent that curious matter of what we might think of as the 'politics' of normative judgement – that is, of the problematic status of 'universal' norms of beauty and excellence, and their implicit connection with relations of political and economic power – Ngugi and his colleagues abolished the Department of English, so that they might radically decenter the place of English language and literature in the study of the larger institution of 'literature'. What Ngugi's faculty did is somewhat analogous to the innovation in cartography effected by the editors of *The Times Atlas of the World*, by placing each country analysed at the very center of the globe, so that the reader sees, say, the United Kingdom as it might appear from, say, the Republic of Kenya. (Gates, 1984, p. 13)

'Culture', and thus inevitably 'cultural diversity', was subordinated, even removed, from many English courses in the otherwise admirable new emphasis in the sixties on personal relevance. It was almost as if the school course 'English' was aiming to fill the gap in schools later filled by pastoral care.

John Dixon, for instance, was an inspiring leader of the revision of the English literature curriculum in the sixties, and his *Growth Through English* (1987) epitomised the strength of the revised approach. Again its title making the point: 'English' equalled literature, the purpose of which in the course was to enable the pupil's personal emotional growth. This personal response model derived from the work of I.A. Richards in *Practical Criticism* (1929) and F.R. Leavis, with their important and re-energising emphasis on responding to the 'words on the page'. At its best this revolution engaged pupils' experiences, emotions and ideas in the literature and led to a deeper understanding. At its worst it led to 'springboard' teaching in which the literature was used merely as 'material' (that give-away term) for a prompt into personal exploration, and even to some teachers almost turning the course into pastoral care.

Frank Whitehead was one of the clearest and most powerful of those redefining the purposes of teaching literature. He developed the personal response model persuasively:

> Herein lies the supreme importance, for English teaching, of those symbolic forms of experience which we call literature. Stories, plays and poems have provided the objective 'third ground' (David Holbrook's phrase) on which we can meet together, to re-enact and later discuss our most intimate hopes, fears, desires and conflicts in a way that is at once vividly personal and yet at the same time securely depersonalised. (Whitehead, 1969, p. 23)

Our properly self-centred, current and personal 'hopes, fears, desires and conflicts' lead us inward, not out to other cultures – though of course many of these personal themes are universal. Frank Whitehead was the spokesperson of many who banished the relationship between literature and art, still less culture:

> It will be clear, then, that literature is assigned a key role in our unified conception of English teaching: not as a subject study ('Eng.Lit,' our cultural heritage), but as a supremely potent mode of significant experience. (ibid. p. 24)

The first problem is that the, as always misleading, word 'subject' is taken to mean the bracketed phrase; secondly, the notion of 'our cultural heritage' is declared unacceptable as one of the educational aims of studying literature; thirdly, there is the worrying use of that 'but'. Why cannot there be a cultural role for studying literature that substantially overlaps with that of offering 'significant experience'. Clearly there will be occasions when we contemplate a cultural artefact of any sort, including a piece of literature, primarily because it is the key to cultural understanding and we can find no experiential response. However, are there not many occasions from Beowulf to poetry from the English literatures of the modern world which we go to for their position in a 'cultural heritage' but in which we also find 'significant experience'?

For instance, I found Konai Helu Thaman's poem 'You, The Choice of My Parents' (Thaman, 1974) because I was trying to learn something of the cultures of the Pacific, but it also moved me as a human exploration.

So obvious is the overlap that it would hardly need pointing out if it had not been that the last quarter of a century's tradition of teaching school literature has been to subordinate the cultural interest. Even that great teacher and anthologiser Denys Thompson, in his fine collection of poetry of the 'preliterate', justified the reading only on the shared humanity, not as a cultural exploration:

> The strength of the poems rests in their closeness to common experience, the fullness of their response to the demands and contingencies of life, and the way in which they are often expressed symbolically. They are not alien and remote from us, or unintelligible, but are near the core of humanity which we share with their authors. (Thompson, 1978, p. 12)

This is true and well put, but again illustrates the curriculum justification for literature only for its experience and self-contained literary values, not its cultural significance.

There was also hidden in this approach an inadvertent patronising disdain of the pupils' own lives, which further distanced literature as art from cultural exploration:

> Throughout almost the whole period of formal education, therefore, the main task of English teaching must be to lay this foundation as well as possible – to ensure that all children gain the widest possible acquaintance with forms of experience in language which are of finer quality than those to which they are exposed in the street and the home. (Whitehead, 1969, p. 28)

The refusal to see literature as exploring cultures has lingered and is more recently echoed in an HMI account of poetry, which is in other ways intellectually cogent: *Teaching Poetry in the Secondary School*. Of course we are moved by the use of Ted Hughes' phrase 'the vital signature of a human being' (HMI, 1987, p. 29), and of course we agree that by studying poetry pupils 'can themselves begin to make sense of the world in which we live' (ibid. p. 33). However, the whole of that booklet exists above and beyond any specific cultural world, and poetry, despite the talk of life, becomes disembodied and a-cultural, existing only as an expression of the personal inner life and blind to faith, ethnicity, environment, economics and culture.

The personal growth or reaction model for education in the arts has rejected not only 'culture', as every meeting with an art is a one-night stand, but rejected also an interest in the artistic work-techniques, biography, economics, individual skills and social pressure that lead to the manifestation of art. The rejection of the critical biography and the mechanics of art creates an unintended curriculum message that works of art come fully formed from the creator, like the packaged vegetables of the supermarket, without a touch of the earth in which they were grown. As Raymond Williams wrote:

> Indeed it is extraordinary how most modern critical theory is a theory of consumption. The extraordinary neglect of the subject of production in modern academic literary thought is attributable to this notion of literature as an object and as existing in the past. (Williams, 1977)

Many examples of arts in schools have been cut off from their roots – culturally, economically and technically. This makes cross-cultural arts considerably harder to plan in a curriculum. If a school has removed the artificer from the artefact, the writer from the written, and the production from the product, the cultural forces that created Indian Mogul painting, Chinese poetry or African sculpture are invisible, and an English course will 'use material' only if it immediately impacts on the pupil's experience, and without using the art to understand the culture that produced it.

The problem created can be seen in the choice of literature offered to pupils. The heritage model is easy to mock – 'from Malory to T.S. Eliot'. The opening up and reviewing of this canon came from the presence of the pupils. For instance, the sensitive realisation of the perception of working-class pupils led to the classroom 'use' of northern, sixties 'working-class' novelists. The presence of pupils of Caribbean background led to the classroom use of Caribbean poetry and narrative (see Marland, 1978). Thus, if there was no pupil-representation, there was no art form! The effect was to introduce some new work but to exclude huge swathes of genre and period.

In destroying the 'cultural heritage' justification for the teaching of the arts, theorists removed the possibility of the arts having a place in the curriculum for 'cultural exchange' or 'cultural diversity'.

Opposed to this dominant personal growth model is the concept so well put by the black feminist writer Audre Lorde, who declares that the antipathetic fears of society ('racism, sexism, ageism, homophobia') result from:

> An inability to recognise the notion of difference as a dynamic human force which is enriching rather than threatening to defined self. (Lorde, quoted in Christian, 1985, p. 208)

In many ways, curriculum planning would be easier if the very tradition of 'English' as a school course did not exist, and 'literature', as in

Ngugi's department at Nairobi, was the conceptual curriculum framework. Then the literature curriculum could be planned as an art to be explored as part not only of the individual's imaginative literary growth but also of a pupil's understanding of cultures.

Literature and cultures

The choice of literature for study serves the curriculum aims of self-understanding, stimulus for the pupil's writing, language exploration, as an art form, and as a cultural exploration. There is a sense in which the core of a school's curriculum, and one encouraged by Section 1 of the 1988 Act, is to be found in the notion enunciated by Alexander Pope two hundred and fifty years ago, 'The proper study of mankind is man'. Translated into a modern curriculum aim: the key study for our pupils is the world's humanity, its peoples, their languages, their verbal arts, their media and the celebration of their cultures in their literatures.

Thus the study of literature needs planning across the curriculum of the school, as part of courses in humanities, languages and arts, as well as in the 'English' course. In that, literature should be studied with a different prime focus at different times, for example the focus may be: thematic, genre, author or cultural.

The overall curriculum plan of the English course would contain a matrix of genre, culture and period. (It is important not to fall into the trap of treating non-European literary traditions as if they had no past or historical evolution.) This matrix would be both a planning device and checklist.

The modules of work would include agreed ones with a cultural focus, for example Chinese, Pacific, Anglo-Saxon (e.g. Crossley-Holland's *Beowulf*, 1987), South Asian. In these the curriculum aim would be to understand the literary culture of a section of the world. It would indeed have something of the old academic approach, in that the pieces would be included partly because they were representative. Of course not all cultures could be explored, but those chosen would be used also to remind pupils of others not chosen. James Banks, the American educator, recommends that the literature curriculum should address the question:

> How does the fiction and other literary works by American ethnic authors reveal characteristics of their cultures? (Banks, 1979, p. 34)

One placing, with which we are most familiar, is within those themes or genres studied for reasons other than those of intercultural exploration. We are used to including short stories by Irish, American or Caribbean writers, but there should be a deliberate plan to include stories from other cultures. I should recommend, for instance, Maori writing such as J.C. Sturm's 'First Native and Pink Pig' (1982) or Patricia Grace's 'Fishing'(1987); South Asian stories as collected by Ranjana Ash (1980) or Madhu Bhinda (1991); some of the great flowering of Singapore writing such as Catherine Lim's 'The Jade Pendant' (1978) or from her other volumes (1980, 1982, 1987) or collected by Robert Yeo (1978), such as S. Rajaratuam's 'The Tiger'; or the Fijian author Subramani (1988); or *Jesus is Indian* by the Asian South African (now living in Yorkshire) Agnes Sam (1989).

Efforts should be made to include cultural forms which are unfamiliar. Most examples of African, Asian or Caribbean writing that have been read in schools are notably literatures using the forms, especially the short story, of the Anglo-European pattern. The experience is black but the form is white. We should also include the Japanese Noh play (for example *The Hundred Nights* and *Kagekiyo* by Seami Motokiyo, or *The Cormorant Fisher* by Enami no Sayemon), Greek drama of the classical period, the Haiku (Henderson, 1967), medieval European poetry and drama, Indian traditional legends. Thus genre can be an organising principle.

So too can a culture, a country or a region, for example the fiction of Latin America, African poetry, Pacific stories, or South-East Asian fiction. The Commonwealth could be a suitable organising idea to meet the criteria of literature 'from other countries and cultures'.

Earlier periods of the literature of the UK should also be included. For instance the Elizabethan play, the eighteenth-century couplet and the nineteenth-century novel. A black British pupil who is denied access to Beowulf, Shakespeare, Crabbe and Pope is being as badly treated as a white monolingual anglophone who is deprived access to Asian, Pacific or Chinese literature.

Language and English

There is clearly no possibility of considering a subject or a course called 'English' in a school without considering language. The language of English is important for the learning of all, for the bilingual students (who make up a significant section of the UK pupil roll), the monolingual anglophones, and of all who are thinking about and responding to the *diversity* of language.

Everyone argues that developing the use and understanding of the English language is a key part of the curriculum of British schools. What is less clearly thought out is the relationship of this to *cultural* understanding. Yet, as a distinguished linguist and historian of black language put it: 'to speak a language means more than to use a certain morphology and syntax; it means to support the whole weight of a culture and civilisation' (Fanon, 1970, p. 13). This must relate a study of language to that of cultures.

If it is accepted that 'to acquire and use a foreign language is to enter another way of life, another rationality, another mode of behaviour' and 'the educational value of foreign language teaching . . . depends crucially on cultural studies' (Byram, 1988, p. 17), it must be equally true of the study of the varieties of English.

The following argues the cultural/linguistic relationship and has substantial implications for the teachers of languages other than English and of the course 'English':

> Language and language variety – dialect or sociolect – is one of the overt signs of cultural identity in daily life. People use language with varying degrees of self-awareness to signal their social identity, and the choice of a particular variety for teaching purposes is significant for the learners' self-projection to native speakers and for his or her understanding of native speakers' cultural and ethnic identity. (ibid. p. 21)

One way of meeting the curriculum challenge is put by James Banks. In his outline of ethnic studies, he suggests that the secondary school course Communication or Language Arts, which is the nearest to our English course, should address the following questions:

> How does the language of an ethnic group express and reflect its values and culture? What can we learn about an ethnic group by studying its symbols and communication styles, both verbal and non-verbal? (Banks, 1979, p. 34)

This in its turn must be related to the linguistic diversity of Britain and yet we can hardly say that we have a national policy towards bilingualism as, say, Canada, Sweden or a number of German *Länder* do (see Marland, 1987). The would-be forward-looking approaches of the Swann Report when speaking of mother tongues, commended 'language maintenance' (DES, 1985, p. 406). The very phrase 'maintenance' is a give-away: a language to be 'maintained' is a language virtually lost. We have been extraordinarily weak in terms of the valuing of languages other than English – and this has ill-served our consideration of English itself.

More recently there has been welcome encouragement from the Prince of Wales for encouraging the linguistic strengths of members of minority ethnic communities in the United Kingdom:

> There is one other area which, it seems to me provides an impor-tant, hitherto untapped source of expertise. We have in the United Kingdom many ethnic minorities with their own strong cultural and linguistic identities. Naturally – and rightly – they are keen to preserve these. This concept of dual identity is as important for those on the Celtic fringes of the United Kingdom as it is for those who come from further afield. It seems such a waste for the rest of us not to take advantage of their knowledge of languages other than English, and to learn from them. (HRH The Prince of Wales, 1990, pp. 11–12)

The teaching of the use and understanding of the English language must be in a context in which seventy per cent of the world's popu-lation is bilingual, and in which 'standard' relates to very many other Englishes. The proportions of bilingual pupils in some parts of England are very high. Figures are detailed in the powerful but simply titled research report, *The Other Languages of England* (Linguistic Minorities Project, 1985). This shows that to be English is no longer necessarily to have English as one's first or strongest language. The figures are worth pondering; for instance, in 1981 proportions of bilingual pupils in five LEAs were: Bradford 17.8%, Coventry 14.4%, Haringey 30.7%, Peterborough 7.4%, Waltham Forest 18.8% (ibid. p. 336). However, as the General Editor's preface puts it: 'There is widespread ignorance of the most basic facts of linguistic diversity in Britain' (ibid. p. xii).

There is a great deal of understandable fear about the requirements of the National Curriculum after the Kingman (DES, 1988) and Cox Reports (DES, 1989b), in terms of specific *understanding* of how lan-guage works. Yet a consideration of cultural diversity without a consid-eration of how language works in those cultures is to avoid the heart of the language study. It is perhaps rare for a culture to maintain that its language embodies as much of its essence as a member of the Islamic faith does of Arabic. However, for everyone language is not merely a personal tool: it is a reflection of a culture and thus a way of understanding that culture.

Discussions about curriculum planning for knowledge about language become easily confused by the assumption that the *only* purpose of gaining such knowledge is to improve the pupil's own *use* of language. There is, though, a complementary aim: language is such an important and interesting aspect of human life that the educated person ought to know something of how it works, be able to consider examples of language in use and have informed views on examples of language. A sympathetic curiosity about the workings of language is surely a proper curriculum aim, and this attitude, knowledge and understanding would be a way of considering cultural diversity.

The first strong official statement came in the Swann Report, which proposed a major revolution in the French-dominated language curriculum:

> We believe that all schools should seek to foster amongst their pupils an awareness of the linguistic diversity of our society and a real understanding of the role and function of language in all its forms. (DES, 1985, p. 249)

The Cox Report, admitting that some rejected the conclusions of the Kingman Report recommending the teaching of knowledge about language, combines the two arguments:

> Two justifications for teaching pupils explicitly about language are, first, the positive effect on aspects of their use of language and secondly, the general value of such knowledge as an important part of their understanding of their social and cultural environment, since language has vital functions in the life of the individual and of society.
>
> Language is central to individual human development; human society is inconceivable without it. Therefore it is intrinsically interesting and worthy of study in its own right. There are important social implications of such knowledge. (DES, 1989b, 6.6-6.7)

A school planning a comprehensive approach to cultural diversity requires a clear curriculum aspect describing the *cultural understanding*, as well as the expressive and communicative, aims of knowledge about language.

Just as a proper curriculum contribution to cultural diversity from the literature and verbal arts aspect of the English curriculum needs to be related to a whole school arts policy, so the contribution of the language aspect of English should relate to the whole school languages policy. Languages other than English – in the past usually called Modern Languages and nine-tenths French – have been taught up to sixteen with little planned relationship to cultural aspects of the curriculum. The interaction of English with other languages in the curriculum has been undervalued. The Prince of Wales argued it well:

> Learning foreign languages provides heightened awareness of one's own culture and civilisation. Goethe, that great German poet, put it very concisely: 'Wer fremde Sprach nicht kennt, weiss nichts von seiner eigenen' (those who know no foreign languages know nothing of their own). (HRH Prince of Wales, 1990, p. 5)

He reminded us that 'languages are inseparable from their culture' (ibid. p. 4). There is a real sense in which all languages are a key manifestation of the cultures they express, and the 'Englishes' of the world are significant expressions of their cultures. As one linguistic historian has said:

> Historical events usually have linguistic as well as political and social results. (Burchfield, 1985, p. 11)

Hence George Steiner's converse analysis: 'History, in the human sense, is a language net cast backwards'!

Our attitude to cultures is closely related to our attitude to their languages, especially to different versions of English. Labov has shown how USA black English was wrongly seen as illogical, and thus the culture it embodied further denied status. A linguistic study of pidgins and Creoles claimed:

> For most of their history, pidgins and creoles have been severely misunderstood by layman and experts alike. These everyday prejudices have exercised a very considerable influence on linguistic thought and continue to be reflected in some scientific writings. (Mühlhäusler, 1986, p. 277)

What could be called ill-informed popular linguistic theory (for there is always an implicit theory even in those with no formal education about language) amplifies prejudice: the pronunciation of words with a silent 't' ('butter') is called 'lazy'; a grammar not requiring subject/object distinctions 'lacking'; and certain ways of expressing negatives 'illogical'.

The study of human life, history, cultures, societies, must include the study of language. The strength of people's attachment to their language can be seen in Belgium and in the rejection of Afrikaans as the linguistic expression of oppression in the Soweto rising of 1976; and many of the pressures between peoples in Eastern Europe have linguistic manifestations.

The multilingual dimension of multicultural education has been comparatively little debated in the profession, and the inclusion within that of the implication for consideration of and knowledge about the versions of English still less. Kingman, Cox and the Statutory Orders include knowledge about language and the varieties of English but they have started only after years of a curriculum vacuum.

There has been a fear of learning *about* from generations of teachers still struggling out of their memories of parsing and clause analysis of their schooldays, and using an anti 'formal grammar' line to object to all technical response to language, including register, structure, aspects of vocabulary, and the semantic and syntactical varieties of English. Currently teachers of dance, craft, design and technology, and 'modern languages' appear to me to be most at ease in bringing techniques and analysis appropriately into the curriculum flow, but teachers of English are less willing. The sensible notion that you learn most by doing has been misunderstood and used to drive out the complementary fact that you learn something by clear analytic understanding. It is ironic that, for instance, mathematics, information technology and sex education have moved towards greater intellectual analysis when the teaching of the English language continues without pondering why things are as they are.

Part of the study of the English language, therefore, (whether in the course 'English' or the course 'languages') should be the varieties of English. Cox and the NCC suggest we study the vocabulary and syntax of dialects. Indeed, the NCC emphasis on 'standard English' is logically not possible without understanding a little of *how* Englishes differ. For instance, just how is the following different from 'standard'. An old Suffolk woman was asked some years ago what she thought of the recently appointed schoolmistress who came from the Shires:

> 'O, har be a bumptious botty bitch, har oon't speak t' th' loikes o' we.' (Claxton, 1968, p. 11)

A major aspect of cultural diversity is given by the new range of the Englishes of the world. Does our curriculum in language or in literature accept the variety?

The emergence of English as a global phenomenon – as either a first, second or foreign language – has recently inspired the idea that we should talk not of English, but of many Englishes, especially in the Third World countries where the use of English is no longer part of the colonial legacy, but the result of decisions made since independence. (McCrum *et al.* 1986, p. 20)

Cox specifically recommends that pupils should be able:

to talk explicitly about: regional and social variation in English accents and dialects; and attitudes to such variations. (DES, 1989b, 6.19)

and points out, very relevantly to our concern:

A sensitivity to this type of variation should contribute towards pupils becoming more tolerant of linguistic diversity, more aware of the richness it can provide and more able to cope with problems of communication. (ibid.)

This study is now required by the National Curriculum (for example DES, 1990, p. 26). This requires the inclusion in the curriculum of analytic concepts and terms. Without an agreed metalanguage, analytic approach and conceptual grasp it is not possible to discuss language. If you cannot discuss language you cannot discuss culture.

The way the Norman-French terms became and remain the vocabulary of the upper strata of our society can be explored by pupils:

calf	veal
sheep	mutton
pig	pork

and the cooking terms of roast, boil, fry. Why are many of the most senior posts worded in a French way: Director General or Attorney General and not phrased in the English word-order of General Director?

A semantic study of English is a study of society and its cultures. The registers of Anglo-Saxon and Latin remain (for example catty and feline, death and mortality, help and aid).

The relationship between the English language and cultural diversity grows out of an understanding, however limited, of language and culture. How does the vocabulary carry associations? How is it that there are so many more words for a woman judged to be sexually loose than a man? That 'housewife' has degenerated to 'huzzy'?

The secularisation of religious terminology is a cultural phenomenon in Europe as cell, rubric, enthusiasm and recluse still show. Rural vocabulary has degenerated as the town took over, with civil and urbane taking higher status, and rustic, lout, boor and bumpkin becoming terms of abuse. (For a detailed discussion see Hughes, 1988.)

The language curriculum should look beyond the cultures of the UK to the other Englishes of the world (some of which, of course, are spoken in the UK as well). Comparisons can be made between varieties of English. The linguistic features of Creole languages are interesting to study because of what they tell us about Caribbean culture as well as about the grammatical varieties of language. In the Creoles which use English vocabulary, the grammatical patterns are easier for us to study than in languages which do not use English vocabulary. The Creoles also demonstrate the conflict between the European masters and the African slaves: the very language is a symbol of that conflict. After Africans from Western and Southern Africa, who spoke languages of the Niger-Congo family, were taken to the Caribbean:

> their mother tongues were suppressed through a system of dividing the speakers of the same languages . . . and a related system of punishments for using African languages including death, the whip, the chain-gang etc. Despite this, the Africans preserved the common core from their related African mother tongues and expressed these grammatical relationships, using the only vocabulary permissible within their respective slave societies, i.e. European language vocabulary. (Dalphinis, 1985, p. 1)

The following two examples show the grammatical structure retained in modern English-vocabulary Creole from the original African language:

Predicative adjective

The language Ewe has the phrase 'è bija', which would be literally translated as 'it red'. This is indeed the English-vocabulary Creole form, and would translate into standard English as 'it is red'. Thus Creole retains the African grammatical structure which does not require the verb 'to be' (ibid. p. 8).

Indication of plural

The use of a plural marker after a noun in Creoles can be traced from, for example, the African language Mandinka to an English-vocabulary Creole. In Mandinka the phrase 'jòng o lu' is literally 'slave the (plural)', which would be translated into standard English as 'the slaves'.

Parallel to that grammatical form and echoing its structure is the Creole 'di man dem', in which 'man' is indicated as being plural by the affix 'dem'. That is literally 'the man (plural)', as in Mandinka, which would be translated into standard English as 'the men' (ibid. p. 9).

In both cases the African syntax pattern has been given a continued life in the Creole.

There are many opportunities for studying the grammar of Creoles and comparing it with English and other languages. For instance, Francine Harper makes the interesting point that Jamaican Creole grammar 'has fewer redundancies' than standard English (Harper, 1979, p. 16).

Our work in schools has suffered from what I call a diversity of specialists: reading, linguistics, modern languages, remedial, English as a second language, mother tongue, information-handling skills, librarians. To produce a synthesis for the pupil is extremely difficult. We need an over-arching approach to language, growing out of and supported by specialisms, not trapped by them. This means a whole school language curriculum across the courses, and relating closely to the curriculum aims towards cultural diversity. Understanding language is both an aid to one's own use of language and a tool for exploring and understanding cultures.

Conclusion

Devising a school curriculum to meet the requirements of Section 1 of the Education Reform Act 1988, to incorporate the National Curriculum and to meet the school governors' aims for the school, requires 'English' to be both school-wide and a course, both of which should include verbal arts and language. The aims of the literature aspect of the curriculum must be for personal growth and imaginative experience as well as for cultural exploration, just as the language aspect must include these for the individual's own communication and to enable pupils better to understand the cultural range of the world. Coherent curriculum planning is required in each school in order to offer 'English for cultural diversity'.

References and bibliography

Allison, B. (1972) *Art Education and Teaching about the Art of Asia, Africa and Latin America*. Education Unit, Voluntary Committee on Overseas Aid Development
   (1980) The relationship between child arts and their cultural foundations. *Journal of Aesthetic Education*, 15, 3, July
   (1985) Cultural dimensions of art and design. *Studies in Design Education Craft and Technology*, 4, 3
   (1987) The training of specialist art and design teachers. *Studies in Design Education Craft and Technology*, 19, 2
   (1988) Art in context. *Journal of Art and Design Education*, 7, 2
Allison, B., Enscombe, M. and Toye, C. (1985) *Art and Design in a Multicultural Society: A Survey of Policy and Practice*. Centre of Postgraduate Studies, Leicester Polytechnic
Arts Council of Great Britain. (1989) *Towards Cultural Diversity*. ACGB
Arts in Schools Project Team. (1990) *The Arts 5–16: A Curriculum Framework*. Oliver & Boyd
Ash, R. (1980) *Short Stories from India, Pakistan and Bangladesh*. Harrap
Banks, J.A. (1979) *Teaching Strategies for Ethnic Studies*. Boston: Allyn & Bacon
Beier, U. (1986) *African Poetry*. Cambridge University Press
Best, D. (1986) Understanding the arts of other cultures. *Journal of Art and Design Education*, 5, 1 & 2
Bhinda, M. (1991) *South Asian Stories*. Longman
   (forthcoming) *South Pacific Stories and Poems*. Longman
Britten, B. (1964) *On Receiving the First Aspen Award*. Faber & Faber
Burchfield, R. (1985) *The English Language*. Oxford University Press
Byram, M. (1988) Foreign language education and cultural studies. *Language Culture and Curriculum*, 1, 1, Spring
Christian, B. (1985) *Black Feminist Criticism: Perspectives on Black Women Writers*. The *Athene* Series, Pergamon Press
Claxton, A.O.D. (1968) *The Suffolk Dialect in the Twentieth Century*. Ipswich: Norman Adlard & Co.
Crossley-Holland, K. (1987) *Beowulf*. Boydell Press
Dabydeen, D. (ed.) (1985) *The Black Presence in English Literature*. Manchester University Press
Dalphinis, M. (1985) *Caribbean and African Languages: Social History, Languages, Literature and Education*. Karia Press
Department of Education and Science. (1975) *A Language for Life* (Bullock Report). HMSO

(1985) *Education for All* (Swann Report). HMSO

(1988) *Report of the Committee of Inquiry into the Teaching of English Language* (Kingman Report). HMSO

(1989a) *The Education Reform Act 1988: The School Curriculum and Assessment* (Circular 5.89). HMSO

(1989b) *English for Ages 5 to 16* (Cox Report). HMSO

(1990) *English in the National Curriculum* (No. 2). HMSO

Dixon, J. (1987) *Growth Through English*. National Association for the Teaching of English

Education Reform Act 1988

Fanon, F. (1970) *Black Skin, White Masks*. Paladin

Garson, S. *et al*. (1989) *World Languages Project*. Hodder & Stoughton

Gates, H.L. Jr. (1984) *Black Literature and Literary Theory*. Routledge

Grace, P. (1987) 'Fishing'. In *Electric City and Other Stories*. Penguin
  (1988) *Matuwhenua, The Moon Sleeper*. Women's Press

Harper, F. (1979) Language and reality. *Roots*, 2

Heath, R.B. (1990) *Trade Winds: Poetry in English for Different Cultures*. Longman

Henderson, H.G. (1967) *Haiku in English*. Rutland

Her Majesty's Inspectorate. (1987) *Teaching Poetry in the Secondary School*. HMSO

Holbrook, D. (1961) *English for Maturity*. Cambridge University Press

HRH The Prince of Wales. (1990) Foreign languages for the new Europe. Typescript of an address given to the Royal Society for the Arts

Hughes, G. (1988) *Words in Time: A Social History of the English Vocabulary*. Basil Blackwell

Lim, C. (1978) 'The Jade Pendant'. In *Little Ironies: Stories from Singapore*. Singapore: Heinemann Asia
  (1980) *Or Else, The Lightning God and Other Stories*. Singapore: Heinemann Asia
  (1982) *The Serpent's Tooth*. Times International Books
  (1987) *The Shadow of A Shadow of A Dream: Love Stories of Singapore*. Singapore: Heinemann Asia

Linguistic Minorities Project. (1985) *The Other Languages of England*. LMT

McCrum, R. *et al*. (1986) *The Story of English*. BBC Publications

Marland, M. (ed.) (1978) *Caribbean Stories*. Longman
  (1987) *Multi-lingual Britain: The Educational Challenge*. Centre for Information on Language Teaching
  (1989) Arts, cultures and the curriculum. *Multicultural Teaching*, 8, 1, Autumn

Mason, R. (1988) *Art Education and Multiculturalism*. Croom Helm

Mühlhäusler, P. (1986) *Pidgin and Creole Linguistics*. Basil Blackwell

Nandan, S. (1985) *Voices in the River*. Vision International Publishers

Naveh, J. (1975) *Origins of the Alphabet*. Cassell

Niven, A. (ed.) (1987) *Under Another Sky*. Carcanet Press

Owusu, K. (1986) *The Struggle for Black Arts in Britain*. Comedia Publishing

(1986) *Storms of the Heart*. Camden Press

Price-Williams, D. (1986) Cross-cultural studies. In B.M. Foss (ed.) *New Horizons in Psychology 1*. Penguin

Rajaratuam, S. (1978) 'The Tiger'. In R. Yeo *Singapore Short Stories 1*. Singapore: Heinemann Asia

Richards, I.A. (1929) *Practical Criticism*. Routledge

Sam, A. (1989) *Jesus is Indian*. Women's Press

School Examinations and Assessment Council. (1990) *GCSE English Criteria*. SEAC

Sturm, J.C. (1982) 'First Native and Pink Pig'. In W. Ihimaera and D.S. Long (eds.) *Into the World of Light: An Anthology of Maori Writing*. Heinemann

Subramani. (1988) *The Fantasy Eaters*. Three Continents Press

Sutcliffe, D. and Wong, A. (eds.) (1986) *Language of the Black Experience*. Basil Blackwell

Tagore, R. (1988) *The World is Beautiful: A Collection for Young People*. The Tagore Centre

Tate, C. (ed.) (1985) *Black Women Writers at Work*. Oldcastle Books

Thaman, K.H. (1974) *You, The Choice of My Parents*. Fiji: Mana Publications

Thompson, D. (1978) *Distant Voices*. Heinemann

The Times Educational Supplement. (1990) 15 June

Welch, J. (1989) *Stories from Asia*. Oxford University Press

Wendt, A. (ed.) (1980) *Lali, A Pacific Anthology*. Longman Paul

Whitehead, F. (1969) Why teach English? In D. Thompson (ed.) *Directions in the Teaching of English*. Cambridge University Press

Williams, R. (1977) Literature in society. In H. Schiff (ed.) *Contemporary Approach to English Studies*. English Association

Yeo, R. (ed.) (1978) *Singapore Short Stories 1*. Singapore: Heinemann Asia

Chapter 10

History and the Challenge of Multicultural Education

John Fines

Why teach history?

As I write, I think about what is going on around the world. Azeris are massacring Armenians, and vice versa; Bulgarians want to deny the Turkish minority their rights; Romania is struggling to face up to its Hungarian and German populations; in France anti-Arab racism is rampant; in South America, the Indian tribes continue to be wiped out on a scale that makes Europe's holocaust look small. I recall the time I spent in an Aboriginal quarter of Sydney more than a year ago.

Why teach history? All these situations are capable of some sort of historical explanation, but can learning about them do any good? Surely it was the teaching of history in Northern Ireland that did most to establish the stereotypes on which hatred and violence have fed. Is it not the greatest arrogance in the world to imagine that history teachers can actually do some good?

Maybe we must consider the matter. There are schools of thought about this. Perhaps the prime responsibility that is placed at history's door in education is that of reminding people about the past, and thereby warning them about man's potential in the future. This function is in part noble, for it insists that we never forget what people have done to each other simply because we don't want them to behave that way in the future. Thus when we record the actions of Nazi war criminals we proclaim to all the truth that you cannot hide from history: Beware, your sins will find you out.

Clearly this function is an important one. When we know of people who stand at school gates delivering pamphlets that aim to show that the Holocaust never happened, we *must* move, and although I would personally find it very hard to agree with the proposition that there are things in history that all children should know (since that would mean shouldering out a host of other things that might prove in the end more important), I could hardly fail to hold up my hand for the teaching of the Holocaust.

And yet, and yet, as the Yanomami choke their way to death in the wake of the gold-hungry invasion of their territory, I wonder at the figure given of twenty million Indians dead as a result of white expansion in Latin America. Should we not be teaching about *that*?

A second function for history that has been seen to be important is in the provision of role models for depressed or oppressed groups. History is indeed full of such examples: Mary Seacole has lived in hundreds of classrooms in the last decade and has continued her good work way beyond her own life span. There are others to be found, and one of the main suggestions of this chapter is that we should continue to hunt through the archives using the new lenses which can see what has been missed.

And yet are we looking for the right things when we search for people who were successful in white society against all the odds? Will this not produce conformist, assimilationist heroes? Is it not those who struggled against the cultural pressures, the social and economic blights, the sniffy hauteur of those who thought themselves heirs to the kingdom that we should put before the children? At least the children deserve a choice.

A third possibility which seems much favoured is to establish a consciousness of a group within the larger society in the past. The message 'we have been here longer than you think, and we have known ourselves, and kept ourselves in times past when it was much harder' is in many various ways a rich one. There are problems here too, for I think that the simple recording of black presence can be merely an antiquarian activity that says nothing and therefore shames itself.

However, there are plenty of occasions when one can feel the power. I recall teaching on the south coast a class of top juniors with just one black girl in it. We were doing a local history topic and I had dug up heaps of resources, including a record of a ship being beached in 1555 just half a mile from where the classroom was now. A pirate couldn't quite get her home and had to run her ashore, and so the local owner of the rights stepped in and an enquiry took place. In the enquiry the pirate declared that when he had taken her there was nothing aboard 'but negurs'. Although all the children were embarrassed by this, I asked them to look more closely at the evidence and read its meaning. If there were 'negurs' aboard when he took it and he beached it as an empty ship, what had happened in between? It took ages, and a mounting sense of shock, to realise the appalling truth that he had thrown the lot overboard to drown in order to get his prize home.

Several weeks later we came across an entry in the churchwardens' accounts about a collection taken up to buy out an Englishman who had been taken by the Barbary pirates. The black girl looked puzzled for a while, and then asked for confirmation: 'Do you mean that Africans came here, to these coasts, and took white men slaves?' She could hardly believe her ears, nor could she restrain a little smile of revenge.

The resources are everywhere, waiting for us to pick them up; we need only to ask the right questions and look in the right places. Every record office, every local collection in every public library in the land contains materials.

The National Curriculum

But into what kind of a context will all this potential work fit?

One of the very basic positions of the National Curriculum in relation to history has been a determined attempt to pull back the content to British history, and to see British history as some kind of machine for assimilation. This in itself is worrying enough, but when you add to it a determination to have a purely content base in the first instance, and to eschew skills and concepts, then the position looks a great deal worse. Without some articulated view of the nature of imperialism, for example, and some notion of how power works in society, how are children to begin to interpret these reams of materials and begin to see a use for them?

In a sense, the push that lies behind the National Curriculum History Working Group involves an understanding that history is a deeply political study and that political standpoints must eventually be taken and so they want the classic definition of 'history with the politics left out'. For this reason they tried to exclude much of the twentieth-century warfare that requires one to take up a point of view in order to study it.

The National Curriculum devotes twenty-five lines to multicultural education, attempting to defend the proposition that the history of Britain is the history of the growth of a nation from many cultures. So that is all right. To be fair, in the Final Report a number of options were put into Key Stages 3 and 4 that would direct pupils' attention to Europe, the wider world and the Americas, but they have retained a heavy British emphasis, with a study of the Empire at its 'zenith', and the Secretary of State in his response has smartly collapsed the wider world and the Americas together. Equally he has suggested that the studies at Key Stage 4 should be more broad and general, leaving many pupils who do not take the full GCSE course with no chance to take such useful courses as 'India and Pakistan 1930–1964' or 'Africa South of the Sahara'. At the time of writing, the NCC is taking advice on the Secretary of State's response to the Final Report, and one hopes that many respondents will note how little attention is given to the real issues of Britain today.

'Immigration' is listed as one topic in 'Britain and the Twentieth Century' in Key Stage 4, but one notes that the much braver Welsh Report has 'Migration and Emigration' as a major option as early as Key Stage 3. The committees seem to have seen English and Welsh children as largely white and unproblematic (and, of course, mainly boys). They have not addressed the pupil who feels both Muslim and British, or who looks forward to a holiday in Bangladesh as a return home, and who sees his or her eating and dressing habits as infinitely more rational then those the school promotes.

It is also clear that the working group sees thinking as something that the pupils will do *after* learning all this information. Unless pupils understand what the learning is for, and where it is tending, they will not do it, and teachers will not have the support of parents and users of the pupils' qualifications in the long run. Only the learners can do the learning, and they need to see exactly how that learning relates to themselves and to their needs.

We cannot answer these with simple responses such as those offered by the National Curriculum Working Group – the problems are too great and too complex. We have a great deal to do if we are to move to a position where our schools are truly serving the needs of today, and to diminish the prospect of racial animosities on the scale that exist in other countries, such as those mentioned at the beginning of this chapter.

History and morality

In searching for a reason for teaching a kind of history that demands thought, the idea of moral justification arises. To admit to such a function leads to trouble whatever the shade of opinion dominant at the time.

No kind of history can be 'balanced' or 'germ-free' in a way that allows us to take a dispassionate position. Nowadays we tend to reject the moral stance as wishy-washy liberalism, rather than the correct, committed position-taking of my juniors, who clearly want to *do* something with their history.

The rejection of liberalism is understandable. Since the outcome of human action is usually quite dreadful, is it not wise to suspect that this was intended by the apparently liberal governors in the first place? If people really did mean to do well by others, surely there should be some signs that things are getting better? Since they are in fact getting ever worse, it suggests that even humanitarians are working in their own interests or those of their class. Hence it is that the helpless get worse damaged and the so-called helpers continue to flourish.

There is a lot to be said for such a gloomy view – especially when we examine the history of racism. Surely the main duty of the historian in this sphere is not to preach but to record, to make sure the horrors of the past, the insults to humanity – slavery, the Holocaust – are not forgotten but are placed before an unwilling public's eyes, to be grieved over.

It is like building a war memorial, stone by stone, a duty of the survivors to remind the future of the suffering of the past and, to a degree, to lay blame where it should be placed. And in examining our reasons for building such a monument, we must ask ourselves what we expect to happen when we have built it. We have built war memorials before and written on them all 'never again' but, somehow, that has not worked. We need in this matter not just the will to do well, but an understanding of how evil came to happen in the first place.

We must find some way of linking the past with the future and discovering the springs of action in history education.

Suspending suspicion – settlers and Aborigines

Perhaps it would help us to understand how evil happens if we were to suspend our suspicion for a while. Suppose we believe that those who set out to do well really do have just that in the centre of their minds, and yet when they fail, what then? If we can find out how good will fails, we will have learned something.

I can illustrate what I mean by using some work of my own in which I set out to find something of what went wrong between the settlers and Aborigines in Australia. I had quite a few useful resources, mainly letters from a missionary who set out to work for the people of Australia and ended up having a huge row with his missionary society and almost everyone else. I asked not just 'What went wrong?' but also 'At what moment did the first thing go wrong?'

We worked through drama, discussion and widespread reading. I must emphasise that in my work I encourage children to think their way towards the beginning of answers to questions posed. Thus, we developed lessons around *their* ideas – some naive, some shocking, but demonstrating a struggle to find useful answers to these questions.

One group wondered if the English had gone out looking for idealised 'noble savages' and had been disappointed in what they found. Others wondered if the white settlers had blamed the Aborigines for their inability to resist the seeds of disaster the white people had brought with them: disease and social problems such as squalor, drunkenness and dependence. I do not mean that the pupils in my class saw the Aborigines as particularly weak or prone to squalor, only that they tried to empathise not only with the Aborigines but also with the settlers and imagine their reactions as the problems built up around them.

Another group compared the different attitudes of the settlers and the Aborigines to property – in which the white people saw their liberty as dependent on the preservation of individual property rights and the Aborigines had no such ideas. Owning everything in common, they saw nothing wrong in taking say, an axe, while the whites believed this to be a hostile act.

In these ways they began to build up a vision of how racism began. Their thoughts were not those of careless or prejudiced people and I believe that they will remember these lessons much better than a conventional session in which I simply taught them what racism is and why it is wrong.

Of all the ideas that came up, the most significant was about the religious goals of the missionaries and settlers. They saw that the missionaries intended to convert the Aborigines into the equivalent of 'good children' and, being very experienced at being children, the class quickly saw the dangers and stupidity of this view. Children, after all, grow up and can disappoint adults.

These ideas seem to me to share two qualities: they are simple and naive and yet they are also attempts at an explanation that promotes understanding of the problem. Here, the learner was not being hectored about the wickedness of the past, but was in a position to invent explanations that promoted thought.

Resources

Now I would like to introduce the reader to the sorts of teaching resources I intend to use in future lessons. They are given in some detail because I think they exemplify rather well the position I am trying to establish in this chapter and they demonstrate that there are ample resources waiting for the teacher who wishes to engage in this sort of work.

An African prince

The first concerns one James Albert Ukawsaw Gronniosaw, an African prince. I had never heard of him until I saw his *Narrative* in a dealer's catalogue. It was once clearly a popular piece of reading. It had first appeared in Bath in about 1770, with an introduction by Walter Shirley (ob. 1786), cousin of Selina Hastings, Countess of Huntington, and a strong Calvinist and hymnwriter. There were many later editions (one in Welsh in 1779). Mine is dated 1840.

The introduction states that it was first 'committed to paper by the elegant pen of a young lady of the town of Leominster' with no intention to print, but its emphasis on Christianity and fortitude was such that it had an appeal to Calvinists, who ensured that it was eventually published.

Born in Bornu in what is now northern Nigeria, James Albert was the grandson of a king. He paints a picture of himself as introspective and anxious, often 'lost in wonder at the work of creation' and enquiring who was the 'Man of Power' who lived beyond the skies.

Indeed, he asked so many questions ('Who was the first man? Who made the first cow, the first lion . . .?') that his family thought him mad. When a trader from the Gold Coast offered to take him for a holiday to his home, they hastily agreed.

Being such a misfit makes James Albert a subject for sympathy, as does his anxiety when the travellers build rings of fire around their encampment to keep out lions. The merchant's companion hated James Albert and kept suggesting that he should be dropped, Joseph-like, into a deep pit, or drowned in a river. It seems that a process of softening up was happening – these were clever slavers, who planned to make their captive leap into slavery.

When they reached the Gold Coast, his rich golden ornaments were polished up and he was sent to see the king who, he was told, planned to execute him personally because he was suspected of being a spy on behalf of his grandfather. In the event he was not executed but, so that he could not return home with the secrets of the Gold Coast, was sold into slavery instead.

After being turned down by a French slaver, because he was too small, he was taken aboard a Dutch ship, where he overheard his master and companion agreeing that if he were not sold, he should be thrown overboard. To save himself, he rushed to the captain and cried, 'Father, save me.' The captain did so – giving two yards of check cloth for him.

He claims to have been devoted to his owner: 'my only pleasure was to serve him well'. He saw the captain's lips move as he read and thought he must be talking to the book, so the book must have the power to talk to him. But when he put his ear close to a page he heard nothing. 'This thought immediately presented itself to me, that everybody and everything despised me because I was black.'

The ship reached Barbados and James Albert was sold first to a young man from New York and then, eventually, to a minister, who taught him to pray. James Albert felt he was about to unravel the mystery of the 'Man of Power'.

He describes how he felt a sense of guilt and how, after reading Bunyan's *Holy War* and other religious books, he remained in a state of despair and attempted suicide. He found some peace in a favourite oak tree, which he used to visit 'whenever I was treated with ridicule and contempt'. Then one day as he prayed, he felt suddenly bathed in a most comforting light and longed to stay there for ever.

His master died suddenly, leaving him his freedom, and six years later he decided to go to England. 'I imagined all the inhabitants of that land were holy', since he had met English visitors like Whitfield and had read holy books written by Englishmen.

He was astonished, on landing at Portsmouth, to hear people cursing on all sides. He met a landlady of a pub, who said she was a Christian. He gave her his watch and £25 to look after, asking her to spend £6 on clothes and giving her a handsome looking-glass from Martinique as a reward. She bought the clothes, but kept the rest of the money. 'I thought it worse than Sodom, considering the great advantage they possessed.'

He took a stagecoach to London, where people charged him 7s. 6d. to show him the way to Whitfield's tabernacle. Safe at last, Whitfield found him a protector, one Betty, a silk weaver of Petticoat Lane. She took on his education and tried particularly to stop him from giving half-guineas to beggars. After a year-long trip to Holland, where thirty-eight Calvinist ministers heard him every Tuesday for seven weeks and authenticated his conversion, he married Betty and moved to Colchester in Essex.

Betty could have done well in London as a weaver, but James Albert writes of riots which he feared the weavers would make him join. These may have been the Wilkes disturbances of 1786.

They moved to Norwich, where sickness and poverty plagued them. When a daughter died both the Baptists and the Quakers refused to bury her. They eventually moved to Kidderminster. James Albert was too old and ill to work but the hard work of his wife and the charity of neighbours supported them.

Why this example?

I give an extensive review of the contents of this slight pamphlet for a number of reasons. Firstly, I think it is worth knowing about, yet it does not appear in any substantial way in literature – Peter Fryer provides an abstract in *Staying Power* (1984, pp. 89–91) and there is a brief account of his English residence in Shylon (1977, pp. 169–71).

Secondly, it shows that material *does* exist, and I think all teachers would value it. Thirdly, it speaks for itself. I believe, particularly with autobiographical materials, that they should be left to whisper their own message direct to the hearer, unimpeded by the historian or teacher's fumbling towards explanation and generalisation.

But, most of all, it raises issues that could be explored in classrooms. The example of James Albert partly explains how abused people come to give themselves up so readily to the control of their torturers: we can tell at once that other terrors have been used to make him not only amenable, but actually ready to run into the arms of the slavers to escape what he believes will be a worse fate. He is grateful to his masters and anxious to serve – which brings us to a second point. Servants do often serve with good will. This is often met with cruelty but it is a feature we should not forget when we come to add up where good will has gone, who put it into the system and why it failed.

The power of religion is never far from James Albert's account (although of course, some of this comes from the elegant pen of the lady from Leominster). What this shows all too well is that the white Calvinists saw James Albert as a 'poor heathen', a lost and sinful child struggling towards God. They delight in the missionary act and warm to the agonies of conversion, seeing him as a pleasingly vulnerable child who, because of good will, struggles to be 'good' for his mentors.

James Albert behaved as a very good child, but he made the mistake of believing that people would do what they said. He gives us the clearest view of his disappointments: though bevies of ministers listened to his story, though a woman of status and skill married him, he still, as a black man, felt the lash of poverty. In Colchester, when his first job ended and starvation lay ahead, he recalls how a farmhand refused him a job and then gave him four very large carrots to help feed his family until more charity came their way. Without charity, it seems, he would not have survived and yet, he notes, there was at least charity.

Jews in London's East End

Well over a century later, one woman observer watched the influx of Jews into London's East End. On 1 February 1895, when she and Sidney had finished their first book, Beatrice Webb wrote in her diary: 'The truth is, I want to give full play to whatever faculty I have for descriptive and dramatic work . . . I am sick to death of trying to put hideous facts into readable form' (Mackenzie, 1982, p. xvii). In July 1893 she had written: 'What is wanted in London is a body of persons who would make it their business to know thoroughly each district. . . London is so huge, and the poor are so helpless' (ibid. p. 89). She wanted to find out from the inside, and so became for a time a rent collector. She learned not just to pity what she saw and to seek remedies, she also began to feel an affinity, even an envy for their carelessness and generosity that in the midst of squalor and despair created moments of joviality and love that were missing in her own life.

On another occasion, having prepared herself with much care as a trouser finisher, a lady down on her luck and needing work, she visited the sweat-shops. The other women saw that her work was poor, but none the less looked after her in various ways:

> I have my cup of tea. The pale weary girl is munching her bread and butter.
> 'Won't you have some?' she says, pushing the papers towards me. 'No thank you,' I answer.
> 'Sure?' she says. And then, without more to-do, she lays a piece on my lap and turns away to avoid my thanks. A little bit of human kindness that goes to my heart and brings tears into my eyes. Work begins again. My friend has finished her trousers and is waiting for another pair. She covers her head with her hands and in her grey eyes there is an intense look of weariness, weariness of body and of

mind. Another pair is handed to her and she begins again. She is a quick worker but, work hard as she may, she cannot make much over 1*s*. a day. (ibid. pp. 248–9)

Beatrice's publication of material like this won her much acclaim; in her empathy for the subject she had steadily moved from straight reporting into a fictive (though truthful) presentation.

Her contribution to Charles Booth's survey on the arrival of the Jews begins unashamedly. 'Let us imagine ourselves on board a Hamburg boat steaming slowly up the Thames in the early hours of the morning.' She describes with a painter's care the men and women, and shows with quick subtle touches the effect of their background and experiences:

> You address them kindly, they gaze on you with silent suspicion; a coarse German sailor pushes his way amongst them with oaths and curses; they simply move apart without a murmur, and judging from their expression, without a resentful feeling; whilst the women pick up their ragged bundles out of the way of the intruder with an air of deprecating gentleness. (Booth, 1902)

She describes those meeting the boat and hints at their stories:

> Presently a boat rows briskly to the side of the vessel; seated in it is a young woman with a mock sealskin coat. She is chaffing the boatman in broken English, and shouts words of welcome and encouragement to the simple bewildered peasant who peers over the side of the vessel with two little ones clasped in either hand. Yes! that smartly dressed young lady is her daughter. Three years ago the father and the elder child left the quiet Polish village: a long interval of suspense, then a letter telling of an almost hopeless struggle; at last passage money, and here to-day the daughter with her bright warm clothes and cheery self-confidence – in a few hours the comfortably furnished home of a small wholesale orange dealer in Mitre Street, near to Petticoat Lane. (ibid.)

Not all faced happy receptions – for those lost souls with none to help them there were the eager touts, offering lodgings, onward tickets for America, taking what little they had and condemning them to the sweaters. The man from the Hebrew Ladies' Protective Society did his best to rescue unaccompanied girls, but most of the incomers were condemned to a life of bitter exploitation and maltreatment – like James Albert they found the holy city of liberal England strangely different from what they had expected.

We could follow Beatrice's account further, it is fascinating, and like James Albert's account would make an ideal source for children to use. It has detail, depth and texture: all the qualities that the brief skim over the surface of a textbook lacks. But it also has a deep sympathy and concern for its subject, and that is what I wanted to bring before you when I started this chapter.

Empathy

There has been much debate among history teachers in England in the past few years about empathy. Some have seen it as an examinable commodity whilst others have seen it as an intellectual and emotional capacity way beyond the grasp of mere schoolchildren. Yet it is clear that if we are to understand in any meaningful way how it was that things went wrong in the past, why they still go wrong for us today, then we must attempt to rethink other people's thoughts, we must try to see the world from *their* position in time and space and circumstance.

As we approach this tangled and thorny problem of teaching pupils about race relations, it seems to me that the empathetic understanding of particular experiences in the past has much to offer as a technique, particularly if we can use rich and detailed resources such as have been displayed here.

And I think something within me urges dispassion in this work so that we can think our thoughts without the pressure of nervousness about possibly getting it wrong, and so that we may look not just at stories of bad and wicked men oppressing others brutally, but also offer examples of those, the oppressed and the oppressors alike, who none the less showed that good will towards their fellow human beings which is, surely, what we all aim for in the end.

References

Booth, C. (rev. edn. 1902) *Life and Labour in London*. London
Department of Education and Science. (1990) National Curriculum History Working Group: *History for Ages 5 to 16: Proposals to the Secretary of State for Education and Science*. HMSO
Fryer, P. (1984) *Staying Power: The History of Black People in Britain*. Pluto Press
Gronniosaw, J.A.U. (1770) *Narrative*. Bath

Mackenzie, N. and J. (eds.) (1982) *The Diary of Beatrice Webb 1*. Virago/ LSE

Shylon, F. (1977) *Black People in Britain 1595–1833*. Oxford University Press

Chapter 11

Geography and Multicultural Education

Geoff Dinkele

'My country is the world'

> My country is the world and my religion is to do good. (Thomas Paine, 1737–1809)

After a period of sustained reading of, and almost daily dips into, the Final Report for National Curriculum Geography (DES, 1990), one's familiarity grows, helped enormously by sharing perceptions with other colleagues. One is struck, sooner or later, by the similarity to the seminal booklet, Curriculum Matters No. 7: *Geography from 5 to 16* (DES, 1986). In particular, the primary phase discussions in the booklet match closely with the proposals for Key Stages 1 and 2 in the Final Report. Curriculum Matters No. 7 lacks the framework of attainment targets, programmes of study and statements of attainment but is an essential companion to the Final Report (and the Statutory Orders).

The scene is incomplete without reference to documentation of multicultural education. Two broad aims of education which appeared in two DES publications in 1981 and 1982 point up a possible foundation for multicultural education. These two aims are:

1 To instil respect for religious and moral values, and tolerance of other races, religions and ways of life.
2 To help pupils to understand the world in which they live, and the interdependence of individuals, groups and cultures.

Many LEAs also make suggestions and offer guidelines as to how these noble aims might be achieved. For instance, the Hampshire policy (1987) includes the following exhortation:

> This policy should permeate the whole curriculum and find expression in all aspects of school and college life!

We may conclude that multicultural education is a cross-curricular dimension, capable of being tracked within an institution and clearly an integral part of a broad and balanced curriculum.

The potential contribution of geography to multicultural education

It is not difficult to see the potential role of geography in multicultural education. Devotees of development education (still struggling to convince teachers that it is heavily PSE and not exclusively 'developing world' studies) will identify readily with the general aims.

Educationalists who believe environmental education to be a cross-curricular theme capable of embracing the lion's share of the curriculum, will regard the aim as subsumed by their menu. Both development education and environmental education have influenced geographical teaching and learning, contributing in various ways to the inputs, processes and outputs of that system. That tension may exist in some eyes between development and environmental education is both predictable and sad. Might it not mirror the basic reasons why multicultural education is regarded as a vital dimension of a person's education?

Geography's contribution to multicultural education will of course be largely in the hands of individual teachers, who need to be well aware of the external influences upon youngsters. It is the teacher who plans and negotiates learning experiences and we must recognise that every educational statement, document and activity reflects a particular educational stance. This could be explicit but, in most cases, is implicit. Walford (1981) has identified four broad 'manners of thinking'; in turn these tend to be associated with teaching and assessment styles. The four 'base positions' are *utilitarian, liberal, child-centred,* and *reconstructionist* and a brief description of each stance follows:

1 *Utilitarian*   This tradition emphasises the preparation of youngsters for survival in society and especially in the world of work. It is concerned with knowledge and skills and gaining qualifications.
2 *Liberal*   Passing on what is considered worthwhile and turning out 'little geographers' typify this tradition, in which teachers are usually willing to adopt new developments in the subject and to try new teaching approaches.
3 *Child-centred*   Teachers who believe strongly in this tradition see

their role as educating the whole person and integrating experiences wherever possible. The stress is upon self-development and autonomy through the provision of experiential and reflective approaches.
4   *Reconstructionist*   Action and participation skills are emphasised in this tradition, which regards education as a potential way of challenging the status quo, asking pertinent questions about issues such as spatial injustice, environmental problems and the distribution of political power and of creating change in society.

It is likely that few teachers embrace one tradition to the exclusion of the other three, but it is important that individuals consider these viewpoints and attempt some self-evaluation. A related question is to ask oneself: 'What is my attitude to my job as a teacher?' An effective multicultural education presence in the curriculum is not unrelated to the outcomes of teacher self-evaluation suggested above.

Now what about the presence of the multicultural dimension in the curriculum? Much can be achieved with limited resources and in a short time; perhaps the most underrated resource are the youngsters themselves. Some teachers find active learning easier to organise and deliver than others and personalities differ as does the climate of a classroom. It has been asserted that prejudice can be reduced by education and laughter – are these common ingredients in every classroom?

One of the concepts through which multicultural education is achieved is obviously that of prejudice. It is worth stating that prejudice is not a demon revealed, demonstrated and articulated by people because they are depraved. Rather, prejudice is a product of situations, problems and circumstances. Many people remain doggedly limited in their own cultures but with help and experience are ready to understand others' points of view. Here is the challenge and it starts in schools.

Confluent education

A significant development in geography has been the emergence of humanistic geography, partly as a reaction to the positivist approaches of the 1970s. This thrust is concerned with people's feelings, perceptions, experiences and fears – in other words, personal and private geographies. Humanistic geography supports the dictum that facts

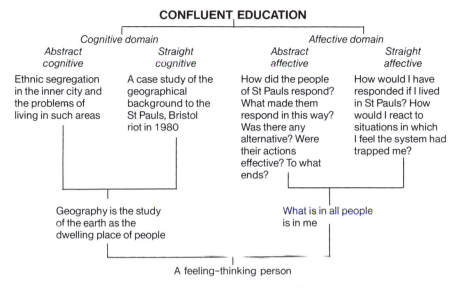

Fig.1   Multicultural geography: a humanistic approach (© Oxford University Press 1983)

without feelings are as dangerous and useless as feelings without facts. A deliberate merging of these two domains (cognitive and affective) of learning is called *confluent education* (see Fien, 1983) and an example is given in fig. 1. This shows the ingredients of a classroom investigation into the disturbances in St Pauls, Bristol in 1980, planned with the ultimate aim of confluent education in mind, that is, to help youngsters become feeling–thinking individuals.

Excursions into the affective domain (feelings, attitudes, beliefs and values) can, properly managed, provide meaningful learning experiences for youngsters in the classroom. A methodology for helping to clarify attitudes, beliefs and values could make a significant contribution to multicultural education.

Ways of exploring attitudes, beliefs and values in the classroom

Here are some suggested activities:

1   *Brainstorming and rounds*   Producing a large number of ideas about a particular topic or issue in a short time, and recording them on the black/whiteboard, overhead projector or flipchart. No comments are allowed during the actual process.

One possible follow-up to a brainstorming session is Rounds.

The intention is to permit each person in turn to express an opinion. Anyone may pass, and no comment is allowed until the round is complete. Teachers can discover what youngsters regard as important and use such leads in their lesson planning.

2   *Writing captions to stimulus material* can be a most revealing activity as responses emerge.

3   *Discussion and decision making over a locational problem*   Qualitative as well and quantitative statements can be made, and feelings may need to be clarified.

4   *Explaining/writing alternative viewpoints to a given statement(s)* is a most effective way of helping youngsters not to accept every statement they come across.

5   *Questionnaires*, when carefully compiled, can be most revealing.

6   *Values probing* is a technique developed by John Fien and Frances Slater (1981), in which students are provided with a non-threatening way to explore what lies behind their attitudes and beliefs – namely their values. It is a child-centred group approach and is designed to encourage tolerance.

7   *Quantitative and qualitative analysis of youngsters' decision making* is another child-centred approach in which the data constitutes the youngsters themselves.

8   *Switching viewpoints to produce cognitive conflict* is a most effective technique when skilfully handled. The deliberate concentration upon one side of an issue is followed by instant exposure to strong reactions against it.

9   *Reactions to a series of news/information stimuli in a conflict situation*   Recorded feelings to a number of items, revealed one by one in chronological order, not only generates interest in the situation but allows feelings and attitudes to be freely expressed.

Drama

A whole range of learning experiences and teaching strategies may be exploited to explore the affective domain and simultaneously help children to gain knowledge and develop a wide range of skills. Consider the multicultural potential of using outside speakers, organising visits and opinion polls, using press reports and brochures, drama and so on. Let us consider an example of using drama.

Imagine a module in a secondary school/college entitled: 'Is it fair?' Part of the classroom activities could include a study of the situation in

South Africa. Rarely absent from the media, can we afford to ignore South Africa in our teaching? Is it not part of a youngster's entitlements?

To avoid indoctrination, the case for apartheid should be explained and explored, along with a selection from the overwhelming range of resources against apartheid. Students need to collect, consider, analyse and make their own judgement on issues, clarifying their own attitudes, beliefs and values in the process.

At the appropriate time, the teacher could pose the situation arising for a family in South Africa. Isobel, the black maid to a white family, the Freelings, is getting married. The wedding is taking place in the black township on the outskirts of the city and Isobel has invited the whole family. Mrs Freeling is a teacher in a white school, Mr Freeling is an accountant, and they have three teenage children, two boys and a girl. Isobel helped to raise the children and has lived with the family, in a detached annexe, for almost seventeen years. She has carried out domestic duties and served the family faithfully, honestly and with affection throughout her stay, and will continue working for the Freelings after her marriage, travelling to work each day from the township.

Given this background, five students sitting around a table can assume the roles of the members of the Freeling family and discuss whether to attend Isobel's wedding or not. The rest of the teaching group will learn as much, and probably more, by being observers and contributing to the discussion afterwards.

There is no excuse for not exploring the South African issue with juniors, not least because there are useful resources available. The Beans series, published by A & C Black, has over forty titles at present and explores the lives of ordinary people over much of the world. From this series, the book *Kwa Zulu, South Africa* (McKenna, 1984) is excellent and could be supported by appropriate or modified resources available elsewhere, especially from development education centres and charity and church organisations. Teaching resources could be regarded as neutral – at least as far as age suitability is concerned – because the important matter is how they are used.

An emphasis upon people

The necessity for focusing upon people in places is obvious. We eat exotic foods, visit distant lands as tourists, drive foreign cars, enjoy media descriptions and films about other people and places and swear by brand goods manufactured abroad. We even donate money to distant cultures we don't understand.

But when it comes to the human beings in these places, and the possibility of direct contact, other forces seem to operate for many people. Fear of strangers and of the unknown, attitudes towards different coloured skins and all manner of manifestation of xenophobia affect our behaviours. The simulation 'Bafa Bafa' (Outsider) – available from Oxfam Youth Department – is an excellent classroom activity for helping youngsters to become more sympathetic to people different from themselves. (Reference to the Geographical Association booklet, *Geographical Education for a Multicultural Society* (Walford, 1985), provides a description of the simulation in action.)

The important thing must be to place oneself in other cultures (real, simulated or imaginary) and be ready to learn from the experience. An ideal unlikely to be achieved in full, would be world-wide exchanges for youngsters. It could be argued that more exchanges for teachers would be beneficial for multicultural education – an idea worth investigating and related to another suggestion which *can* be realised with determination and support. (It often exists informally and fortuitously.)

A seminal booklet appeared in 1988, entitled *A New Approach in Primary School Linking Around the World*. Written by Cherry Mares and the late Rex Beddis, it is inspirational, advocating class and teacher links and relating the substance of the link to the curriculum. The feasibility study carried out by Avon LEA involved over 120 class-to-class links with forty countries around the world. Among the many themes for linking was environmental responsibility.

The National Curriculum

The Final Report for Geography offers many opportunities for multicultural education. Proposals for Key Stages 1 and 2 are in harmony with the advice given in Curriculum Matters No. 7.

> *Lower Primary* (KS 1): Begin to develop an interest in people and places beyond their immediate experience.
> *Upper Primary* (KS 2): Study some aspects of life and conditions in a number of other small areas in Britain and abroad which provide comparisons with their own locality.

Such investigations of unfamiliar (not necessarily interchangeable with distant) places must be welcome in the primary phase for the following reasons:

1   Children are curious about other people and places.
2   We must help them to make sense of the world around them.
3   It contributes to the growth of their geographical literacy.
4   Such studies both strengthen and complement the local perspective.
5   Opportunities arise to counter misconceptions, stereotyping and prejudice.

The emphasis must be upon real people and real places as opposed to country studies which can represent a decidedly abstract and mind-emptying experience for youngsters prior to Key Stage 3. Imaginative, diverse, up-to-date, topical, relevant and appropriate resources need to be provided by both teacher and pupils to support investigations so that place studies become alive. Visual images will figure strongly and they can be a powerful input to multicultural education.

To stress the commonality of humankind, teachers often refer to human needs. These statements tend to be material needs, the conditions that need to be met for survival. It is true that the absence of these conditions threatens survival and without them no higher goal is feasible, but once survival is assured, the next question is: survival for what? That question is about quality of life and the non-material side of life. The philosopher David Spangler regards human needs as different hungers – biological, emotional, mental and spiritual – and it is the last level in which the well-being of others, society and the world emerges. Unity and harmony with the earth figure strongly in the spiritual level too and introduce an often neglected aspect of environmental education.

This last excursion into human needs was intentional for it is essential to introduce such approaches to youngsters as their global reference system takes shape. There is more to geography than the ultimate Statutory Order and the challenge is to incorporate such materials with the mandatory programmes of study.

Key Stages 3 and 4 perpetuate the opportunities to introduce pupils to the reality of cultures and ways of life in other countries. Ethnic and cultural issues should arise during investigations of themes and places, when the approaches of confluent education could be invaluable. We must be careful at all times to balance objectives-led and assessment-related curriculum development with humanistic ingredients and elements. These are less easy to measure, but they are part and parcel of meaningful education.

References and bibliography

Schools often ask, 'What two resources would you recommend to support geography and multicultural education?' My deliberations usually focus upon a book and a calendar. The former is *Teaching Geography for a Better World* (Fien and Gerber, 1988) and the latter is The New Internationalist Third World Calendar, which is published annually by The New Internationalist magazine. Displayed prominently for regular reference, the attractive, colourful and provocative pictures, backed by useful information, provide direct, and more importantly indirect, support for the curriculum. The calendar also reminds one that time is precious in the classroom and in life itself.

Department of Education and Science. (1981) *A Framework for the School Curriculum*. HMSO

  (1982) *The School Curriculum*. HMSO

  (1986) Curriculum Matters No. 7: *Geography from 5 to 16*. HMSO

  (1990) *Geography in the National Curriculum*: Final Report. HMSO

Fien, J. (1983) Humanistic geography. In J. Huckle (ed.) *Geographical Education: Reflection and Action*. Oxford University Press

Fien, J. and Gerber, R. (eds.) (1988) *Teaching Geography for A Better World*. Oliver & Boyd

Fien, J. and Slater, F. (1981) Four strategies for value education. *Geographical Education*, 4, pp. 39–52

Hampshire Education Authority. (1987) *Education for a Multicultural Society*. HEA

Mares, C and Beddis, R. (1988) *A New Approach in Primary School Linking Around the World*. Avon Education Department/Tidy Britain Group Schools Research Project

McKenna, N.D. (1984) *Kwa Zulu, South Africa. Beans* series. A & C Black

The New Internationalist. N.I. Publications, 55 Rectory Road, Oxford, OX4 1BW

Walford, R. (ed.) (1981) *Signposts for Geography Teaching*. Longman

  (1985) *Geographical Education for a Multicultural Society*. Geographical Association

Chapter 12

Language and Cultural Diversity

Rosamond Mitchell and Christopher Brumfit

The need for a single policy

The general purpose of this volume is to take stock of progress towards the goal of education for cultural diversity by the late 1980s, and to look forward to the development of policy for the 1990s and beyond. In this chapter we shall consider the language curriculum from this perspective, in the broadest sense, taking account of the needs of both monolingual and bilingual pupils in a multilingual society, and considering requirements for the learning and teaching of English, of community and heritage languages, and of modern foreign languages.

The current National Curriculum proposals for language have fragmented this whole area into a series of separate language programmes, with an overwhelmingly dominant place for English (and, arguably, for standard English at that). We consider that in order to take account of children's language development in an all-sided way and properly reflect the cultural and linguistic diversity of contemporary society, this trend must be resisted, and a coherent single policy be developed for the language curriculum, interpreted in its widest sense.

In the period since 1985, the language curriculum has been influenced by a variety of important initiatives. As far as linguistic minorities are concerned, the Swann Report (DES, 1985) has arguably had a significant negative influence on the status of community and heritage languages in state schools, while on the other hand promoting the mainstreaming of provision for English as a second language (ESL). The Calderdale Report on separate provision for bilingual students (CRE, 1986) has also had a profound influence on policy in this area. Nationally there has been a significant effort to integrate ESL support into the curriculum mainstream (see Bourne's review of current policies and practices, 1989). However, it is the 1988 Education Reform Act which has the greatest potential for influencing the school language experiences of all children, whether monolingual or bilingual, through its wide-ranging proposals for curriculum, assessment and the Local Management of Schools (LMS).

In reviewing the present position and immediate policy issues, we will consider four main aspects of the school language curriculum:

1   The place of children's first/home language(s) in school (whether standard or non-standard English or another community language).
2   Access for all children to standard English.
3   The development of children's knowledge about language ('language awareness').
4   Access to modern foreign languages.

First/home languages in school

In the primary school, only children speaking English as their home language are at present assured of continuity between home and early school language experience. The Swann Report (DES, 1985) took the view that the use of other community languages as media even for early school learning would be ethnically divisive, and interpreted such research evidence as was available (mostly non-British) as showing no clear-cut academic benefits deriving from bilingual school experience. This nationally important report therefore argued that the first language development of bilingual children should be relegated to community efforts outside the school.

These conclusions (which mysteriously are not applied by Swann to Welsh, at least in Wales) may be criticised on a range of grounds (and have been: see Hamers and Blanc, 1989). It is notoriously difficult to attribute enhanced educational achievement to any particular innovation; but such British research evidence as is available on bilingual provision is encouraging rather than the reverse (for example Fitzpatrick, 1987). It is also perfectly possible, given appropriate staffing, to run British-style primary classrooms with a mix of bilingual and monolingual children, and respond appropriately to the language needs of both (for example Mitchell *et al.* 1987). If the prime educational concern is for continuity of development between home and school, rather than for a hiatus potentially threatening to confidence (and perhaps also to cognitive development), the Swann hostility to bilingual schooling must be seen as profoundly mistaken. Moreover, it has had a clear blighting effect on the development of any coherent national policy on the issue.

Work to support children's bilingualism has continued to develop slowly at primary level but typically as a series of local initiatives, funded on 'soft' money, with staff on short-term contracts and limited resources (Tansley and Craft, 1984). A small number of nationally or European Community (EC) funded short-term projects (Tosi, 1984; Tansley, 1986) has only supplemented local efforts. It remains to be seen how much of this local work survives the impact of the National Curriculum in primary schools, with its one-sided expectations for attainment in English.

As far as secondary schools are concerned, there has been a gradual development of GCE/GCSE programmes in a number of community/ heritage languages (Broadbent *et al.* 1983); this was of course the one form of school provision for these languages positively advocated by Swann. Under the terms of the Education Reform Act, in future all children must study one so-called 'modern foreign language' between the ages of eleven and sixteen, and the Secretary of State has the power to specify a list of languages which may be offered in this particular curriculum slot. In a circular (DES, 1989c), the Secretary of State identified two lists of languages which could be offered. The first list consists of all the officially recognised languages of the European Community. The second list includes a number of languages of international importance (for example Russian and Japanese), plus a number of the most important British community/heritage languages. The two lists have different statuses; a school can offer a language from the second list in National Curriculum time only if it is also offering a language from the first list (so that a choice of languages is available).

While the existence of two lists with different degrees of recognition may appear at best unnecessarily bureaucratic and at worst discriminatory, the scheduling of community/heritage languages in this way may at least be interpreted as an implied commitment on the part of central government to positive resourcing, for example in development of materials and teacher training. However, one single working group was established in summer 1989 to devise an outline curriculum for all languages taught within the National Curriculum framework; it remains to be seen whether this group can persuade the National Curriculum Council to accept a language learning programme which is sufficiently flexible to accommodate the relatively sophisticated needs of children studying a community language in which they already have everyday fluency, alongside those of complete beginners starting a genuinely 'foreign' language. Its Report does, however, propose that the two lists should be amalgamated and pupils be allowed to choose non-EC languages providing they specifically opt out of EC languages (DES, 1990, pp. 147–8).

Access to English

The Cox Report on the teaching of English was published in 1989 (DES, 1989a). As far as its programmes of study were concerned, this Report reflected current liberal consensus on good classroom practice; there was much emphasis on process and on the use of (English) language for a diversity of authentic purposes. Issues relating to the development of bilingual children's English competence were treated in a separate chapter, which advocated mainstreaming and the development of appropriate language awareness among all pupils. However, the levels of attainment against which pupil progress was to be assessed were specified in terms which had evident potential for discrimination against ESL users and indeed against all users of non-standard varieties of English.

This is most strikingly the case for the proposals for the assessment of 'Speaking'. Sociolinguistic research over the last twenty years or so has made it abundantly clear that a rich variety of styles and norms for speaking persists even within monolingual English-using society, and that the way we speak is a complex indicator of social identity and group membership. Competent adult speakers are highly diverse in what they try to do with spoken language and how they accomplish it. Yet the Cox Report proposed one single strand of stylistic development (with the illustrated lecture as its pinnacle!) as the target for all.

In addition, though the Report stopped short of proposing that all children should become active users of spoken standard English, it is hard to see how the highest 'levels of attainment' in the Report can be reached if they do not, at least for some purposes. The Report also failed to recognise the technical problems of objective assessment of spoken language skills (again, there is a substantial research literature documenting how teachers' and assessors' own linguistic stereotypes and prejudices can colour such judgements: see review by Edwards, 1982).

As we have seen, the report of the Calderdale inquiry (CRE, 1986) stimulated the mainstreaming of ESL provision in the mid to late 1980s. This happened in the absence of any substantial research evidence regarding the most effective types of provision and, in particular, on how ESL and other teachers might form the most productive partnerships. Without such guidance, it is unsurprising that Bourne's recent inquiry (1989) unearthed mainly organisational changes but rather little substantial experience as yet of integrated mainstream classroom practice. At a local level there is evidence of active developmental effort, for example through the work of groups such as Hampshire's Multilingual Action Research Network (1988). It remains to be seen what the impact on ESL support of Local Management of Schools (LMS) will be; disturbing reports continue to appear of bilingual children being mainstreamed into special educational needs classes (for example Daley, 1989), and a clear danger exists under LMS for this trend to be intensified.

Language awareness

It has been a fairly longstanding theme among proponents of education for multicultural diversity that all pupils should develop an appreciation of the nature of language as a variable system and some familiarity with, and respect for, language varieties other than their own. Materials to foster classroom work of this kind were produced during the 1980s for primary schools (Houlton, 1985) and for secondary schools (Raleigh, 1981; Hawkins, 1984). The impact of such initiatives in schools has, however, been patchy.

More recently, government policy initiatives have sought to promote a more systematic and explicit study of language in all its aspects, in the expectation that the development of such 'knowledge about language' will have a positive impact on children's language proficiency. The issue of promoting awareness of language variation has survived as one aspect of this new emphasis, though expressed at times in somewhat patronising terms:

> It should be made clear to English-speaking pupils that classmates whose first language is Bengali or Cantonese . . . have languages quite as systematic and rule-governed as their own. (DES, 1988, ch. 4 para. 3)

The Cox Report contained extensive and systematic proposals for the study of language variation, but with the important limitation that only variation *within* English was taken into account. The Modern Foreign Languages Working Group (DES, 1990), which was also given a brief to promote 'language awareness', has not diverted this English-centring to systematic concern for bilingualism and multilingualism. Its chapter on bilingual learners is concerned with language choice and attainment issues (pp. 153–9), and language awareness is played down in the proposals.

Modern foreign languages

Under the National Curriculum proposals, it is likely that for most children, whether monolingual or bilingual, the main experience of second language learning in school will remain a five-year programme studying a European language from scratch, which is for them a truly foreign language. To what extent is this foreign language study contributing to 'education for cultural diversity' and what potential does it have for making such a contribution?

In principle, this element of the National Curriculum can be seen as potentially offering one of the main opportunities for all pupils to be introduced to a culture other than their own, to learn to analyse it and to develop an appreciation of difference. But under the present GCSE framework, with its one-sided concern for the development of 'relevant' communication skills, mainly in face-to-face tourist encounters, this opportunity is largely wasted (Byram, 1989, ch. 7). Byram quotes a Danish commentary on the images of France presented in textbooks current in the late 1970s:

> The learner is presented with a picture of a France populated by unworried and friendly middle-class people; they have no economic problems, no housing problems. The learner does not see the French at work: shopping and spare-time occupations preponderate . . . There are no social or political problems; there are no blacks, no Arabs, no immigrant workers, no unemployment, no minority groups of any kind. To sum up, all the language course material gives a socially and ideologically one-sided picture of France and the French. (Risager and Andersen, 1978 quoted in Byram, 1989, p. 16)

The picture presented in French coursebooks popular in the majority of British schools today is not significantly different; furthermore, coursebooks still typically focus largely on French in France and ignore the status of French as a first or second language in other parts of the world. Here again, a profound rethinking of the purposes of foreign language study will be necessary if a serious contribution is to be made to preparing pupils for life in a culturally diverse society, both national and international.

A way forward?

It is possible that the National Curriculum may show itself to be sufficiently unworkable to be repealed or substantially modified within the next ten years. However, it is more likely that we shall need to find ways of operating within its constraints in order to ensure that it does not work against the best interests of all learners. One ray of hope may be found in the recognition in recent discussion of cross-curricular needs (DES, 1989b). It is clear that there is widespread concern over the compartmentalisation of the curriculum into traditional subject categories (Bash and Coulby, 1989).

Accepting that there will have to be some flexibility in the implementation of the National Curriculum between now and 2003 (when it will at last be operational throughout the system), what sort of strategy should we adopt?

A language charter

One procedure would be to try to obtain widespread agreement for a language charter for all learners. The argument for the concept of a 'charter' is that this enables us to define what is desirable and to express a commitment to realising those goals, in so far as resources and circumstances permit. The charter would provide a frame of reference against which the commitment of each school or education authority could be measured.

An attempt to define such a charter was made in a lecture in 1986 (Brumfit, 1989) and follows closely the general categories of our discussion in this chapter. The intention in drafting it was to produce a formulation for language development throughout the education system which would be:

- equally beneficial to each individual (and thus would not advantage English speakers at the expense of others);
- sensitive to the most authoritative research on language acquisition and education;

- realisable, at least to some degree, for every learner;
- responsive to the linguistic needs of British-educated learners for the foreseeable future.

The charter thus proposes the following:

It is the policy of _____ (enter name of school, college, or education authority) to attempt to the maximum extent possible within available resources to enable all learners:

i   to develop their own mother tongue or dialect to maximum confident and effective use;

ii to develop competence in a range of styles of English for educational, work-based, social and public-life purposes;

iii to develop their knowledge of how language operates in a multilingual society, including basic experience of languages other than their own that are significant either in education or the local community;

iv to develop as extensive as possible a practical competence in at least one language other than their own.

It is our belief that the development of these four strands in combination will contribute to a more effective language curriculum for Britain in the twenty-first century than emphasis on any of them separately at the expense of the others.

The detailed justification for this structure for a charter was spelled out in the original lecture (Brumfit, 1989). Its major innovation is a determination to see English, ESL, home dialect, community languages, and foreign and classical language development as part of a single coherent strategy. It thus directly confronts the separation of foreign languages, English and Welsh in the National Curriculum. None the less, it is not incompatible with a sensitive working out of National Curriculum requirements, as our earlier discussion has indicated. It is also, however, defensible in relation to the larger concerns of this book. Our concern for language policy should not prevent us from seeing ourselves as part of the broader educational movement. How do we fit into this?

A strategy for the future will have to depend on two separate general approaches, because there are two different issues to be addressed.

At a specific level, there is a need for members of linguistic minority groups to ensure, through political activity, that their democratic rights as individuals and as groups are not ignored in local or national policy making. All members of society can assist and support this work, but the lead is best taken by those who are directly affected and who are most closely in touch with the parents and language-users whose case is being pressed.

At a more general level, there is the necessity for the whole of British education to be responsive to linguistic and cultural diversity. In the long run the needs of minority groups will be best met only in this context, for the majority of the active members of the nation has to be supportive of national policy before it will be effectively implemented at all levels. Using a strategy like a national charter thus becomes very important. Because it is couched in terms which apply to every single learner resident in Britain, it does not diminish some people's rights at the expense of others. Because it is responsive to the latest current research, it is intellectually defensible. Because each element is being addressed to some extent already by teachers and community leaders, it is realisable, at least in part. But above all, if there is a statement of commitment made at this level of specificity, we can at least agree on what are the criteria for effective language development and argue case by case over whether such development is being appropriately resourced. Finally, it is a democratic, bottom-up strategy. Individuals and institutions will commit themselves to such a charter because they wish to implement it at a local level. Affecting national educational policy will become then a result of the pressure from many local groups.

We are thus in a position to argue that alongside specific concerns of specific groups we should place the policy of the society as a whole. The country needs an effective and just policy, in its own right, and also as a means for minority groups to obtain their own effective and just policies as part of the national policy. We need to fight on both fronts simultaneously and a charter of this kind will enable us to do so. Without alternative and flexible structures, the rigidity of the National Curriculum will become stultifying; charters of this kind will guide implementation, without necessarily undermining the official statements, while at the same time enabling a sensitive and well-informed alternative to be developed as change inevitably takes place.

References

Bash, L. and Coulby, D. (1989) *The Education Reform Act, Competition and Control*. Cassell

Bourne, J. (1989) *Moving into the Mainstream*. NFER-Nelson

Broadbent, J. *et al.* (1983) *Assessment in a Multicultural Society: Community Languages at 16+*. Longman for Schools Council

Brumfit, C.J. (1989) Towards a language policy for multilingual secondary schools. Keynote lecture to CILT European Community Pilot Project Seminar, September 1986. In J. Geach (ed.) *Coherence in Diversity*. Centre for Information on Language Teaching and Research

Byram, M. (1989) *Cultural Studies in Foreign Language Education*. Multilingual Matters

Commission for Racial Equality. (1986) *Teaching English as a Second Language: Report of a Formal Investigation in Calderdale LEA*. CRE

Daley, C. (1989) 'The education of linguistic minority children in mainly white schools: a cause for concern.' Unpublished M.A. dissertation, University of Southampton

Department of Education and Science. (1985) *Education for All* (Swann Report). HMSO

   (1988) *Report of the Committee of Enquiry into the Teaching of English Language* (Kingman Report). HMSO

   (1989a) *English for Ages 5 to 16* (Cox Report). HMSO

   (1989b) *National Curriculum: From Policy to Practice*. HMSO

   (1989c) *Modern Foreign Languages in the National Curriculum*. HMSO

   (1990) Modern Foreign Languages Working Group: *Initial Advice*. HMSO

Edwards, J. (1982) Language attitudes and their implications among English speakers. In E.B. Ryan and H. Giles (eds.) *Attitudes Towards Language Variation*. Edward Arnold

Fitzpatrick, F. (1987) *The Open Door*. Multilingual Matters

Hamers, J.F. and Blanc, M.H.A. (1989) *Bilingualism and Bilinguality*. Cambridge University Press

Hawkins, E. (1984) *Awareness of Language: An Introduction*. Cambridge University Press

Houlton, E. (1985) *All Our Languages*. Edward Arnold

Mitchell, R. *et al.* (1987) *Report of an Independent Evaluation of the Western Isles' Bilingual Education Project*. Department of Education, University of Stirling

Multilingual Action Research Network. (1988) *Languages Matter No. 1*. Southampton: Curriculum Development Centre

Raleigh, M. (1981) *The Languages Book*. ILEA English Centre

Tansley, P. (1986) *Community Languages in Primary Education*. NFER-Nelson

Tansley, P and Craft, A. (1984) Mother tongue teaching and support: A Schools Council enquiry. *Journal of Multilingual and Multicultural Development*, 5, 5, pp. 367–85

Tosi, A. (1984) *Immigration and Bilingual Education*. Pergamon

Chapter 13

Religious Education and the Education Reform Act

David Naylor

In order to consider the potential contribution of religious education to the development of a multicultural society, it will first be necessary to clarify the rationale for the subject. This chapter will then assess the extent to which it remains possible for the subject to stay in the forefront of developments in the field of multicultural education. This will necessitate a close scrutiny of the relevant clauses of the 1988 Education Reform Act that will provide the legal framework for the subject in the foreseeable future.

A rationale for religious education

Any subject finding its place on the agenda of schools does so on the basis of value judgements. In the case of religious education, the value judgement the professional RE teacher in our multicultural society would wish to defend might be stated as follows. Religion remains at the heart of most cultures. In their ideal form, religions incorporate a total world-view and have been and, in many cases, continue to be the power house of civilisations. The teachings of the major world faiths have been pivotal in the development of human societies. They represent the human need to seek meaning and to base life on principles perceived as having been revealed or uncovered in the religious quest. The search for meaning remains an essential human characteristic and those involved in the quest have an entitlement to be given access to the answers some people have found to the perennial questions about human existence in the world.

The phenomenon of religion is complex and many sided, its exploration requires a collection of methodologies matched to its complexity. Hence religious studies, emerging only comparatively recently in the academic world, is by its nature poly-methodic. The student of reli-

gion requires a conglomeration of ill-assorted fragments of other subjects (history, philosophy, sociology, psychology, and so on) stitched
together into a sort of crazy academic patchwork quilt! (See Sharpe,
1975.) It is not surprising that this situation creates a division between
the specialist teacher in the secondary school and the non-specialist
teacher, whether primary or secondary. The approach has been variously labelled as 'non-confessional', 'non-dogmatic' or 'phenomen-
ological'. Alongside its development and propagation through groups
like the Shap Working Party and extensive publications, have been a
variety of educational developments. Especially important in this context are those developments concerned with matching knowledge and
skills to the needs, capacities and interests of pupils at particular stages.
Regrettably, usable research in the area of the development of
capacities either to understand religion or to achieve religious understanding is thin on the ground and both syllabus making and assessment arrangements have proceeded on the basis of experience and
hunch rather than research.

The approach to RE developed in Hampshire from the late 1970s
has been widely influential in that it has been adopted by twenty other
local education authorities. In trying to pursue a non-confessional
approach and at the same time to avoid over-sophistication, it con-
sciously restricted the field of enquiry in most schools to the study of
Christianity and at least one other faith.

The intention, which may displease some of the purists in the field of
multicultural education, was not only to make the task manageable for
teachers, but to concentrate on skills and above all attitudes to world-
views usually different from the pupils' own (mainly secular) perspectives. As *Religious Education in Hampshire Schools* (1978) puts it:

> The task of teachers is two-fold. First, to foster in their pupils a
> reflective approach to living. Second, to engage their pupils in a
> dialogue with living faiths in such a way that the reflective process
> is broadened and enriched. (p. 26)

This is a tall order and it is only realistic to admit that achievement
remains mixed. The main cause of failure is a misunderstanding about
the nature of the enquiry, alongside unease about the extent to which
education is or should be an initiation into a culture. How is it possible
to educate for pluralism without encouraging either agnosticism or
mere adoption of the status quo? It is not only the classroom teacher
who is baffled by this question, but the boffins of the subject who write
chapters like this one. Where there is understandable confusion and

uncertainty, it is hardly surprising that some settle for Bible stories while others assume that religious education is really moral education and set about trying to make the pupils 'good'. This is of course a laudable aim, but it can leave pupils seriously ignorant about religion and even lead them to the dangerous assumption that morality has to be derived from a religious world-view.

The serious study of religion in schools is a comparatively recent event. In the early sixties few schools had specialist teachers. It is not surprising therefore that much clarification and development needs to go on in the form of in-service education and publishing of educationally worthwhile material. Many authorities, but by no means all, have encouraged these activities and the achievements have been considerable. Into this arena, however, has been thrown the 1988 Education Reform Act. Its impact has brought the subject into public debate but, emerging as it did from a generation of peers in the House of Lords with little or no understanding of either the social context of most schools or thinking about the subject in educational terms, its effect has been to add mud to muddy water.

The National Curriculum and the Education Reform Act

The first draft of the Education Reform Bill made scant reference to RE: it simply referred to the clauses of the 1944 Act and in so doing ignored almost half a century of intensive and creative debate. However, when the Bill reached the House of Lords, Baroness Cox and a group of allies, seeing that children had been sold short on religious education, laid the blame for this at the feet of syllabuses they regarded as a 'mishmash' of world religions. Their solution was to insist that religious education should be 'predominantly Christian'. Although this form of wording was ultimately rejected (thanks mainly to the Bishop of London), the idea received wide publicity and has lodged in the minds of many teachers.

The subtle and flexible form of wording which finally surfaced in the Act in relation to RE stated that any new agreed syllabus that followed the enactment of the 1988 Act:

> shall reflect the fact that the religious traditions in Great Britain are in the main Christian whilst taking account of the teaching and practices of the other principal religions represented in Great Britain.

A further subtlety of the Act concerns the position of RE in relation to the National Curriculum. Even the high-powered management course mounted by HMI presented the situation in a misleading way by referring to core subjects, foundation subjects and basic curriculum RE. The legislation actually states:

> The curriculum for every maintained school shall comprise a *basic curriculum* which includes:
>
> *a*   provision for religious education for all registered pupils at the school; and
> *b*   a curriculum for all registered pupils at the school of compulsory school age (to be known as 'The National Curriculum').

The semantics are vitally important. A more accurate reading at all levels could have generated discussion and a plethora of papers labelled 'The Basic Curriculum' rather than 'The National Curriculum'. The difficulty is compounded by the fact that while the core and foundation subjects have national working parties, the RE curriculum, for historical reasons, is in the hands of local Standing Advisory Councils for RE (SACRE). SACRE has responsibility for attainment targets, programmes of study and assessment arrangements. All such bodies comprise four groups: representatives of the Church of England, of other religious denominations, of teacher organisations, and elected members of the LEA. Core and foundation subjects have nationally selected educational heavyweights to develop the curriculum but the ambiguous position of RE leaves it with institutionalised amateurism. Fortunately, in practice, there is much delegation to working parties of teachers.

Ways forward

In spite of this burden of historical accident and tradition, the Act provides a useful basis for development by legitimising much current practice. Firstly, the name of the subject is officially changed from religious instruction to religious education. Such change signals the acceptability of the presuppositions of an educational approach referred to earlier. Secondly, by stating that RE 'shall reflect the fact that the religious traditions in Great Britain are in the main Christian whilst taking account of the teaching and practices of the other principal religions represented in Great Britain', the potential for making a contribution to multicultural education is formalised. Significantly, the reference is to Great Britain rather than to the locality of particular schools. This form of words should prevent schools in white areas ignoring the multicultural aspects of RE on the grounds that 'we have no problem here'.

Hence, the potential for development is provided, the powerful mythology can be broken down and the struggle for adequate time and resources can be won against the pervasive emphasis on the National Curriculum at the expense of not only the basic curriculum but the whole curriculum. Fortunately RE is served by a small but able band of advocates who will need to work their way tirelessly through the range of potential misunderstandings.

Collective worship

Perhaps a more insidious threat to multicultural approaches will be the clauses on collective worship. Here again the Act is infinitely more flexible than the media's misrepresentations of it have made out. Put simply, the question raised by the notion of worship is, 'How is it possible to be involved in an open quest in the classroom and constrained within theistic assumptions in the Hall? The resolution of this dilemma requires a level of sophisticated argument which it is unrealistic and unfair to expect of the general practitioner.

Close and detailed study of the Act shows that educational and social factors are taken seriously. For instance, schools are free to make decisions about timing and grouping. The Act only requires that *most* collective worship in any one term should be Christian. The latter phrase is subsequently elaborated to mean reflecting Christian *belief* (rather than Christian worship). There are however two non-negotiable features, one helpful, the other distinctly unhelpful.

First is the requirement to match the collective worship to the age, aptitude and family background of the pupils. Since the parents of the vast majority of pupils in school choose not to place worship on their annual, let alone their daily, agenda, the school will for the most part be seeking to develop those aspects of worship which are most basic, for example stillness and reflective thinking. In reflecting broadly Christian belief they can focus on such qualities as compassion, self-sacrifice, forgiveness, humility, mercy, tolerance, honesty, respect etc., none of which is exclusively Christian. Humanists and all major religions also espouse such qualities. Clearly, within these qualifying clauses, there is scope for a multicultural approach, the only problem being the degree of professional confidence required to articulate and defend it.

The second and more intractable feature is the requirement that collective worship should be *daily*. It is instructive to reflect that even the most pious religious adherent does not worship collectively every day, and yet the Act requires this of all pupils and students from five to eighteen. The creative interpretation of the Act commended in this chapter is difficult to sustain on this one issue especially for the secondary age-range.

The Act in practice – a case study

This chapter has surveyed the potential contribution of RE in a situation of cultural diversity. Despite the room for misunderstanding in the debates between teachers, governors and parents, engendered both by the complex and controversial nature of the subject and by the Education Reform Act, many schools are finding scope to fulfil their multicultural ideals. The following case study shows the way in which a Southampton school has worked within the legal framework to achieve a workable approach to both RE and collective worship with parents, governors and local faith communities.

The Bevois Town First and Middle School serves an extremely diverse community near Southampton city centre. The term 'minority cultures' is largely inaccurate when applied to Bevois Town as 45 per cent of the pupils are of Asian background (40 per cent from the Sikh community, 42 per cent Muslims and the remainder from a small Hindu group).

The cultural, linguistic and religious mixture within the school has a direct bearing on the nature of the RE and collective worship that is organised. Additional factors further influence religious education provision:

1   Some of the ethnic minority children attend their religious establishments after school for instruction in their own faith.
2   Some of the children come from families who have no declared faith and are anxious for the emphasis in school to lie heavily upon religious *education*, not religious *instruction*.
3   At the moment *none* of the parents of the children, of any religious faith, have requested that their child(ren) be withdrawn from RE or collective worship.
4   Religious leaders who have visited the school have agreed that the current multifaith approach is an acceptable reflection of the mixed community status.

5   No member of the teaching staff has yet indicated that they do not
    wish to participate in collective worship or to withdraw from
    involvement in religious education.

The details above are merely factual statements and do not fully
acknowledge, or give credit to, the carefully developed and nurtured
relationships between the different cultural groups which the school
has achieved over the years. The rich and varied background experiences and the cultural diversity enjoyed by the children are seen as a
distinct advantage. It enables the school to 'live' multicultural education day by day, not least in the opportunities taken each week for collective worship.

Elements within the new Reform Act *may* indicate that the school
should move towards a more disparate, fragmented assembly and RE
arrangement, with children of different faiths meeting separately.
Should this happen, it would undoubtedly run counter to the 'playing
and working together' creed that has been, and is, the hallmark and
pride of Bevois Town School.

Consultation procedures: staff, governors, parents and local religious leaders

In seeking to arrive at policy decisions that were best suited to the
school and also remained within the requirements of the law, the
headteacher took steps to consult with a range of interested groups.

STAFF

All members of the teaching staff completed a short questionnaire to
indicate their views regarding RE and collective worship. As with any
mixed group of people, their responses reflected a variety of personal
and professional standpoints. Approximately half the staff thought
assemblies should contain more elements of the Christian faith and
more aspects of other faiths in general, though some teachers thought
this should appear as part of classroom RE. Generally, the staff were
familiar with the contents of the Hampshire handbooks on RE; not so
many had studied the booklet *Religious Education in Hampshire Schools*. RE
is approached in a variety of ways, class by class: (a) appearing as a separate topic, (b) taking its place as an integrated discipline within a broad-
based study area, (c) as part of a health education programme of work
or (d) during relevant discussions with the children in their daily social
interactions.

GOVERNORS

Lengthy discussions among the Board of Governors also met with a variety of responses. A number of governors had been present at school assemblies and approved of the multifaith arrangements that existed in the school. Governors' attendance at assemblies in general increased as they wished to become familiar with the pattern of collective worship that had been established. The governors encouraged the headteacher to canvass responses to this issue from the parents, and they discussed results along with data from the staff questionnaire. The Board met specially to debate RE and collective worship and their recommendations to the headteacher were reflected in the policy decisions that were taken.

PARENTS

The parent body was invited to contact any governor of the school, or the headteacher, concerning the present arrangements, and to offer their opinions regarding any change they thought might be necessary in the light of the Education Reform Act. A number of parents responded, either by letter or by speaking directly to governors. Of the viewpoints expressed, a considerable majority indicated that they wished the present status quo at Bevois Town to be preserved. There were written anxieties from two parents concerning the possible factionalism that could be caused by specialist religious assemblies. One Muslim parent wrote:

> I personally agree that religious education plays an important part in developing and inspiring a moral awareness amongst our children. This I believe is due to the fact that secular education leaves a vacuum that can only be filled by religion. However, we have to bear in mind that the children in Bevois Town School have a background of various religions. Therefore, it would be incumbent upon us to devise a solution which is beneficial and not offensive to the desire of the pupil/parents of different religious backgrounds . . . what is needed is to extract the *moral teaching* of religions as a unifying factor for the betterment of our society.

This parent, along with a verbal response from another parent, advised the school against discussing the concept of God and engaging in collective prayer. One Christian parent wrote:

> We would encourage you to view Mr Baker's Act as a positive step

in restoring Christian education in this country . . . whilst we respect other people and their faiths, we do not believe that it is a matter of integrating all faiths under one roof or 'hat' . . . It may be that various faiths can co-exist in school.

Clearly a small number of parents felt strongly enough about religion in Bevois Town to express their views to the governors and/or the headteacher. The religious standpoints were diverse but not necessarily in opposition to each other. A carefully formulated RE collective worship policy should seek to meet with acceptance by as many parental viewpoints as possible – but it was accepted that it may not be possible to please everyone. Perhaps the most important outcome of the parental response was that over ninety per cent of the parents did not express any viewpoint. One could perhaps conclude that the vast majority of parents did not support a change of approach in the school (other than that decreed by law), or were not concerned about this matter.

LOCAL RELIGIOUS LEADERS

As part of the normal RE and collective worship provision at Bevois Town, representatives from a variety of religious faiths and denominations visit the school, more often than not to lead assemblies and share with the children some basic elements of their faith. During discussions with these religious leaders it appeared that, although some faiths have very specific advice to give to educational establishments about what constitutes acceptable practice for the children of their religion, there was an awareness of the multifaith, multicultural aspects of the community, and a wish to encourage the present efforts both to unite groups spiritually and to celebrate the diversity of the faiths in school.

Requirements and advice from Hampshire Education Authority

Individual schools are not expected to be entirely self-contained and the advice to all schools from the RE Adviser was particularly pertinent to the situation at Bevois Town:

COLLECTIVE WORSHIP

Worship has to do with worth and worthiness. It is the recognition, affirmation and celebration of the 'worth-ship' of certain realities and values, held to be of central importance to the community which worships.

> Clauses [within the Act] . . . should enable schools to pursue a policy which is compatible with an open approach to religious education [as outlined in the County document]. (HEA, 1978)

The Act makes it possible for collective worship to be matched to the age, aptitude and family backgrounds of the pupils. It simply requires that *most* acts of worship should be broadly Christian and leaves the *extent* to which they reflect this broad tradition and the *ways* they are reflected to schools and colleges. Throughout the Act *educational* factors point the way to an interpretation which can enrich the life of the school, while respecting the integrity and honesty of both teachers and pupils, whatever their personal standpoint. *Collective* (not corporate) acts will leave open the possibility of a variety of responses. Any interpretation which failed to match these educational principles would not be compatible with widely agreed policies on RE adopted in Hampshire over the past decade.

RELIGIOUS EDUCATION

> Although the context of religious education will vary from place to place, its content will be drawn largely from the study of Christianity in its many forms, this being the religious faith which has most influenced our culture. However, it is no part of the responsibility of a county school to promote any particular religious standpoint, neither could an exclusively Christian content do justice to the nature of the subject. A syllabus relevant to the needs of our children must also provide an introduction to other religious commitments and world-views found in contemporary British society. (ibid.)

Therefore, following (a) the identification of specific issues to which the Act requires conformity, (b) consultation with various interested parties, (c) the examination of existing LEA documentation and (d) a consideration of existing practices within the school, Bevois Town adopted the following policy during the Spring Term 1990:

The policy

COLLECTIVE WORSHIP

1 There will be a daily act of collective worship, as defined by the RE Adviser. The usual pattern throughout the week in school will be as follows:

Monday – Class- or year-based assemblies, to be taken at any time during the day.

Tuesday – First and Middle school assemblies, usually taken by the headteacher or deputy head, in the morning.

Wednesday – a.m. First and Middle school assemblies, which will involve members of staff and/or headteacher, and usually contain an element of singing. The songs selected for use will embody elements of RE already existing in the school.

Thursday – a.m. First and Middle school assemblies, taken by members of staff within the confines of this policy agreement.

Friday – Usually a.m. Whole school assembly, which usually gives the opportunity to classes or groups of children to share their recent experiences. They will seek to conform to the definition of 'worship' given by the RE Adviser.

2 Resources utilised by the teaching staff will include:
   a   stories from the Bible and other religious books
   b   literature from a variety of faiths
   c   stories, myths and legends of a high moral tone that will enable us to achieve our RE objectives
   d   programmes produced by the BBC and ITV networks with religious themes
   e   life-stories of people who have positively influenced the history of mankind
   f   current affairs news items judged to have religious content relevant and suitable for our children.

3 During any given term, the majority of collective acts of worship will mainly be of a broad-based Christian character, as defined by ERA and interpreted by the LEA. This school views such an assembly to be one which may or may not refer directly to the Christian faith, but which *will* contain elements that embody such aspects of Christianity that will support the spiritual development of our children.

4 Unless requested in writing by individual parents, *all* children will attend collective acts of worship designed for their age group.

5 As many religious faiths will be represented at any one gathering, along with children who have no religious faith, the whole group will not be invited to pray. However, it *will* be customary for the assembly leader to engage those present in an act of quiet reflection.

6 Bevois Town School will continue to celebrate the major religious festivals throughout the year and involve as many children as possible, from all faiths, in these rewarding activities.

7 Religious leaders from different faiths will be invited to lead collective acts of worship, within the confines of this policy.

8 Parents, governors and representatives of local religions may visit assemblies on request, except for Friday assemblies which are open to *any* member of the community.

9 Groups of children may visit religious establishments for the purpose of specific acts of worship. Parents will be informed of these off-site activities.

10 All collective acts of worship will adhere to the educational principles by which the school is managed.

RELIGIOUS EDUCATION

1 The school adopts the aims and objectives for RE that are set out in the document, *Religious Education in Hampshire Schools*.

2 Bevois Town will incorporate the study topics that appear in the LEA documents, *Paths to Understanding* and *Following the Paths*, where they are found to be appropriate to year groups within the school.

3 Curriculum guidelines will exist in a separate document form which details the allocation of RE topics to various year groups throughout the school, and gives further advice regarding the integration of RE in general topic work.

4 The teaching staff regard that this subject requires special attention during general classroom activities, and will seize the opportunity to widen the context of any learning situation to encompass elements of moral or spiritual worth.

5 All aspects of RE will adhere to the educational principles by which the school is managed.

REVIEW/MONITORING PROCEDURES

1   Following final consultations with the Board of Governors and with local religious leaders, it is intended that this policy be adopted and implemented as soon as is practicable. The headteacher along with members of staff with special responsibilities in this area, undertake to monitor the nature and character of the acts of collective worship and to ensure compliance with the LEA interpretation of ERA. It is intended that the policy be reviewed annually and any changes made where necessary. Representatives of local religious faiths and any parents should have access to this policy and all related documents. Their views regarding this policy are welcomed.

2   It is hoped that the policy decisions outlined in this document are acceptable to the parents and to the religious faiths within the community. The headteacher and governors of Bevois Town reserve the right to apply to SACRE at any time for exemption from some elements of ERA for some pupils. Nevertheless, they feel that close observation of the working principles proposed by the policy will cause that step to be unnecessary. The primary aim of the school is that the precious interfaith and intercultural relationships that exist can be preserved, to the advantage of the educational development of its pupils.

References

Education Reform Act 1988
Hampshire Education Authority. (1978) *Religious Education in Hampshire Schools*. HEA
   (1980) *Paths to Understanding*. HEA
   (1986) *Following the Paths*. HEA
Sharpe, E.J. (1975) The one and the many. In N. Smart and D. Horder (eds.) *New Movements in Religious Education*. Temple Smith

PART 3:   Equality of Opportunity

Chapter 14

Caribbean-heritage Pupils in Britain: Educational Performance and Inequality

Peter Figueroa

This chapter focuses on Caribbean-heritage pupils, but also provides some information on 'Asians'. It is often said that 'Caribbean' pupils underachieve academically in Britain. More fundamentally, however, they are unequal in the British education system – as indeed are the 'Asians'. Will the Education Reform Act help rectify this situation?

Reviews of the research

Monica Taylor (1981) has carried out the fullest review of research about Caribbean-heritage pupils in British schools. This was commissioned by the Committee of Inquiry into the Education of Children from Ethnic Minority Groups, which was established in March 1979. The Committee stated its brief in terms of the 'underachievement of West Indian Children' (ibid. p.3).

Taylor concludes that 'there is an overwhelming consensus: that research evidence shows a strong trend to underachievement of pupils of West Indian origin' (ibid. p. 216). This stark conclusion is made even though she acknowledges that 'the picture is complex, with minor inconsistencies, more important ambiguities and even contradictions at almost every turn'. But she considers these to be mere 'niceties'.

This chapter draws on some of the materials from Peter Figueroa (1991) *Education and the Social Construction of 'Race'*, Routledge and (1984) Minority pupil progress, in M. Craft (ed.) *Education and Cultural Pluralism*, Falmer Press.

In another review of the literature, Sally Tomlinson (1983, p. 130) says that the main issue has been 'achievement'. She claims too that:

> Research concerning the educational performance of children of West Indian origin is extensive and . . . there are enough large-scale studies using total samples of over 600 children to counter charges that the research is small scale and biased. (ibid. p. 28)

She then identifies twenty-five studies with total samples of over 600, seven with total samples of between 100 and 600, and twelve with total samples of less than 100. Unfortunately, when she goes on to discuss the large-scale studies, she does not make clear the size of the Caribbean sub-samples – although that, surely, is what mainly counts in relation to the situation of Caribbean pupils. In fact in some of these studies the number of Caribbean respondents is very small. Besides, Tomlinson fails to mention several small-scale studies, while some of the large-scale studies involve double-counting so that the impression she gives that most of the studies are large scale is misleading.

Tomlinson concludes that 'children of West Indian origin . . . do underperform and underachieve in comparison with "white" and "Asian" minority groups' (ibid. p. 44). Again this unqualified conclusion is reached even though the complexity of the issues and some of the limitations of the research are indicated.

Likewise giving much attention to the 'underachievement' of pupils of Caribbean background, the Swann Report concludes:

> there is no doubt that West Indian children, as a group and on average, are underachieving, both by comparison with their school fellows in the white majority, as well as in terms of their potential, notwithstanding that some are doing well. (DES, 1985a, p. 81)

This constant harping on 'West Indian underachievement' needs to be questioned both on empirical and on conceptual grounds. It could itself represent a handicap by contributing to the stereotyping of Caribbean pupils as 'non-academic'.

In fact the research that has been carried out is limited and open to many criticisms. Besides, much of the available data would be better conceptualised as educational inequality rather than as underachievement. Moreover, not all the findings support the prevalent thesis and more attention should be given to Caribbean achievement.

Limitations of the research

What are some of the main limitations and shortcomings of the existing research? Despite Tomlinson's claims (1983, p. 130), much of the research on Caribbean pupils is small scale.

Besides, many of the studies, even many of the larger-scale ones, relate to areas with substantial minority ethnic populations. These are often conurbations and inner city areas, which tend to be deprived areas where children generally perform less well than on average nationally. Although almost half of the Caribbean population lives outside Greater London (CRE, 1978), many of the studies were carried out in London. Moreover, much of the research has used 'opportunity samples'. It is therefore not safe to assume that the findings are representative. We have little information about the performance of Caribbean pupils outside the inner city areas and in schools where 'good practice' is the norm.

Furthermore, in comparisons between Caribbean pupils and others, especially white pupils, adequate controls are often not built in so as to ensure that like is being compared with like – in terms, for instance, of learning opportunities. In one of the few studies where such controls were introduced, Bagley (1971) found that the mean Caribbean IQ score was slightly higher than that of white pupils.

Another set of basic problems concerns the measures and instruments used in many of the studies, including the large-scale ones. Where standardised tests are used there is often a problem of the population on which the test has been standardised. In particular, how often do those populations include a representative sample of Caribbean-heritage pupils? Indeed, some of the studies within the educational priority areas' action research of the 1960s (Barnes, 1975 and Little, 1975) employed the Illinois Test of Psycholinguistic Abilities, and used USA norms!

On the other hand, teacher assessment is often relied upon, for example in categorising pupils as 'West Indian' or not, and in measuring attainment or linguistic competence. But this must raise serious doubts about the reliability and validity of the resulting data, especially given the stereotypes, ignorance, confusion and even prejudice and racism on the part of many teachers (see for instance Green, 1972; Brittan, 1976; Driver, 1977; Edwards, 1979; Tomlinson, 1982; Carrington, 1983; Figueroa and Swart, 1986 and Wright, 1986).

For instance, Brittan (1976) on the basis of a national sample of 510 primary and secondary school teachers found a strong tendency for

'West Indian' pupils to be stereotyped negatively. Mabey (1981) found that teachers tended to rate eight-year-old Caribbean pupils negatively. For example, teachers thought that most of the Caribbean pupils had negative attitudes towards school. Yet researchers have found on the contrary that Caribbeans are positively orientated towards education (see for instance Hill, 1968; Evans, 1972; Figueroa, 1974; Jelinek, 1977; Dawson, 1978 and chapter 16 below). Figueroa (1991) in a case study of white Postgraduate Certificate of Education students has found that they had little contact with or knowledge about Caribbean people; yet expressed stereotypes about them, stereotypes that tended to be of a non- or anti-academic nature.

One other important question that has not so far received much attention with reference to teacher assessment of ethnicity, is to do with how teachers categorise Caribbean-heritage pupils who are not Afro-Caribbean. It does not seem to be generally realised that a large proportion of people from the Caribbean do not fit the usual image in Britain of the 'Jamaican' or the 'West Indian'. Smith and Tomlinson (1989, p. 236) found that teachers often had problems in categorising Caribbean-heritage pupils.

Teacher assessment

An early example of a large-scale study which relied on teacher assessment was carried out in 1966 in fifty-two Inner London Education Authority primary schools with a large proportion of 'immigrants' (ILEA, 1968a). This investigated 11+ transfer, and over half of the 1,068 'immigrant' pupils transferring were Caribbean. Tomlinson (1983, p. 29) says that this study 'probably had most impact on practitioners and on general beliefs about the educational under-performance of some minority groups', especially Caribbean pupils, who obtained the worst combined English, mathematics and verbal reasoning scores. Bagley (1968) criticised the methodology used and raised the question of the extent to which this study bolstered the ideology that 'coloured' children were intellectually inferior, thus possibly contributing to the educational underrating of Caribbean pupils.

All three measures used in this study were problematical, as Figueroa (1984, p. 23) has commented. The scores for English and mathematics were based on teachers' assessment. But as the study itself showed, the teachers saw 'immigrant' children as culturally disadvantaged, strange and with 'linguistic' problems – whereas of course they were simply culturally different, strange to the teachers and speakers of languages other than standard British English. Caribbean pupils in particular, many of whom in the 1960s would have spoken an English-based Creole, were probably seen by teachers as speaking 'bad' English, since many teachers would not have realised that Creole is a separate language with its own structure (Bailey, 1966; Le Page, 1981), and with a valuable oral tradition as well as a substantial body of first-rate literature.

In addition to English and mathematics, the ILEA study also tested 'verbal reasoning'. This of course was done in the medium of standard British English. Naturally, children who were not competent in that dialect were at a disadvantage. It is essential to distinguish competence in standard British English – which is of course highly desirable in England – from verbal ability. In general, tests of 'intelligence' tend to be culturally, ideologically and socially biased (see for instance Karier, 1976 and Kamin, 1977).

The Swann Report

The data set out in the Swann Report (DES, 1985a), based on a more recent large-scale study, also face problems of possible bias. These data consist of CSE and GCE examination results for 1978/79 and 1981/82 in five LEAs with substantial proportions of ethnic minorities. But these school-leaving examinations, like most other tests of attainment in Britain and like the tests of 'ability' mentioned above, also assume competence in standard British English – as well as familiarity with many cultural phenomena or contexts that might be foreign or remote to many minority ethnic pupils. It is therefore difficult to know, as far as minority ethnic children are concerned, to what extent these examinations measure competence in standard British English and familiarity with particular cultural contexts more than mastery of particular bodies of knowledge and particular related skills.

It should furthermore be noted that the five LEAs studied probably accounted for something under half of all minority ethnic school leavers. The question therefore also arises as to the representativeness of the data.

Besides, teacher assessment was relied on to place the pupils into ethnic categories, and this often took place 'several months' (ibid. p. 61) after the pupils had left school, thus bringing into question the accuracy of this categorisation. Also, the broad categories used in presenting the data – 'Asians', 'West Indians' and 'all other leavers', without even any differentiation between boys and girls – are unsatisfactory. 'Asians' include 'other Asian' children for whom 'a more precise category was either not appropriate or was not known' (ibid. p. 110). Does this category therefore include Vietnamese, Chinese and even Indo-Caribbeans, that is, descendants of the indentured labourers introduced to the Caribbean from the Indian sub-continent during the nineteenth century? (Nearly half of all Trinidadians, for example, are Indo-Caribbeans.) Also, 'the small numbers of African or undifferentiated West Indian/African leavers' were added to the category of 'all other leavers', which included leavers whose ethnicity was not known (ibid p. 110). One must wonder how many Caribbean pupils that do not fit the usual stereotypes were excluded from the 'West Indian' category.

These Swann data (ibid. pp. 113–16) indicate that a large proportion of 'West Indians' obtained graded results at CSE and GCE O-level, but that these tended to be lower grades: their results were well below average on the higher grades (Table 1). With such CSE and GCE O-level results it should not be surprising that the Swann data also show poor Caribbean A-level results. For the reasons given above, however, the accuracy and especially the representativeness of these data cannot be taken for granted. In any case how they are to be interpreted and accounted for remain important questions.

Public examinations in ILEA

Kysel (1988) reports on a more recent large-scale study. She analyses results for CSE and GCE O-level examinations taken by fifth-year ILEA pupils in summer 1985. The Caribbean pupils did well in the middle bands of grades but their higher-grade results were below average (Table 2). Similarly, their average performance scores (along with those for the Bangladeshi, the Turks, the Arabs and the white British) were below the mean for the group as a whole (Table 3). These scores were calculated by awarding points in the following way:

Grades:	O-level	A	B	C	D	E	-	-	U
	CSE	-	-	1	2	3	4	5	U
Points:		7	6	5	4	3	2	1	0

It would seem that a score of zero was also assigned where no exam was taken.

	Asians		Carib- beans		Others		Totals in the 5 LEAs		Totals for England	
	'79	'82	'79	'82	'79	'82	'79	'82	'79	'82
1. CSE & O-level										
English:										
Ungraded/Not taken	31	28	31	25	30	25	30	25	21	18
Lower grades	47	51	61	60	41	46	44	48	45	47
Higher grades	22	21	9	15	29	29	26	26	34	36
Mathematics:										
Ungraded/Not taken	38	33	47	45	40	32	40	34	32	27
Lower grades	41	46	47	47	42	47	42	46	45	45
Higher grades	21	21	5	8	19	21	17	20	23	26
All examinations:										
Ungraded/Not taken	20	19	17	19	22	19	21	19	14	11
Less than 5 higher grades	63	64	80	75	62	62	64	63	66	66
5 or more higher grades	17	17	3	6	16	19	15	18	21	23
2. A-level										
No pass/Not taken	88	87	98	95	88	87	90	88	87	86
At least one pass	12	13	2	5	12	13	10	12	12	14
Base Numbers	466	571	718	653	5,012	4,718	6,196	5,942	693,840	706,690

Source: DES 1985a adapted from Tables 4, 5, 6, and 7, pp. 114–116.
Notes: These figures are based on a 10% sample, and refer to maintained schools;
CSE = Certificate of Secondary Education;
O-level = Ordinary level of the General Certificate of Education (GCE);
A-level = Advanced level of the General Certificate of Education (GCE);
Higher grades = A–C at O-level, and 1 at CSE.
Lower grades = other graded results.
– = Less than .5%

Table 1   Examination results of school leavers in five LEAs and in England as a whole 1978/79 and 1981/82 (percentages)

Kysel also had some information on the fifth formers she studied, going back to the time of their transfer from primary to secondary school. She found that a larger proportion of the Caribbean pupils than of the group as a whole had been considered by their primary headteachers, on the basis of teacher assessment, as below average on verbal reasoning. This teacher-assessed verbal reasoning corresponded

	No exams taken	Percentage of pupils in each group gaining:					No. of pupils
		No grade	1+ *CSE* *(4/5)*	*1+CSE (2/3)* or *O (D/E)*	*1-4 CSE (1)* or *O (A/C)*	*5+ CSE (1)* or *O (A/C)*	
Turkish	21.3	4.1	10.8	19.5	31.7	2.6	268
Bangladeshi	35.7	6.0	12.0	24.3	17.7	4.2	333
Caribbean	13.8	3.0	13.4	37.9	27.3	4.6	2,981
Arab	16.5	7.7	7.7	30.8	30.8	6.6	91
White British	21.8	3.5	8.8	26.9	28.7	10.3	10,685
African	15.5	1.2	9.9	32.4	30.8	10.3	426
African Asian	10.5	0.6	3.7	27.2	33.3	14.7	162
Other n.i.e.	12.1	2.4	6.2	23.7	38.9	16.7	1,483
Pakistani	8.7	0.9	8.7	26.4	37.7	17.7	231
Indian	6.3	0.8	5.3	26.4	34.9	26.4	398
All	19.0	3.2	9.3	28.7	29.5	10.2	17,058

Source: Kysel 1988 adapted from Table 1.

Notes: CSE = Certificate of Secondary Education;
O = Ordinary level of the General Certificate of Education (GCE);
(1), (2/3), (4/5) = Grade 1; Grade 2 or 3; and Grade 4 or 5 in CSE;
(A/C), (D/E) = Grade A, B or C; and Grade D or E in GCE O-level;
'1-4 *CSE (1)* or *O (A/C)*' means that at least 1 and not more than 4 passes were obtained in any combination of CSE Grade 1 or GCE O-level grades A, B or C;
n.i.e. = not included elsewhere. White British includes Irish.

Table 2   Examination results of fifth formers in the Inner London Education Authority, Summer 1985 (percentages, ranked on 5 or more higher-level passes)

	Score	N
Bangladeshi	8.7	333
Turkish	11.9	268
Caribbean	13.6	2,981
Arab	14.0	91
White British (including Irish)	15.2	10,685
African	16.9	426
Greek	17.6	243
South East Asian	19.1	300
Pakistani	21.3	231
Other n.i.e.	21.3	940
African Asian	22.7	162
Indian	24.5	398
All	15.6	17,058

Source: Kysel 1988 adapted from Table 2.

Note: n.i.e. = not included elsewhere.

Table 3   Average performance scores of fifth formers in the Inner London Education Authority on GCE O-levels and CSEs, Summer 1985 (ranked)

more closely with the Caribbean CSE and O-level average performance score than did the results from tests of reading and mathematics, which would have led one to expect a better performance than one actually found.

Kysel therefore concludes that the verbal reasoning categorisation by teachers 'does provide a useful measure of primary attainment against which examination results can be assessed' (ibid. p. 88). However, it is also possible that the poor Caribbean examination results are, at least in part, a consequence of the placement in the depressed verbal reasoning categories. Alternatively, or additionally, both the below-average verbal reasoning categorisation and the below-average examination results might be a function, at least partly, of negative or narrow stereotypes and expectations, including negative judgements about Caribbean speech.

The most recent data for ILEA are comparable to Kysel's data and paint a similar picture (ILEA Research and Statistics, 1990b). These are the summer 1987 CSE and O-level results for 18,314 sixteen-year-olds in 116 out of 141 voluntary and county secondary schools (Table 4). The average performance scores (Table 5) were calculated using the same points system as above.

This study shows that on average the pupils of Indian, Pakistani and continental European backgrounds obtained the best examination results in 1987, while those of Bangladeshi, Turkish and Caribbean backgrounds obtained the worst. The English, Scottish and Welsh (ESW) pupils constituted more than half of the research sample but their examination results were a little below average.

These data too are problematic in several ways. Since the ethnic categorisation was apparently done by the schools, it may contain a substantial error factor, especially in the case of Caribbean pupils. It is not clear, for instance, how Indo-Caribbean pupils were classified. It is also revealing that the ESW category was apparently used exclusively for *white* British pupils.

Furthermore, the report tells us nothing about the large proportion, almost one-fifth, of schools excluded from these data. Could it be that most of these schools contained relatively few black pupils and/or that the ESW pupils in these schools were performing relatively well?

Another point is that the data relate only to sixteen-year-old pupils. However, black pupils often stay on at school and obtain good examination results when older, as for example Mabey (1985) and Rutter (1982) have shown. The data also do not control for important factors such as social class or previous educational treatment. Finally, no

	No exams taken	No grade	Percentage of pupils in each group gaining:				No. of pupils
			1+ *CSE* (4/5)	1+ *CSE* (2/3) or *O* (D/E)	1–4 *CSE* (1) or *O* (A/C)	5+ *CSE* (1) or *O* (A/C)	
Caribbean	13.5	3.2	10.9	36.0	31.4	4.9	2,758
Bangladeshi	34.5	6.6	9.0	23.2	21.6	5.0	776
Turkish	25.6	2.6	10.9	20.5	33.7	6.7	312
Black n.i.e.	20.4	2.2	8.1	23.1	37.6	8.6	186
Arab	17.2	4.3	11.8	20.4	36.6	9.7	93
ESW	22.0	3.2	7.6	26.5	29.9	10.8	10,233
White n.i.e.	20.0	2.3	5.7	24.0	34.9	13.1	175
African	16.2	1.5	8.3	27.7	33.0	13.2	530
Irish	18.5	2.5	6.6	27.2	31.0	14.2	1,240
Greek	15.8	1.9	8.4	20.0	38.6	15.3	215
S.E. Asian	19.7	1.5	4.7	23.1	34.8	16.2	402
Pakistani	10.2	2.8	9.8	23.6	36.6	16.9	254
Indian	12.7	0.5	3.0	23.0	41.4	19.5	440
Euro. n.i.e.	12.0	1.7	5.0	23.4	36.6	21.3	700
All	20.0	3.0	7.9	27.3	31.0	10.8	18,314

Source: Inner London Education Authority Research and Statistics 1990b Table 6.
Notes: ESW = English, Scottish and Welsh;

S.E. Asian = South East Asian;
Euro. = European;
See also notes to Table 2.

Table 4   Examination results of 16-year-olds in the Inner London Education Authority, 1987 (percentages ranked on 5 or more higher-level passes)

	Score	N
Bangladeshi	9.9	776
Turkish	13.1	312
Caribbean	14.3	2,758
English, Scottish and Welsh	15.7	10,233
Black n.i.e.	16.0	186
Arab	16.8	93
African	17.6	530
White n.i.e.	18.1	175
Irish	18.2	1,240
Greek	18.5	215
South East Asian	18.8	402
Pakistani	20.6	254
European n.i.e.	22.5	700
Indian	22.8	440
All	16.1	18,314

Source: ILEA Research and Statistics1990b adapted from Table 8.

Note: n.i.e. = not included elsewhere.

Table 5   Average performance scores of 16-year-olds in the Inner London Education Authority on GCE O-levels and CSEs, Summer 1987 (ranked)

national conclusions should be drawn from this study, since it is restricted to Inner London.

Some educational achievements

Whatever their limitations, however, much of the available data suggest that Caribbean pupils are on average badly placed within the British education system and are receiving much poorer results than they should be. Nevertheless there is also evidence of educational achievement, and of ability, although these findings too have their limitations.

Driver (1980) has produced data which indicate that the West Indians he studied, especially the girls, were getting somewhat better GCE O-level and CSE results than their white British school peers. It is interesting that Driver's study is the only one which Taylor (1981, pp. 113–22) subjects to a minute and searching critical analysis. Nevertheless, she concludes that 'it is clear that not all pupils of West Indian origin are underachieving and . . . some are indeed attaining relatively high results' (ibid. p. 122).

In a study of twelve non-selective Inner London schools between 1976 and 1978 Rutter (1982) also found evidence of Caribbean pupils doing better than white pupils in CSE and GCE O-level examinations. Craft and Craft (1983) have also produced some limited evidence of Caribbean pupils doing very well at the highest levels.

There is evidence, too, of good performance on ability tests. For instance, Stones (1979) found that, when thirty Caribbean and thirty white British children in a Midlands inner city school were taught with materials based on the principles contained in the Raven's Matrices Test, the performance of these two groups on this test differed little from each other. In a study referred to earlier, Bagley (1971) took trouble to control a range of factors by studying fifty carefully matched pairs of white British and Caribbean pupils in London. Both groups performed above average on a Stanford–Binet intelligence test, with the Caribbean children scoring somewhat better (105.7) than the white pupils (103.2), although the difference was not statistically significant.

'Underachievement' or inequality?

Not only do many Caribbean pupils do very well in the British education system, to speak constantly of Caribbean 'underachievement' as do most reports and reviews is also misleading for other reasons. First of all, the conceptualisation of the findings in terms of 'under-achievement' assumes that the instruments used to measure ability or attainment or to make comparisons between individuals or groups are valid, unbiased and culture-fair. Where comparisons are made, there is also an implicit assumption that the parties being compared have had similar or comparable learning opportunities and experiences. As we have seen, both of these assumptions are problematic. Besides, the notion of 'underachievement' tends to direct one's focus on to individuals and their characteristics, and to make ill-founded deficit or pathological assumptions about their culture and social background.

The situation of Caribbean-heritage pupils in the British education system needs to be seen in terms of inequality and not simply of 'underachievement'. (See also chapter 16 below.) Thus Caribbean pupils are over-represented at the bottom end of the education system: in educationally subnormal (ESN) and non-selective schools (ILEA, 1967 and 1968b; Coard, 1971; Townsend 1971, p. 56ff; Fethney, 1973; Figueroa, 1974, Table 2 7–9 and Tomlinson, 1982); in lower streams and non-examination classes (for example Townsend and Brittan, 1972); in disruptive units (Tomlinson, 1982); and among pupils suspended or expelled (ILEA Research and Statistics, 1990a).

Bagley (1982) also found some indication in his re-analysis of data from the National Child Development Study that Caribbean pupils are allocated fewer resources than many others. Townsend (1971) and Little and Willey (1981) likewise point to unequal standard British English language provision for Caribbean-heritage children compared with 'Asians'. Stone (1981) has suggested that often Caribbean pupils are not given fair educational opportunities and rigorous teaching. Wright (1986) has produced evidence which suggests that Caribbean pupils are treated unequally in the process of allocation to bands and examination sets. Similarly, in the study already referred to, Kysel found:

> some indication that when there was a mismatch between the VR [verbal reasoning] band in which a pupil had been placed by teachers and that based on test performance, Caribbean pupils were more likely to be placed in a lower VR band . . . while ESWI [English, Scottish, Welsh and Irish] pupils were more likely to be placed in a higher VR band than their test scores would suggest. (Kysel, 1988, p. 88)

The way Creole speakers were dealt with in the third and last of the ILEA language censuses (ILEA Research and Statistics, 1989) is symptomatic of the failure to address equitably the situation and needs of Caribbean pupils – even though they are seen as one of the most problematic groups of school children. Although a lot of trouble was taken to identify accurately the languages spoken by the more than 280,000-strong school population, no account was taken of dialects of English or of English-based Creoles, except for Krio, spoken in Sierra Leone, eighty-nine speakers of which were recorded. The largest identified group of pupils speaking a language other than English were 20,113 Bengali-speakers, and the next largest were 4,625 Turkish speakers. But we are left with no idea of what proportion of the approximately 37,000 Caribbean-heritage pupils had an English-based Creole or a non-standard dialect of English as their first language.

Understanding the situation of the Caribbean pupils as one of educational inequality is not to gainsay the possible importance of individual characteristics and background, such as self-esteem, motivation and parental support. Many factors contribute to the situation and performance of Caribbean-heritage pupils. However, using inequality rather than underachievement as the key concept, points one's attention to structural realities, dominant frames of reference, discrimination, and institutional processes and racism.

Educational inequality is related both as cause and effect to inequality in the society at large, of which it is part and parcel. It must be understood in terms of that wider inequality, of the characteristics, perceptions and behaviour of the majority population, of the way the education system works and of school processes, rather than simply in terms of the characteristics and home background of Caribbean pupils.

The inequality of the Caribbean-heritage population and the existence of racism in the wider society have been documented in chapter 1 above. Several studies have also identified racism among teachers, student-teachers and pupils (see for instance Figueroa, 1974 and 1991; Brittan, 1976; CRE, 1988; Kelly and Cohn, 1988 and Tattum and Lane, 1989).

However, the notion that racism might be a significant contributor to the poor educational situation of many Caribbean heritage pupils has been questioned, even though it is strongly held by many in the Caribbean community (Select Committee, 1977) and was accepted by the Rampton Committee (DES, 1981). Thus Lord Swann states at the beginning of this book that 'Asian' children, like 'West Indian' children, are subject to racism and yet achieve on a level with white children, so that 'the explanation of underachievement as being solely, or very largely due to racism in schools, was immediately suspect'.

It should be noted that Lord Swann was not questioning the existence of racism, but the extent to which it can account for Caribbean 'underachievement'. Nevertheless, the argument with reference to 'Asians' falls down on three counts. Firstly, some 'Asian' groups – for example, the Bangladeshi – actually do rather badly within the education system (Taylor with Hegarty, 1985). Secondly, even among those groups of 'Asians' who achieve well compared with their peers locally, it is not at all clear that they are doing as well, nationally, as white pupils from similar social class backgrounds. Thirdly, the images commonly held of 'Asians' are rather different from those held of Caribbean people. For instance, 'Asians' are often stereotyped as hardworking, well-behaved, submissive and non-English-speaking, whereas Caribbean people are often stereotyped as happy-go-lucky, lacking concentration, noisy and rebellious (Tomlinson, 1982; Figueroa, 1989). In other words the racist frame of reference concerning 'Asians' is rather different *in content* from that regarding 'West Indians'. Hence, it should not be surprising if racism works differently in the two cases.

The unequal structural realities, and the processes and frames of reference integral to them, are fundamental, not only in accounting for the situation and performance of Caribbean pupils, but also in understanding the dominant modes of perceiving, conceptualising and relating to this situation and this performance. The constant emphasis on Caribbean educational 'underachievement' can itself be seen as integral to the unequal location of Caribbean people within the society and to the dominant negative and narrow frames of reference regarding them.

The Education Reform Act and the future

Will the Education Reform Act meet the needs of the Caribbean-heritage pupils and promote their educational achievement? As pointed out in chapter 1, ERA does offer some positive opportunities. Also, National Curriculum working groups were specifically required to take account of the ethnic and cultural diversity of the school population and of the society.

However, we also saw in chapter 1 that problems remain with the provisions of ERA. In fact, multicultural considerations have so far been marginalised – and anti-racist ones largely ignored. It is also odd that the concept of equal opportunities tends to be used in National Curriculum Council documents only in relation to gender. The main exceptions to this are in Curriculum Guidance Nos. 3 and 8 (NCC,

1990a and 1990b) and in the final Modern Languages proposals (DES and Welsh Office, 1990), where the notion of equal opportunities is used across the board, and where multicultural and even anti-racist issues are dealt with. Even *Better Schools* brought the issues into sharper focus than is often the case in NCC documents:

> The Government's policies are designed to reduce under-achievement wherever it occurs, to remove the educational obstacles which hold back particular groups of pupils, and to support the work of the education service in preparing pupils for an ethnically mixed society and in working towards racial [sic] harmony.
> . . . curricular policies . . . should ensure that what is taught . . . is meaningful to all pupils. Teaching approaches need to take account of all pupils' backgrounds so that the pupils may . . . learn by drawing upon their own experience . . . all pupils need to understand, and acquire a positive attitude towards, the variety of ethnic groups within British society. (DES, 1985b, p. 61)

Unless the situation and needs of the Caribbean-heritage – and indeed 'Asian' – pupils are specifically addressed, and unless the issues discussed in chapter 1 above of cultural diversity, inequality and racism (both direct and indirect) are faced up to in a concerted manner, the provisions of ERA cannot be expected to meet those needs and to respond adequately to that situation. It is essential that specific steps be taken to ensure that the curriculum, the pedagogy, the books and the other teaching materials, as well as the assessment and allocation procedures are equitable and anti-racist in practice, promote the highest academic standards for all and foster open-mindedness, a constructively critical spirit, autonomy, equality, collaboration, mutual respect and friendship. In particular it is essential that NCC standardised assessment tasks, teacher assessment and GCSE and A-level examinations be linguistically and culturally sensitive and fair, avoid all forms of ethnicism and racism, and incorporate a wide range of content, contexts, points of view, approaches, methods, formats and styles.

But, however rich the curriculum may seem on paper and however equitable the assessment and allocation procedures, little can be achieved without the teachers (and other personnel in the education system) being informed, competent and committed. Pre-service and in-service education are therefore essential to raise awareness, question and shift assumptions, extend knowledge and develop skills, sensitivity and commitment in the fields of cultural diversity, equal opportunities, anti-ethnicism and anti-racism.

References

Bagley, C. (1968) The educational performance of immigrant children. *Race*, 10.1
(1971) A comparative study of social environment and intelligence in West Indian and English children in London. *Social and Economic Studies*, 20.4, pp. 420–30, December
(1982) Achievement, behaviour disorder and social circumstances in West Indian children and other ethnic groups. In G.K. Verma and C. Bagley (eds.) *Self-concept: Achievement and Multicultural Education*. Macmillan
Bailey, B.L. (1966) *A Transformational Grammar of Jamaican Creole*. Cambridge University Press
Barnes, J. (ed.) (1975) *Educational Priority: Curriculum Innovation in EPAs*, vol. 3. HMSO
Brittan, E. (1976) Multiracial education 2. Teacher opinion on aspects of school life. Part 2: Pupils and teachers. *Educational Research*, 18.3, pp. 182–91. NFER-Nelson
Carrington, B. (1983) Sport as a side-track: An analysis of West Indian involvement in extra-curricular sport. In L. Barton and S. Walker (eds.) *Race, Class and Education*. Croom Helm
Coard, B. (1971) *How the West Indian Child is Made Educationally Subnormal in the British School System*. New Beacon Books
Commission for Racial Equality. (1978) *Ethnic Minorities in Britain: Statistical Background*. CRE
(1988) *Learning in Terror: A Survey of Racial Harassment in Schools and Colleges*. CRE
Craft, M. (ed.) (1981) *Teaching in a Multicultural Society: The Task for Teacher Education*. Falmer Press
Craft, M. and Craft, A. (1983) The participation of ethnic minority pupils in further and higher education. *Educational Research*, 25.1, pp. 10–19, February. NFER-Nelson
Dawson, A.L. (1978) The attitudes of black and white adolescents in an urban area. In C. Murray (ed.) *Youth in Contemporary Society: Theoretical and Research Perspectives*. NFER
Department of Education and Science. (1981) *West Indian Children in Our Schools* (Rampton Report). HMSO
(1985a) *Education for All* (Swann Report). HMSO
(1985b) *Better Schools*. HMSO
Department of Education and Science and Welsh Office. (1990) *Modern Foreign Languages for Ages 11–16: Proposals of the Secretary of State for*

Education and Science and the Secretary of State for Wales. HMSO

Driver, G. (1977) Cultural competence, social power and school achievement: West Indian secondary school pupils in the Midlands. *New Community*, 5.4

(1980) *Beyond Underachievement: Case Studies of English, West Indian and Asian School-Leavers at 16 Plus.* Commission for Racial Equality

Edwards, V.K. (1979) *The West Indian Language Issue in British Schools.* Routledge

Essen, J. and Ghodsian, M. (1979) The children of immigrants: School performance. *New Community*, 7.3, pp. 442–29

Evans, P. (1972) *Attitudes of Young Immigrants.* Runnymede Trust

Fethney, V. (1973) Our ESN children. *Race Today*, 5.4, pp. 109–15

Figueroa, P. (1974) 'West Indian school-leavers in London: a sociological study in ten schools in a London borough. 1966–1967.' Unpublished Ph.D. thesis, London School of Economics, University of London

(1984) Minority pupil progress. In M. Craft (ed.) *Education and Cultural Pluralism.* Falmer Press

(1989) Student-teachers' images of ethnic minorities: A case study. In S. Tomlinson and A. Yogev (eds.) *Affirmative Action and Positive Policies in the Education of Ethnic Minorities*, vol. 1 of International Perspectives on Education and Society, Greenwich, CT: JAI Press Inc.

(1991) *Education and the Social Construction of 'Race'.* Routledge

Figueroa, P. and Swart, L.T. (1986) Teachers' and pupils' racist and ethnocentric frames of reference: A case study. *New Community*, XIII. 1, pp. 40–51, Spring/Summer

Green, P.A. (1972) 'Attitudes of teachers of West Indian immigrant groups.' Unpublished M.Phil. thesis, University of Nottingham

Hill, D. (1968) 'The attitudes of West Indian and English adolescents in Britain.' Unpublished M.Ed. thesis, University of Manchester

Inner London Education Authority. (1967) *Immigrant Children in ESN Schools: Survey Report.* ILEA Research and Statistics Group, November

(1968a) *The Education of Immigrant Pupils in Primary Schools*, Report 959. ILEA, February

(1968b) *The Education of Immigrant Pupils in Special Schools for ESN Children*, Report 657. ILEA, September

Inner London Education Authority Research and Statistics. (1989) *1989 Language Census*, RS 1361/89 (report written by J. Sinnott). ILEA, December

(1990a) *Suspensions and Expulsions from School – 1987–88*, RS 1270/90 (report written by J. Davies). ILEA, March

(1990b) *Differences in Examination Performance*, RS 1277/90. ILEA, March

Jelinek, M.M. (1977) Multi-racial education 3. Pupils' attitudes to the multi-racial school. *Educational Research*, 19.2, pp. 129–41. NFER-Nelson

Kamin, L.J. (1977) *The Science and Politics of I.Q.* Penguin

Karier, C. (1976) Testing for order in the corporate liberal state. In R. Dale, G. Esland and M. MacDonald (eds.) *Schooling and Capitalism*. Routledge

Kelly, E. and Cohn, T. (1988) *Racism in Schools: New Research Evidence*. Trentham Books

Kysel, F. (1988) Ethnic background and examination results. *Educational Research*, 30.2, pp. 83–9, June. NFER-Nelson

Le Page, R.B. (1981) *Caribbean Connections in the Classroom*. Pamphlet of Guidance for Teachers Concerned with the Language Problems of Children of Afro-Caribbean Descent. Mary Glasgow Trust

Little, A. (1975) The educational achievement of ethnic minority children in London schools. In G.K. Verma and C. Bagley (eds.) *Race and Education Across Cultures*. Heinemann

Little, A. and Willey, R. (1981) *Multi-ethnic Education: The Way Forward*. Schools Council

Mabey, C. (1981) Black British literacy: A study of reading attainment of London black children from 8 to 15 years. *Educational Research*, 23.2, pp. 83–95. NFER-Nelson

(1985) 'Achievement of black pupils: reading competence as a predictor of examination success among Afro-Caribbean pupils in London.' Unpublished Ph.D. thesis, University of London

National Curriculum Council. (1990a) Curriculum Guidance No. 3: *The Whole Curriculum*. NCC, March

(1990b) Curriculum Guidance No. 8: *Education for Citizenship*. NCC, November

Rutter, M. (1982) Growing up in Inner London: Problems and accomplishments. Inner City Lecture, London, IBM/North Westminster, 4 October

Select Committee on Race Relations and Immigration. (1977) *The West Indian Community*. HMSO

Smith, D.J. and Tomlinson, S. (1989) *The School Effect: A Study of Multiracial Comprehensives*. Policy Studies Institute

Stone, M. (1981) *The Education of the Black Child in Britain: The Myth of Multiracial Education*. Fontana

Stones, E. (1979) The colour of conceptual learning. In G. Verma and C. Bagley (eds.) *Race, Education and Identity*. Macmillan

Tattum, D.P. and Lane, D.A. (1989) *Bullying in School*. Trentham Books

Taylor, M.J. (1981) *Caught Between: A Review of Research into the Education of Pupils of West Indian Origin*. NFER

Taylor, M.J. with Hegarty, S. (1985) *The Best of Both Worlds . . .? – A Review of Research into the Education of Pupils of South Asian Origin*. NFER-Nelson

Tomlinson, S. (1982) *A Sociology of Special Education*. Routledge

(1983) *Ethnic Minorities in British Schools: A Review of the Literature 1960–82*. Heinemann Educational Books

Townsend, H.E.R. (1971) *Immigrant Pupils in England: The LEA Response*. NFER

Townsend, H.E.R and Brittan, E.M. (1972) *Organisation in Multi-Racial Schools*. NFER

Wright, C. (1986) School processes – an ethnographic study, In J. Eggleston, D. Dunn and A. Malidu *Education for Some: The Educational and Vocational Experiences of 15–18 Year Old Members of Minority Ethnic Groups*. Trentham Books

Chapter 15

Traveller Education: Structural Response to Cultural Diversity

Pat Holmes

Organisation and structure are the keys to the creation of an education system which can cater for cultural diversity. Gypsies and Travellers are an important group to address in relation to organisational issues, as their mobility and life-style have been, and still are, used to marginalise and exclude them from the 'system'. Solutions that are inclusive of them can ultimately be useful to everyone.

Starting-points

The starting-point must be the recognition of Gypsies and Travellers as an ethnic group, of which the tradition of mobility is one identifying feature. Gypsies and Travellers have always been historically a viable and effective mobile workforce providing skills and services to the settled communities. The places they traditionally camped were returned to year after year in order to ply their trades and work across a planned area of operation. This camp tradition is reflected in the road and lane names we know today such as Gypsy Lane, Gypsy Hill, and so on. As with all ethnic groups, these traditions are subject to change from outside as well as from within.

In the 1960s there were economic and social developments which had a significant impact on how the Gypsies and Travellers were reintroduced to 'education' after a virtual post-war absence. With the mechanisation of farming, the growth of the towns and the expansion of the commuter belt, the community began to be squeezed out from their regular work patterns and stopping places. The 1960 Caravan

I would like to thank Margo Gorman, Principal Officer, Save the Children Fund, North West, for valuable discussions around these issues; also my colleagues at West Midlands Education Service for Travelling Children and The Partnership Project for their skills and enthusiasm for developing good practice.

Sites and Control of Development Act gave local authorities the power to provide and run sites for Gypsies and laid down minimum standards for amenities. Hundreds of Gypsies were driven off private sites under this legislation and it is believed many more were driven off by local council harassment of non-Gypsy landowners, forcing them to move Gypsies off their land.

Legislation enacted at the end of the 1960s should have changed all this. The 1968 Caravan Sites Act (Part II refers to Gypsies and became law in April 1970) placed a duty on every local authority to provide adequate accommodation for Gypsies residing in or resorting to their area. However, in 1990, above forty per cent of Travellers still had no legal place to stay, despite the Secretary of State for Environment having powers to direct a local authority to provide a site by Statutory Instrument. Under this law, Travellers are also subject to a system of inhabiting sites in designated areas which amounts to a restrictive quota system for their community in a given area.

Pont d'Avignon – a bridge that goes only half-way

In the mid to late 1960s, when Travellers were more visible in the towns and cities, living on open or derelict land and seeking to adapt to new work opportunities, they drew the attention of human rights groups and other voluntary organisations who initiated attempts to respond to their educational 'needs'. Voluntary welfare and education support operated on the camps and volunteers attempted to act as a bridge between families and generally inflexible services. Volunteers also took on family problems and attempted to resolve them on their behalf at DHSS, health departments, clinics, housing departments etc. These volunteers tended to operate in vehicles brought on to sites or in the family caravan/trailer, bringing reading and writing to Traveller children. The work of the volunteers highlighted the need for a more organised and inclusive response by the statutory bodies to provide education for Traveller children.

In some areas LEAs responded by funding the continuation of provision on Traveller sites – often in mobile units. Some had a hazy commitment to bridge children into school once they had reached a social and academic level that would enable them to enter school equally with their settled peer group. In reality, it often acted as a bridge for the teacher from mainstream society into Traveller culture, but rarely operated the other way round. Recent intercultural exchanges have led to the affectionate label 'Pont d'Avignon' for these initiatives in recognition of another bridge that only went half way.

The rationale for keeping Traveller children out of school was based on one or all of the following:

- their mobility which prevented them from attending school;
- their lack of formal education which caused them to be 'behind' their settled peers;
- the intention of preserving and protecting their culture in the belief that it would be threatened by mainstream schooling;
- the hostility of the settled community towards them.

The response of most mainstream schools did nothing to allay the fears of volunteers or Traveller families. Those Traveller children who made their way to school were all too frequently hived off into special schools. Those who went into schools with some support were generally withdrawn from the classroom and seen as empty receptacles into which undiluted '3Rs' could be poured to 'bring them up to the standards of their settled peers'. The inability of children to respond to this method was put down as their failure and thus more candidates for special schools were moulded. It is not surprising, given the independence and self-respect of most Gypsy children, that many of them were insulted by these approaches and opted out altogether.

Tackling the mainstream

Throughout this experience there were those people in voluntary groups and in education who believed that the rights of Traveller children to a broad, balanced and relevant curriculum could best be delivered by the extensive resources of mainstream education and that the task was not only to assert children's rights to education and to provide support for the individual child and family, but to support and create awareness in schools and policy makers about the specific experiences, skills and needs of Traveller children and their families. It is worth noting that the National Gypsy Council has maintained its commitment to the above throughout.

Today, despite some measured improvement, basic access to accommodation, health care, welfare rights and education remains difficult and sometimes impossible for Traveller families and they continue to be excluded from the organisation of society on the basis of their cultures, life-style, traditions, and the myths and negative stereotyping about them that abound. Just a glimpse of the obstacles and dilemmas many Traveller families face daily reveals discrimination such as the following:

- regular eviction from unofficial camps;
- gross underprovision of legal stopping places/sites;
- they are frequently refused treatment by family doctors and clinics;
- hospital appointments' systems frequently fail to accommodate mobile and/or largely illiterate communities;
- some headteachers and school governors employ delaying tactics such as elaborate and lengthy enrolment procedures with regard to Traveller children in the hope they will move on before entry;
- other schools simply refuse to admit them despite the law;
- some LEAs have unwritten percentage notions of how many Traveller children they will allow into a school;
- other schools do not facilitate their entry at all, preferring to provide education in isolation from the resources and social setting of mainstream education;
- when Traveller children do go into school the children are sometimes marginalised and excluded from the curriculum and social community, and support teaching is still provided in the traditional remedial-type setting, for example away from the classroom;
- the children and parents of the settled community often behave in a hostile manner towards Traveller children, demanding their removal from school, and where this demand is not met, they remove their own children from the school.

As few as 40–50% of primary-aged Traveller children attend school and at secondary level there is a reduction to around a disturbing 10% . . . Those attending regularly are but a small proportion of the total. (HMI Discussion Document, 1983)

This was endorsed by the Swann Report, *Education for All*, which stated that:

Whereas with the other groups of children whom we have been considering we have been chiefly concerned with their needs within schools, many of the particular educational needs of Travellers' children arise because of difficulties of gaining access to the education system at all. In many respects the situation in which Travellers' children find themselves also illustrates to an extreme degree the experience of prejudice and alienation. (DES, 1985)

In theory, Travellers' rights to education are recognised. Under the Education Act 1980, LEAs have a duty to make arrangements to provide parents with a choice as to which school they wish their children to attend. The duty extends to all children residing in or resorting to its area whether permanently or temporarily and regardless of legal status. DES Circular 1/81 in confirming the 1980 Act stated: 'the duty thus embraced in particular Traveller children including Gypsies'.

Furthermore, central government, through the DES, substantially assists LEAs to meet the costs of educating Traveller children. Initially it enabled LEAs to recoup expenditures incurred on Traveller education from the DES No Area Pool Fund, at rates of 75 and 100 per cent. From April 1990, under Section 210 of the Education Reform Act 1988, the Government replaced the No Area Pool Fund with the New Specific Grant for Travellers and Displaced Persons (75 per cent recoupable) in respect of all educational provision for Traveller children.

Why then is progress so slow in advancing Traveller children's rights to education in an atmosphere free from prejudice and discrimination? The answer would appear to lie in the lack of any coherent strategies on organisation and structures. This is now further complicated by the new funding programme, ERA and Local Management of Schools.

The regulations governing the new Specific Grant embraced a wider educational field of students than the former No Area Pool Fund. They included, for the first time, opportunities for grant support for pre-school provision for Traveller children; post-sixteen vocational training and adult literacy projects. In addition, the range of Travelling communities on whom the grant was focused was extended to include the newly emerged mobile groups from the settled community ('New Age'/'New Travellers').

Despite the progressive promise in the regulations for the new grant, LEAs have had to compete for financial support for an initial three-year performance indicator-related, project-based period of work in Traveller education. Work which those in the field identified as developmental in character, was deemed to be 'project-based' by the new regulations. This has serious implications for long-term planning and quality of staffing. The total grant (£8.1 million) was not sufficient to support the existing provision in spite of expectations to the contrary raised by the new regulations.

A total of seventy-six LEAs applied for grant assistance from April 1990. Sixty LEAs with existing provision received a percentage of their submission of which the staffing, transport and school uniform elements of the bid were prioritised by the DES. Fifteen LEAs who had previously failed to provide equal education opportunities for Traveller children and who had been encouraged to redress the situation by submitting proposals under the new Specific Grant regulations, were left without any funding assistance at all. Hopes that the new Specific Grant would substantially progress the existing patchy provision towards a more organised, structured and consistent response nationally were dashed.

A further DES Circular (10/90) with a revised proforma for information for the next stage of submissions under the new Specific Grant, which was issued in the summer of 1990, did little to redress this situation although a further million pounds was identified specifically for 'new' work.

The Education Reform Act and Traveller children

The implications of ERA for Traveller children are complex. Many aspects appear promising but there are serious reservations around some of the, as yet largely unknown, elements such as testing and assessment. The key issues for Traveller children in the new framework are:

1   access to schools;
2   access to the National Curriculum;
3   respecting, reflecting and including the culture, life-style, skills and experience of Travellers in the hidden and open curriculum;
4   continuity of education through enforced mobility and planned mobility;
5   achievement.

Since the Education Act 1980, which removed all artificial barriers to parental choice of school, the only ground remaining on which a school can refuse to register a child is where there are insufficient places. Even that may be appealed, leading to the possible increase of places in the school to meet the parental demand. One suspects, however, that the all-too-common reluctance and delay in some schools registering Traveller children will continue until the detail of the legislation becomes commonplace in the negotiation skills of those supporting the access of Traveller children to schools, or indeed in Traveller parents' own knowledge as they independently support the continuity of education for their children.

Under ERA, pupils are entitled to a curriculum which is:

broad, balanced and relevant to his/her needs and which

(a) promotes the spiritual, moral, cultural, mental and physical development of pupils at the school . . .

(b) prepares pupils for the opportunities, responsibilities and experiences of adult life.

It is not enough for such a curriculum to be offered by the school; it must be fully taken up by each individual pupil. These principles will need to be rigorously applied and returned to regularly for examination of what is offered to all children, including Traveller children, to ensure that the curriculum addresses their needs and experiences. Schools which exempt individual Traveller children from the National Curriculum under general or special needs criteria, for example, are still required to provide those children with a broad, balanced curriculum relevant to their needs. Under the provisions of the Act, schools would do better to concentrate on developing access to the National Curriculum for Traveller children than to seek 'special needs' status for their regular life-style of mobility.

In theory, Traveller children will be able to access the National Curriculum at their own level of learning. Teachers' skills in differentiated learning will enable children to access and achieve it in practice.

Local Management of Schools currently presents problems for schools receiving Traveller children who are mobile, enter a number of schools each year and appear in only one or none of these schools on the day that budgets for the schools are calculated on a per capita basis. In effect, schools can cope in terms of consumable stock for a small number of children who may register mid-year. However, schools receiving groups of Traveller children from time to time throughout the year may need access to centrally held contingency funding to support them in providing short-term-stay Traveller pupils with appropriate writing books, pencils etc. This would positively assist the continuity of education for Traveller children and small schools in particular.

Requirements for schools to develop more appropriate ways of recording children's achievements and the key stages at which children are operating could also prove a positive continuity strategy for the learning of Traveller children.

Little is known as yet about how prescriptive and exclusive the National Curriculum may emerge in some schools or about how prescriptive and exclusive testing and assessment will be nationally and/or locally, given an atmosphere of competition between schools for financially attractive client groups.

ERA is the most radical piece of education legislation since the 1944 Education Act. As referred to here, it could potentially be supportive to progressing the education of Traveller children. However, the overwhelming pressure from the changes that are required means that areas where progress was being made, for example in response to the Swann Report, have been marginalised. The emphasis of ERA is on opening up opportunity, not on the equality of that opportunity. Yet it is the equality of opportunity that needs to be addressed urgently with regard to Traveller children and, indeed, all children.

The experience of the strengths and limitations of multicultural and anti-racist education in the UK should provide fertile ground for the growth of 'interculturalism' as described in Council of Europe documentation and referred to in chapter 2 of this book. With an intercultural approach it is possible to draw on the best of multicultural and anti-racist values and strategies and to take them further. Without a recognition of the interaction and interdependence, which the concept 'interculturalism' implies, we must be prepared for contradictory demands, individual provision, segregation and, ultimately, social conflict.

Strategies and structures

Strategies to enable Traveller children to gain meaningful access to schools and to promote continuity of education are needed if the relationship between Traveller families and schools is to progress. Class teachers need the support to develop an awareness, ethos, curriculum and resources which value and include Traveller children. Staff engaged in this support should be involved in raising awareness, promoting the positive image of Travellers as members of society and demonstrating practically the implications of equal opportunities within the context of education across the hidden and open curriculum. We need the richness of the exchange of knowledge and skills between communities and services to inform ethos, practice and management. With education for a culturally diverse community there is room for everyone on equal terms. We need an organisation that is socially constructive and not just preventive of conflict.

It is important to work with Traveller parents to develop and broaden their understanding of education beyond the '3Rs', and to support them in extending their knowledge and developing positive expectations of education. Support staff working with schools, Traveller parents, colleagues and other agencies in this way can have a positive impact on social attitudes surrounding the situation, which can in turn inform wider audiences.

The West Midlands Education Authorities Service for Travelling Children has welcomed the moves towards interculturalism as it confirms trends that have been developing in their work for some time. The Service is a structural but flexible response which supports the inclusion of Gypsy and Traveller children in local schools in the communities, through which they move or in which they settle. It operates across ten authorities of the West Midlands region with a team consisting of a co-ordinator, field welfare staff, advisory/support teachers and administrative staff.

The Service's work is essentially to locate families and support the positive development of their links with schools and other services and to support schools in developing appropriate responses to meet the needs of Traveller children. Schools are offered advice, strategies and resource support which will respond to and reflect children positively, and will constructively challenge prejudice, discrimination or inequalities, in the curriculum and in the school.

The Service is concerned with strategies for improving the continuity of education for Traveller children. Two key strategies are:

1   the operation of transport support where needed;
2   an education record transfer system.

The latter gives validity to the educational experiences of Traveller children as they move between schools and between LEAs. It also raises teacher expectation by providing an information base of children's experience to build on.

Frequently Traveller families provide their homes and themselves as resources for photographic work for illustrated information presentations or as the basis for the development of early learning resources, and they occasionally agree to speak to class teachers or a group of children about themselves and their experiences. The Service's regional resource centre is well established with a comprehensive library on Gypsy history, development, interests and children's books. Staff engage directly with parents, children, students, teachers, governors and staff from other service agencies, combining together to promote a positive image of Travellers as part of the community.

The multiplicity of problems faced by Travellers in gaining access to accommodation, health care and other services, can tempt educationalists into the areas where other service providers are inactive. This can lead to inappropriate practices by professionals, the dilution of skills and the second-rate delivery of their own service to families. This is not what an interagency approach should be about. The West Midlands Education Authorities Service for Travelling Children liaises with the National Gypsy Council, who negotiate increases and improvements in site provision. It also works with a variety of health and welfare services for the benefit of Traveller families. In an attempt to extend this interagency approach and to develop a more co-ordinated response to health services and the wider child welfare field, a partnership has been set up with district health authorities and the Save the Children Fund. The project aims to develop and demonstrate successful interagency approaches and to transfer lessons learnt, throughout the region.

Traveller children and the hidden curriculum

In order that the ethos of a school is welcoming, inclusive and con-firming of all children, we need to examine closely the hidden curricu-lum to ensure that there is no mismatch between what we say we want and how we organise to achieve it. The hidden curriculum is about the organisation of the school, the things not overtly taught. It comprises messages conveyed by how the school and classrooms are organised and managed, and the behaviour and attitudes towards children and colleagues; it is about teaching styles and the status given to equal opportunity issues. In fact, all those things not taught by the open cur-riculum.

At the institutional level, a negative hidden curriculum can be crippling to children, operating against them becoming happy, active and confi-dent learners. At the personal attitude and behaviour level it can be conducted in a way that denies the child's whole existence, rendering children confused and constantly misreading what is required of them, to their detriment.

We cannot assume anything about a Traveller child's experience of the hidden curriculum. For children from families largely without any history or tradition of formal education, Traveller children have little to draw on in terms of picking up clues about what is expected of them in school. Teachers need to be explicit and organise so that children can be supported and successful rather than being constantly caught out by unclear messages and made to feel a failure. Measures to include Trav-eller children in this way demonstrate a sensitive, flexible, confident and respectful school – one that is good for all children.

The assumption made by some teachers that Traveller children have learning difficulties as a result of their lack of schooling often means children are inappropriately assessed, inappropriately placed and inappropriately responded to in terms of a learning programme and resources. Traveller children generally have simply lacked the opportunity to learn. Individually valued and with an appropriate learning programme, progress can be immense over a startlingly short period of time. All children need to be seen as individuals, assessed in terms of their own experiences and skills. If learning is individually valued, teachers themselves would feel more confident about assessing and meeting individual needs. Classroom management strategies that promote collaborative learning and encourage children to become co-operative and independent learners would enable teachers to foster a classroom ethos where each child is valued and where children respect each other.

Cultures in the classroom

Liking a child, having sympathy with her or him and being pleasant is an important start but it is not enough. We have to be active in planning strategies and programmes to support and enable children to learn and operate successfully.

The teacher needs to consider both the individual personality of the child and the background that he/she brings into the classroom. This is not just an issue of ethnicity; the male/female divide is probably the most fundamental 'cultural' issue in any classroom. Add to that the potential diversity that may exist, for example black, white, working class, middle class, majority English, Irish, Afro-Caribbean, Asian, Chinese, Vietnamese, Gypsy/Traveller. Of course it does not stop there – there are further dimensions, for example the black British dimension or in the case of Gypsies and Travellers the Irish, English, Scottish, Welsh dimension to their ethnicity. The experiences of first- and second-generation immigrants are different again. The group most often overlooked in all this diversity is the white majority English group. They are not usually seen as an ethnic or cultural group but as the norm by which all other groups are judged.

There are often many layers of unconscious racism in operation and it does not restrict itself to its most tangible form in its response to skin colour. Racism towards whites is apparent in the treatment of the largest minority group in England, the Irish. Irish Travellers face double discrimination from their experience as a minority within the

Gypsy/Traveller community and in the wider community – as Travellers and Irish.

One can begin to see how dangerous forcing a single culture on a class of children can be. It is when the experiences of children are ignored or suppressed and a single culture is imposed, that children are excluded and marginalised and disadvantaged by not belonging to it. It should not surprise us then when children become disaffected and conflict results. In the long term, it disadvantages all children.

In imposing a single culture, teachers ignore the wealth of expertise in the children's experience of their own culture and fail to see this as a valuable resource in the classroom. Utilising children's experiences is the most essential element of child-centred education and fundamental as a starting-point from which children can develop new and broader experiences, perspectives and skills. Using child-centred approaches:

- gives the child a good self-image;
- presents a positive image of the child to others;
- confirms your respect and the value that you place on the child's experiences;
- gives the child confidence to contribute and participate in a constructive way towards new experiences and learning.

In looking at the intercultural implications, the shift in focus from multicultural to intercultural requires that educators are the ones in need of change, in need of cultural re-examination. It has far-reaching implications for individuals and for management, organisation, curriculum and development. Although there is no point in reinventing the wheel, there are necessary processes of learning that everyone has to go through in order to understand the interaction between cultures.

Reflecting Traveller culture in the classroom is not about imposing images of the way we perceive them. It is about creating an environment in which Traveller children feel confident in sharing their experiences through all areas of the curriculum. It is also important to have an ongoing dialogue with Traveller families to help broaden their perceptions of how children learn and to listen to their needs and experiences and learn from them.

Many teachers, in good faith but in ignorance, can reduce Traveller culture to museum status by projecting as current romantic images of vardos, camp-fires, peg-making and the idyllic freedom to roam aimlessly. These characteristics are further elevated into the image of the 'true Romany', based on false notions of racial purity. The distinction between living culture and history or heritage needs to be seen as a dynamic one.

In this context, the history and heritage of Travellers is important and, given access to it, will become increasingly important to the Travellers themselves as they become literate and reclaim their history. Their culture, however, is the here and now and in the classroom; the child has the key and is the expert. The only way to access Traveller culture is through the children and their families. They are the ones who own it. If we take it from them and make it an academic subject we are dangerously close to setting up a situation in which we cause children to fail in their own culture too.

This is not to say that it is not possible to generalise in a way that positively reflects a given culture, but, when these generalisations become static picture-book stereotypes, then we can be sure we are not responding profoundly to the children in our community today.

Working beyond marginalisation

Given a secure and supportive learning environment children can develop confidence in sharing what is unique, important and personal to them. This approach to teaching, if adopted, will help children understand themselves and where they are within the community.

Every child in our multicultural society needs the confidence and support of having intercultural skills to operate effectively in order to develop understanding and respect for themselves and for others. This approach promotes this and also enhances their own life choices. A model which finds a place for everyone in the classroom and the wider society on equal terms will be more successful than one which pushes some to the periphery and marginalises, devalues and renders exotic their experiences.

It cannot be emphasised enough that education which can meet the needs of minorities is also capable of responding more efficiently and effectively to the needs of society in general. Interculturalism can offer us new possibilities for improving the quality of educational responses to all children. It is worth remembering that most of these ideas in themselves are not new. What has been lacking are the structures and strategies that would create a framework which could respect and safeguard equal opportunities for all sections of the community.

References and bibliography

Bagley, C. and Verma, G.K. (1982) *Self Concept, Achievement and Multicultural Education*. Macmillan

Banks, J.A. (1981) *Multiethnic Education: Theory and Practice*. Boston: Allyn & Bacon

Craft, M. (1984) *Education and Cultural Pluralism*. Falmer Press

Department of Education and Science. (1981) Circular 1/81. HMSO
   (1983) HMI Discussion Paper: *The Education of Travellers' Children*. HMSO
   (1985) *Education for All* (Swann Report). HMSO
   (1990) Circular 10/90. HMSO

Jones, C. and Kimberley, K. (eds.) (1986) *Intercultural Education: Concept, Context, Curriculum Practice*. Project No. 7: *The Education and Cultural Development of Migrants*. Council of Europe, Council for Cultural Co-operation, Schools Education Division

Leigeois, J.P. (1987) *School Provision for Gypsy and Traveller Children: A Synthesis Report*. Commission of the European Communities

Lynch, J. (ed.) (1981) *Teaching in the Multicultural School*. Ward Lock

Modgil, S. *et al.* (eds.) (1986) *Multicultural Education: The Interminable Debate*. Falmer Press

National Gypsy Council. (undated) Report: *Discrimination*. NGC

Rex, J. and Moore, R. (1967) *Race, Community and Conflict*. Oxford University Press

Tomlinson, S. (1985) *Ethnic Minorities in British Schools: A Review of the Literature*. Heinemann

Chapter 16

The Post-Sixteen Education of Young Black Britons

John Eggleston

'Education for some'

If there is a single theme that runs through our report,* it is the determination of very large numbers of young people from ethnic minority groups to persevere with their education in the hope of improving their prospects and obtaining their desired occupations. This persistence shows in many ways: in attention to homework and extra schoolwork, staying on, attending Saturday schools, colleges of further education and part-time courses and the keen desire to enter higher education. Sadly it is reinforced by fears of failure to obtain work and by discriminatory experiences in Youth Training Schemes (YTS).

There are social processes in both schools and society at large that counteract the efforts of young black people. In schools, both at and below sixth-form level, we found evidence that ethnic minority pupils may be placed on courses and entered for examinations at levels significantly below those appropriate for their abilities and ambitions. Within the hidden curriculum of some schools lurk lower expectations by teachers for their black pupils. Teachers may be unwilling to acknowledge the existence of these processes, or even to redress them where they are aware of them. Black adolescents often demonstrate the self-fulfilling prophecy by reacting with manners, speech and behaviour that appear to justify the differential in expectations that surrounds them. And when the schools fail them, young black people can find it difficult to enter colleges of further education.

Beyond school, the study found that the effects of racial discrimination upon employment prospects were severe. Even when young

---

*This chapter is based on a report of the study of black and white fourteen- to eighteen-year-olds in England, published in John Eggleston *et al.* (1986) *Education for Some*, Trentham Books.

black people did obtain appropriate qualifications, they did not obtain jobs in equal proportions to whites either before or after participating in YTS or similar schemes.

The study was based on a cohort of 593 black and white young people, including 157 pupils of South Asian and 110 of Afro-Caribbean ethnic origins attending two comprehensive schools in each of the following cities: Bedford, Birmingham, Bradford and London. Most were born in Britain; almost all had lived here for more than five years.

The report's findings

Aspirations

In their fifth year at school, more black than white young people were expecting to undertake a one-year sixth-form course, usually to enhance O-level or CSE stocks. A greater proportion of Afro-Caribbean pupils wanted to go to colleges of further education. More respondents of both white and South Asian backgrounds were expecting to take GCE A-levels, and the latter group were more likely to be envisaging spending three further years so doing.

A high proportion of all groups expected to resit their fifth-year public examinations in the following year in school or college.

The occupational levels to which both Afro-Caribbean and white boys aspired were very similar. Boys of South Asian ethnic origin were more likely to want professional and intermediate non-manual occupations than others. Black girls wanted rather higher occupational levels than white girls, but almost all girls hoped to do non-manual work. Young people from all groups seemed likely to hope for occupational levels higher than their parents and those of their communities as a whole. The correspondence between occupational levels reportedly advised by respondents' parents and those planned by pupils themselves was close for white and Asian pupils. Afro-Caribbean respondents generally aspired more highly than their parents advised.

Books and pamphlets, parents and careers officers were claimed to be the most helpful sources of careers advice. But young people of Asian backgrounds reportedly found their parents, and particularly their mothers, less helpful than others and their parents were also less likely to have visited their children's schools to discuss schoolwork or future opportunities – though it is notable that few parents were reported as having met their child's careers officer or discussed careers at school. A third of all pupils also claimed not to have talked to a careers officer, and only half to have talked to teachers about staying on at school or the qualifications needed for employment. The latent racist stereotyping of much careers literature, particularly in the illustrations, gave grounds for concern. Few photographs of black professional workers were found, whereas a generous supply of black manual workers was visible.

Examinations

In public examinations at sixteen-plus, there were few differences in the results achieved by pupils of white and South Asian ethnic origin, though girls of the former and boys of the latter group gained, overall, slightly higher grades. Afro-Caribbean girls achieved grades similar to white boys, but Afro-Caribbean boys received the lowest grades in the cohort even though they were only half as likely to be entered for any GCE 0-level as other ethnic groups.

These differences in examination performance do not necessarily reflect the abilities of the young people. Furthermore, the ethnographic study of two additional schools in a further LEA by Cecile Wright, suggests that certain factors might operate to the disadvantage of Afro-Caribbean pupils in some schools. If teachers hold views antagonistic to particular racial groups and if, in any resulting conflict, such teachers are supported by the authority structure of their schools, the consequences are likely to be detrimental to the attainment of most if not all pupils of that group. If racial prejudice operates among teachers, examination achievements can indicate even less adequately than usual the young person's occupational capacity.

Finding work

Of our respondents who had left school, whites were more likely to be employed; they also spent less time before getting their first job and had held more jobs overall. The black unemployed were much more likely than whites to wish they had stayed at school or college and appeared more bothered about being unemployed.

Continuing education

Black respondents in continuing education were willing to invest a great deal of persistence in the pursuit of qualifications. Half of those leaving school after a one-year sixth-form course were intending to go on to college, compared with less than one-fifth of whites. About a third of respondents of South Asian origin and Afro-Caribbean girls were envisaging spending at least three years before taking A-level examinations, and a greater proportion were hoping to get A-levels. Black students were on similar levels of course in both schools and colleges – with about one-third taking vocational examinations in schools and taking or aiming to take A-levels in colleges. White students were distributed differently. Few were taking vocational courses in schools or A-levels in colleges of further education.

Afro-Caribbean young people had apparently found it difficult to get into college, while those who had actually succeeded, did so only after more applications and more rejections than whites, and generally only by obtaining details of college opportunities by informal and incomplete methods rather than directly. Many subtle factors negatively influenced the enrolment and staying power of black students. White secretarial staff at the enrolment desks seemed to find it easier to help white students than black; lecturers on vocational courses were often uninhibited in their racist comments. We found little awareness of special 'access' programmes to either college or higher institutions. A high proportion of all black students and almost two-thirds of Asians hoped to enter higher education. But we found uncertainty among almost half our respondents, who thought they may perhaps have missed opportunities and that their education might make no positive difference to their future. Whilst some black students, mainly those of Asian origin, displayed considerable faith in the ability of education to get them a better job, more than half of the black students were prepared to admit the possibility of not getting a job at all and would have preferred to be in a job rather than at college.

Interpretation of these findings is not straightforward, for the vast majority of all intending leavers were looking only for work they really wanted to do and expressed reluctance to take just any available job. While the prospect of a job may have seemed more desirable to some than continuing to study, the need to attain an appropriate job was seen as sufficient reason for continuance. For many black students, an entirely justifiable fear of unemployment may have served to reinforce their dedication to and persistence in education.

It is the distress associated with unemployment and the insecurity of jobs accorded little respect which many young black people, having shared their parents' experiences, are seeking to avoid in their struggle for qualifications and skilled or non-manual occupations. Yet continuing education alone can by no means remove ethnic or most other forms of discrimination from the labour market. As Lord Scarman has indicated, this is a far wider social problem, but one of great urgency.

> Eliminating discrimination will take time. It would be disastrous, however, if there were to be any more doubt than at present exists among the ethnic minorities about the will of government, employers, trade union leaders and others in a position of authority to see this through. There are already signs among some black youths, despairing of an end to white discrimination, of a disturbing trend towards a total rejection of white society and the development of black separatist philosophies. (Scarman, 1981)

Recommendations

In the report we made recommendations to a number of educational institutions of ways in which they could improve their educational provision for pupils and students from minority ethnic groups.

Schools

Black pupils give the schools a major vote of confidence by staying on in very large numbers and should be more actively rewarded by schools.

Curriculum and organisation for the sixteen plus years should take full account of their ambitions, motivations and their uncertainties. The opportunities are great; students are present by choice rather than obligation and, in many cases, there are smaller class sizes, allowing more individual teaching. Yet schools sometimes offer little more than a repeat performance of the situations which have already failed these pupils. Something more imaginative than a programme of GCSE resits is desirable and possible: pre-A level courses, vocationally oriented courses and some components of the new spectrum of technical and vocational, community and recreational opportunities could be devised, in consultation with the students, to help them to maximise their own resources and those of the neighbourhood.

Procedures of allocation to sets, streams, bands and other work and ability groups should fully recognise not only the existing achievement, but also the potential of the students. Faulty allocation due to labelling can lead to faulty achievement and it seems to be Afro-Caribbean children who suffer most as a result of this process in schools.

Schools should carefully examine their procedures for examination entries and allocation to examination groups to ensure fair treatment for all racial groups, and that each individual pupil is allowed and enabled to attain optimum qualifications.

The school curriculum should offer all children the best chance to identify and develop the most marketable skills appropriate to their chances in the labour market. Schools should seek to develop the confidence and capacities of their minority group pupils. Schools need to be aware of the thin dividing line between emphasising strengths and building upon them, and identifying differences and stereotyping them. Schools must not 'ghettoise' their ethnic minority pupils by providing them with a 'soft option' curriculum; this can do no more than substitute high attainment in non-marketable skills for low attainment in mainstream marketable skills. We recommend schools to deliver a curriculum that is relevant to the potentials of black and white children and which recognises their full range of capabilities.

The best interests of all children are served by careful recording of achievement which can be used for enhanced diagnosis and guidance and the identification of potential.

Schools should examine their strategies of punishing pupils, whether 'in school' or by exclusion from it and withdrawal of support for employment or continuing education. 'Bad behaviour' can be a means of communicating frustration with discrimination, limited achievement and low status. Whatever its cause, formal punishment can often reinforce negative racial stereotypes and lower the expectations of achievement of black pupils, especially when they perceive that they are receiving unequal treatment.

Unless and until children are able to use standard English, schools may hold them back from demanding and rewarding courses. This contrasts strikingly with most British universities and polytechnics where overseas students with modest command of English regularly obtain Masters and Ph.D. degrees, their fluency increasing as they work in their chosen subject. We recommend schools to consider similar approaches with ethnic minority children, in relation to bi-dialectalism as well as bilingualism.

All schools developing Technical and Vocational Educational Initiative (TVEI) programmes should pay particular attention to the ways in which black children may benefit. TVEI could well provide pupils with more marketable attainments than the more conventional exam courses we monitored, and many aspects may be specially relevant to the needs of some black children. Schools offering work experience programmes should pay particular attention to familiarising employers and would-be employers with the full potential and capabilities of black children. Recent work undertaken for the Training Commission shows how incomplete is the communication between schools and black parents about TVEI (Eggleston and Sadler, 1988).

Anti-racist guidelines issued by LEAs can point the way to understanding the feelings and sensitivities of the ethnic minority groups more fully and should be taken seriously by schools. Teachers who are still racist should be given a clear opportunity to consider whether or not they are still suitable to be members of the profession. All teachers and pupils should be educated to handle racism in a way that helps both black and white children to be unharmed by it and, ultimately, to diminish it.

Teachers should recognise their responsibility for providing encouragement and support to all pupils. Many young black children have a realistic appraisal of their capacities but lack confidence in their own judgement, and their teachers then fail to give them the reassurances they give white children, more through the 'hidden curriculum' than overtly. 'Diagnostic' guidance must be offered sensitively so that correct guidance is not, for the best of reasons, ignored.

Further education

Young black people in our sample were twice as likely to go to college as whites – this was even more true of Asian boys and Afro-Caribbean girls. Yet there was much evidence of ignorance and uncertainty about the opportunities provided by further education.

Further education establishments should present the opportunities they offer more clearly and directly to both black and white young people, who seemed to rely on street and conventional wisdom. Link courses, open days and better promotional material are needed about both full-time courses and the part-time courses favoured by many young black people whether or not they work. A modest programme of access courses developed by Ken Millins as part of a DES project based at Ealing College of Higher Education, demonstrated how careful bridging could provide a path between low formal attainment and university and polytechnic education. There seems a similar need for access provision to bridge the much smaller gap between low or non-existent school attainment and further education, which would be more effective than a further year of resits in the schools. We recommend further education establishments to take the initiative in developing such courses in liaison with the schools, and also to re-evaluate their presentation of course content so as to offer young people a far fuller choice at sixteen plus.

They should present themselves as first-chance institutions for those for whom school may have been irrelevant or an experience of failure, not just as venues for a second chance at exams. Further education establishments, too, need to reappraise their views about the potential achievement of young black students.

The careers service

The careers service is a major influence on the educational and vocational experience of young people of ethnic minority groups but there was much evidence of the inconsistent delivery of the service to young black people.

A more intensively targeted and carefully planned and monitored approach to guidance and placement on schemes and other forms of continuing education of young black people is needed.

All careers services should be required to adopt clear and uniform statistical procedures to ensure a true local and national database. Our report draws attention to a number of statistical, technical and attitudinal practices which obscure or distort the picture of the young people's position in the labour market.

There is a central need for the careers service to provide complete coverage on the instance of 'missing persons', particularly of young black people who, having left school, had neither obtained work, YTS entry or registered as unemployed. This would serve the interests of the young and of society at large. (We found a 'missing' figure of twenty-five per cent in some areas.)

Young people should be better prepared for interviews by the careers service, which should find ways for young people to learn about the world of work before their interview. Careers interviews are necessarily brief, so optimal delivery of careers advice demands full and early liaison with schools. If the careers officer has to administer 'reality shock', there will be no time to explore real aspects of guidance.

Some young black people, isolated as they are from the job network, need a longer time-scale to identify their opportunities. The careers service should therefore start preparing school leavers earlier in the year in order to assure equality of opportunity in applications for all categories of employment available for school leavers. We recommend that the careers service refines its procedures for not only recognising but also acting upon evidence of discrimination so as to correct it.

We also recommend that the service institutes more effective procedures for monitoring referrals to training schemes and employment interviews, in order to assist young black people to receive equal opportunities in acquiring both marketable skills and paid employment. In-service training within the careers service is needed and should be extended to include appropriate aspects of race-awareness training.

The careers service literature needs to be comprehensive and readily available to all young people. The literature should avoid stereotypes of racial differentiation in employment.

Local Education Authorities

All LEAs should develop guidelines for their institutions and staffs aimed at eliminating discriminatory, prejudiced and racist behaviour. Our evidence suggests that some teachers need reminding of the implications and consequences of their behaviour in their work with children from a range of ethnic groups. Such guidelines should seek to implement our report's recommendations to schools and colleges and can provide a frame of reference against which discriminatory behaviour can be judged.

All LEAs should develop strategies for schools to identify learning materials which convey discriminatory messages and, in particular, literature which differentiates occupation roles in terms of ethnicity and colour. Such materials should not be in use to influence occupational decisions by young people, whether black or white.

LEAs need to develop a range of access routes for entry to their further education establishments, aimed at bridging the gulf between low-achieving young people in the schools and their aspirations for entry to further education.

Developments of this kind and the associated developments we have recommended for the schools cannot take place without the support of LEAs. They should take steps to ensure that their whole advisory service (and not just those members specifically concerned with multi-ethnic education) is fully aware of what is needed and seek to implement changes. This could include the development of relevant in-service courses, guidance and counselling to individual teachers and to school staffs as a whole and an alert presence in the schools. Without a committed local inspector or advisory service there can be little coherent or effective change.

The Department of Education and Science

The DES could also contribute to improving matters for school leavers of ethnic minority groups.

The School Examinations and Assessment Council should take into account the position of candidates from ethnic minorities when reviewing criteria for public examinations and in establishing arrangements for age-related testing of the National Curriculum through the Standardised Attainment Tasks (SATs).

The National Curriculum Council should guide schools in delivering a curriculum that is applicable to and equally available for all their pupils, and ensure that it is effectively directed to identifying and developing their marketable skills.

A concerted programme of in-service training is needed for teachers and careers officers concerned with the placement and guidance of young people from ethnic minority groups. This should involve the employers with whom the placements are made. The pre-vocational programmes initiated in Circular 8/83 and Circular 4/84 courses should be fully implemented and developed.

The DES and HMI should give urgent attention to ways in which schools might develop the opportunity presented to them by the young black students who are continuing their education in the schools after the minimum leaving age.

Continuing pressure on teacher training establishments will be needed to ensure that all students develop an appropriate sensitivity and perceptiveness for working with minority group adolescents. All students should be given the experience of good practice in multiracial schools and colleges, and HMI should help identify such placements. Training establishments must also be encouraged to identify and enrol a far higher proportion of black students, and be helped to establish arrangements to do so.

All published reports by DES and HMI, ranging from those on individual schools through to major reports on curriculum and organisation, should be written with an awareness of the special problems identified in our report, and should offer alleviatory strategies specific to the establishments under review.

The Training Agency

Ethnic monitoring should be given high priority by the Training Agency (TA; previously the Manpower Services Commission) and should include evaluation of the participation in, and employment out-comes of, their schemes; the level of black participation should be measured especially in schemes based on employment and those which give opportunity to experience 'extended interviews' with poten-tial employers. Care should be taken to ensure that no racial discrimi-nation, whether overt or covert, is practised by colleges, managing agents, or by employers used for placements. We recommend that agents and employers take advice from the Commission for Racial Equality to ensure that discrimination does not occur.

In the Special Groups Division, with its concern for minority groups, the TA and its officers should take particular care to dissociate the notion of special needs from that of racial disadvantage.

Effective delivery of equal opportunities through the YTS will require the area officers of the TA to undertake detailed local monitoring of publicity and recruitment procedures and their results.

TVEI, particularly with the sixteen-plus age group, could enhance the educational and vocational achievements of young members of the ethnic minority groups, but only if the TA pays particular attention to the performance of young black people.

Conclusions

A few of the changes we suggest involve additional costs and resources, which would be justified even in present economic conditions. But most involve changes of perception and attitude on the part of the indi-viduals and require no new money.

Schools and colleges cannot fundamentally change the labour mar-ket, but they can certainly enhance the employability of their young people and might even develop pupils' entrepreneurial skills, enabling some, ultimately, to create their own employment opportunities. Schools and colleges alone cannot eliminate the structural racism in society but they can help to create a more just and equitable distribution of opportunities in society.

References

Department of Education and Science. (1983) *The School Curriculum* (Cir-cular 8/83). HMSO
(1984) *The In-service Teacher Training Grant Scheme* (Circular 4/84). HMSO

Eggleston, J., Dunn, D. and Anjali, M. (1986) *Education for Some.* Trentham Books

Eggleston, J. and Sadler, E. (1988) *The Participation of Ethnic Minority Pupils in TVEI.* Training Agency

Scarman, Lord (1981) *Report of an Inquiry into the Brixton Disorders 10–12 April 1981.* HMSO

Chapter 17

Dealing with Racist Incidents in Schools

Paul Zec

> A rabbi prayed to God, in a state of hopeless agitation.
>
> 'Lord,' he said. 'What am I to do? My son, my only son, has just come to me and told me that he's going to convert to Christianity. The son of a rabbi! Oh, the shame he is bringing on his family! Please help me.'
>
> God spoke to the rabbi, and in a voice of great weariness, said: 'Huh. *Your* son! And what about *mine*?'

Is that an offensive joke? It seems, after all, to mock Christianity and Judaism simultaneously, and might even be taken to be sacrilegious. It certainly draws attention to the conflict that may flow from human perceptions of human differences. Given that the racist joke is one of the commonest forms of 'racial' abuse, was I not tactless in introducing a chapter on dealing with racist incidents with a story that looks rather like a racist joke?

I think not. If humour is a vehicle for racist abuse, it must be taken seriously. But where humour seeks to mock, not the characteristics of 'others', but the insularity and prejudices of all of us, it can soothe rather than inflame and can therefore be a weapon against prejudice. That particular story has, I believe, just that function. But then I would say that, wouldn't I? It is a Jewish story, and I am Jewish.

I do not claim to be an expert on dealing with racist incidents. Fortunately, however, there are no experts; nor could there be. Why not? Firstly, because there is no objectively correct definition of a racist incident: any such definition is bound to be stipulative; secondly, because different perceptions of what constitutes a racist incident arise partly from irreducibly different moral and social values; thirdly, because those values will in turn lie at the heart of any recommendation con-

I am grateful to Marie Montaut for providing me with an example of good practice from her own school and for helping me with some references.

cerning policy or procedure or effective strategy for dealing with racist incidents.

Racist incidents and ethnic diversity

Why discuss racist incidents in the context of education for ethnic (or cultural) diversity? The reason must be that there is a clear connection between three types of failure in and by our educational system: failure to make our schools sufficiently free from racial prejudice – particularly as this issues in racial abuse, of which, in the main, black and Asian youngsters are the victims; failure to provide adequate educational opportunities for young people of ethnic minority origin; and failure sufficiently to develop in young people generally the knowledge and attitudes that are appropriate to life in a diverse society. And that is to say nothing of the context of inequality, division and conflict in our society which is reflected in the educational system.

In this chapter I shall first summarise very briefly some public evidence of the nature and scale of (apparently) racially-inspired violence, harassment and abuse in our schools. I shall follow that with some observations about the discourse which embodies public/professional concern in this area, particularly in order to demonstrate some of the tensions embedded in the discourse. Finally, I shall offer some tentative conclusions of my own. These in turn will include some suggestions about what might count as satisfactory interethnic relationships in schools; a brief discussion of factors which may influence those relationships (and, perhaps, reduce the likelihood of racial incidents occurring); and some recommendations about dealing with incidents when they do occur.

Violence and abuse in British schools

Although, as I shall make clear later on, what counts as a racist incident is open to considerable disagreement, there is plentiful evidence of *interethnic abuse* in schools and colleges, whose motivation is apparently racist. There is also evidence that such abuse is not taken sufficiently seriously by local education authorities and by those who work in the institutions themselves. Much of the evidence has been collected in the Commission for Racial Equality publication *Learning in Terror: A Survey of Racial Harassment in Schools and Colleges* (CRE, 1988).

The Home Office Report *Racial Attacks*, published in 1981, is perhaps the best place to begin the story, dealing as it does with the general picture of racial abuse in Britain. The Report estimated that:

> Asians were 50 times more likely than whites to be the victims of racially motivated attacks, and West Indians 36 times more likely. (Home Office Report, 1981, quoted in CRE, 1988)

That early Report did in fact include evidence about racial abuse in and around schools, calling on LEAs to issue guidelines for dealing with it.

Despite having been much criticised for equivocation on some issues, the Swann Report (DES, 1985) was unequivocal, both in drawing attention to the nature, scale and significance of racial abuse in schools, and in refusing to accommodate racial abuse within the general category – familiar to all who have worked in schools – of pupil's inhumanity to pupil. For example:

> We believe the essential difference between racist name-calling and other forms of name-calling is that whereas the latter may be related only to the individual characteristics of a child, the former is a reference not only to the child but also by extension to their family and indeed more broadly their ethnic community as a whole. (DES, 1985, quoted in CRE, 1988)

Although interethnic violence – at school or elsewhere – attracts most media and political attention, the most ubiquitous form of racial abuse is, of course, name-calling. Tessa Cohn's study of 549 pupils in six schools in the London Borough of Barnet (Cohn, 1987) revealed both the widespread use among those pupils of racist names, including those which reflected simple xenophobia as well as anti-black, anti-Asian and anti-Jewish stereotypes, and a considerable degree of awareness among those very pupils of the nature and significance of name-calling.

> 'I think names to do with a person's race are the worst', 'prejudiced names', 'names connected with your family', 'names to do with colour'.

> *Boy, 16* (called 'yid'): 'I can't stand it. I take it as an insult to my family.' (Cohn, 1987)

Cohn found that 'racist' (her quotation marks) name-calling was common; increased with the age of the pupils; was more frequent than abuse on the basis of sex or other attributes, and was a weapon used more by boys than by girls.

So far, the assumed context has been urban and multi-ethnic. Racial abuse in the absence of large numbers of its objects is, of course, pervasive and no less repugnant. Akhtar and Stronach (1986) give an 'account of racism [that is] commonplace rather than exceptional' in first and middle schools in Norwich:

> as we will see, racism *is* a problem in Norwich. And – away from the special circumstances of inner cities and mass unemployment – Shahnaz Akhtar's research reveals something of the quietly endemic nature of racism in English society. (Akhtar and Stronach, 1986)

And having picked out evidence from an area of relatively low ethnic minority settlement, we should not of course forget what is perhaps the most ubiquitous racist abuse of all: that which is expressed in the total absence of its objects – that is to say, in the 'white highlands' of Britain

The fatal stabbing of an Asian boy by a white fellow-pupil at Burnage High School in Manchester in 1986 provides the unhappiest, and most sensationalised, evidence of racial abuse in schools. Apart from the intrinsically horrifying nature of the incident itself, the Burnage tragedy's importance lies in the questions it threw up about attitudes, policies and strategies regarding interethnic relationships. The balance of evidence from the Macdonald Inquiry (Macdonald, 1990) and from further elucidation by members of the Macdonald committee presents a picture of a school policy against racism pursued in an insensitive and undemocratic way. The Inquiry also revealed polarised attitudes among teachers, many of whom could not or would not recognise the racial dimension in the scenario of conflict among pupils, and regarded attempts to address issues of racial equality in the school as 'loony left' ideas. Some teachers, it was found, actually subscribed both to the practice of racist name-calling and to the general ethos of macho aggression which apparently pervaded the school.

So it would appear that Burnage reflected the worst of two worlds: on the one hand an ill-thought-out policy of anti-racism, imposed in an authoritarian fashion; and on the other hand a climate of attitudes among staff which effectively, at least, nourished intolerance among pupils; and all this against a background of the exclusion of white pupils and the white community generally from participation in dialogue and policy development concerning racial and other aspects of equality.

The discourse of interethnic relations

Cohn's study of pupils and teachers in Barnet led her to the view that:

> teachers are inclined to regard [the issue of racial abuse] as
> unimportant, outside our province, or one where any acknow-
> ledgement is too dangerous to contemplate . . . if, as teachers, we
> never acknowledge what is quite evidently going on in our schools
> and playgrounds, we are seen by our pupils to be condoning the
> racism which many of them experience daily (Cohn, 1987)

Akhtar and Stronach found three different 'patterns of evasion'
among teachers and heads when confronted with evidence of racial
abuse among pupils: 'There is no problem'; 'There is a problem, but it
is not serious'; and 'There is a problem, but it is not a racial one'. The
last of these was found to be the most common.

> Teachers, and sometimes parents, tended to shy away from racial
> interpretations of relations between the white and the non-white
> children . . . They feel it better to play down [an] incident itself and
> to make general and positive appeals for tolerance. (Akhtar and
> Stronach, 1986)

The implicit criticism here concerns the *discourse* of interethnic relations in schools. Because of the emotive meaning of the term 'race' –
the negative feeling which the word evokes through its association with
racism – it is uncomfortable to acknowledge cases covered by the term;
it is particularly uncomfortable because we have learned to believe that
we live in a society whose moral foundations include the principles of
tolerance, fairness and equality of opportunity; and it is yet more
uncomfortable, because we should like to think that the moral licence
which Victorian Britain gave to racism has long since expired. In short,
we all abhor racism; many of us would therefore wish to reclassify its
apparent instances. But in doing so we could just be redescribing that
which we should prefer not to confront.

At the risk of sounding sanctimonious, I shall align myself with that
critique. But equally open to criticism is any tendency to discuss racial
abuse in schools in isolation from its context:

> Burnage showed that issues of race inequality were tied up with
> gender inequality and macho behaviour, highlighting the need to
> tackle these as well – for racism cannot be isolated from other
> forms of inequality in our society . . . If we are to avoid more mur-

ders in our playgrounds, we need to find ways of genuinely engaging with crucial issues of equality. (Epstein, 1989)

A further potential difficulty in this discourse – as in any social analysis – is that of ignoring agents' self-descriptions. It has become widely accepted that, in seeking to understand a social situation, it is essential to listen to how its actors describe it, and their position in it. Thus, my theorising about the professional practice of dealing with racial incidents must take into account the perceptions of the practitioners. The latter, it might be said, are in turn under an equivalent obligation to frame *their* discourse in the light of the perspectives of those who are caught up in such incidents – black pupils, or Bengali parents, for example. It follows that, for example, schoolteachers should have the time and the physical conditions to allow them to be as effective as possible in generating their own discourse – a discourse which is sensitive in the ways I have suggested – as theorising practitioners. The maintained education service does not on the whole provide those opportunities.

In talking or writing about racial incidents or interethnic relationships, then, we must be careful not to misdescribe them, or ignore their context, or fail to listen to the meaning they have for the agents concerned. With that in mind, we might turn briefly to an illustration of the general problem of defining terms.

What counts as a racial incident?

A white friend of mine has a teenage daughter whose mother is Afro-Caribbean. She is an intelligent, sensitive and physically tough young woman. In the school playground she was subjected to substantial verbal abuse by a small group of female fellow-pupils of African origin. Among the taunts was the accusation that her mother was a white-man lover (I have cleaned up the language). She finally became very angry and subjected her tormentors to physical threats; some fighting took place, broken up before it became too serious. My friend told me that he believed that the African group had become 'fed up' with his daughter's overbearing behaviour and had, perhaps, resorted to racial abuse simply because it was, in the circumstances, the only effective way of finding a vulnerable spot. In his view this was a conflict situation in which, because of the ethnicities involved, racist terms were available as weapons. *Racism* as such was not, he believed, the motive. But his daughter believed it was. Was this a racial incident?

In this chapter so far I have already mapped out a number of perspectives from which one might examine situations such as this. Let us use them. Firstly, the point of view of the actors. Just to focus on the 'victim' for the moment: it is typical of adolescents (is it not?) to see situations as falling *wholly* under categories – not partly in and partly out. The ability to handle abstract ideas, and to conceive of moral rights and wrongs, is still developing. Adolescents wield a broad brush. Thus the insults are just 'racist'; there is no grey area, no room for doubt or for alternative explanations. And – lest what I have said appear patronising – the way my friend's daughter sees the situation must be taken seriously. It can, and should, be understood in its context, but should not be dismissed. The same should apply to the actors in any equivalent situation.

Secondly, the social context: do the neighbourhood, the school staff, LEA and school ethos, ethnic mix in the school, interethnic relations in the school generally, local activities of extreme right-wing political groups and other factors add up to a climate of legitimation of racism to any appreciable extent? That must make a difference to how one ought to perceive an incident of the kind I exemplified.

Thirdly, the values and personal/professional priorities of those who have responsibility in relation to such incidents: why, as a head or teacher, might I want to play down or point up the racial nature of the situation? What kind of framework is there and should there be in the LEA and the school which links racial equality/inequality to other principles and issues? And what opportunities might such a framework create for treating racial incidents as an item within a broader agenda?

Fourthly and finally, at the level of pure definition: at the beginning of this chapter I ruled out the possibility of such definitions; but were I to be reading it I should probably want to say to its author, 'Come on; there must be central cases of racial incidents, irrespective of context, special interests, individual perception and the like. What do those central cases have in common?'

My answer has to be that a racial incident is any case of abusive behaviour which (as in the case exemplified) uses supposed racial categories as a weapon and as justification. As such (and this is more important than the definition I have just given) a *racial incident* is to be distinguished from *racism*. It is a mistake to assume that racial abuse is always and necessarily evidence of racism; it is also a mistake to assume that where there are no racial incidents, there is no racism. Racism is a feature of social and institutional structures, and thus of power-relations. Racial incidents may be more likely to occur in a relatively democratic school, in which there is an active policy of equality of consideration for all and open discussion of racial and cognate issues, than in a school run on authoritarian lines where those conditions are absent. The latter type of school, which may exhibit those features which justify the label 'racist', could be relatively effective at keeping the lid on racial incidents.

Consequently, while I should not want in any way to minimise the importance of racial incidents, I am if anything more interested in the rather broader focus of the quality of interethnic relationships in a school where one or more ethnic minorities are represented.

Ethnicity and race

One final point about definitions: those who are most caught up in racial incidents are people who are to be correctly characterised by their *ethnicity* (that is, a combination of social and cultural experience, and received and self-attributions) and not merely by their genetic inheritances or 'race' – even though that distinction fails to be accepted or even understood by perhaps a majority in British society.

It is important always to remind ourselves that, while we cannot avoid using the term 'race' and its derivatives in our discourse of opposition to racism and racial abuse, part of what we are fighting against is the use of the bewitching powers of language to legitimise prejudice and discrimination. In short, our opposition to racism must, where appropriate, include questioning the very conceptual categories which are part of racism's stock-in-trade.

The heart of the topic

I turn now to a brief discussion of each of three substantive questions which seem to be at the heart of this topic, and on which the small amount of research carried out by my colleagues Gajendra Verma, George Skinner, Deborah Gewirtz and myself has emboldened me to make one or two judgements. The questions are:

1   What counts as good race relations (or, as I should prefer to say, interethnic relationships) in a school?
2   What are the factors likely to influence those relationships?
3   What operational principles should govern action in dealing with racial incidents?

It would be premature to say anything about the research currently in progress. However, in 1988 we carried out a pilot study of two maintained, co-educational, multi-ethnic comprehensive schools – one in Lancashire and the other in London. One school (A) contained a roughly 50/50 mix of white and South Asian pupils; the other (B) was more genuinely *multi*-ethnic, in that six major ethnic groups were represented – Afro-Caribbean, Greek and Turkish Cypriot, Indian, Bangladeshi and white Anglo-Saxon.

What are good interethnic relationships?

Although it should be stressed that the main point of the pilot study was to test our research instruments, it is worth mentioning here that the study did reveal some interesting variations in perception among staff both within and between the two schools. In school A there appeared to be a low level of interaction between white and Asian pupils, as well as (in the teachers' view) a very low incidence of intergroup hostility and very infrequent occurrence of individual incidents. Yet name-calling, using racial categories, *was* very frequent at that school. Asian pupils reported that they experienced name-calling 'many times a week' and that 'you get called Paki even when you are just walking down the corridor'.

It is interesting that most staff at that school seemed to exclude name-calling from the category of racial incidents. It is even more interesting that most staff and pupils interviewed described race relations in the school as good or quite good. The relationship between general levels of interaction, frequency of incidents other than name-calling (for example bullying, fights etc.), and name-calling, clearly warranted further exploration.

In school B there seemed to be a much higher level of positive (that is, friendly and collaborative) interaction between pupils from different ethnic groups. This was the school with the greater ethnic variety. At the same time, there appeared to be a higher frequency of ugly racial incidents other than name-calling, but less name-calling, than in school A. Here also, there was a greater plurality of views among the staff than at school A on what exactly constituted a racial incident. For some in school B, name-calling certainly came into that category and did so because it underlined their determination to challenge it unequivocally. For others, name-calling was seen more as part of all pupils' repertoire of uncivilised behaviour. Furthermore there also seemed to be a much broader variety of perception among the staff in school B about the state of interethnic relationships in their school, than in school A. Some teachers in school B took the view that relationships were – all things considered – very good. Others felt that there were undercurrents of hostility which the school – and particularly the management – wished to keep submerged as far as possible.

Both teachers and pupils who were asked about it said that there was one group in the school which was getting a raw deal: newly arrived Bangladeshi children. There had been considerable short-term friction between them and some white and other South Asian pupils; in general (it was admitted) they were, at best, ignored – and found to be irritating because of their incomprehensible use of mother tongue (the latter, in fact, was seen as an irritant in both schools). Most pupils interviewed at school B had positive things to say about the state of interethnic relationships, not least in terms of the evidence they provided of a high incidence (compared with school A) of interethnic friendships and task-related groupings.

I have done no more than pick out some possibly suggestive material from our pilot study which is at least relevant to the question of what constitutes good interethnic relationships. Distilling the experience of our study, and on the basis of reflection, I should want to say that good interethnic relationships are more than the mere absence of overt hostility or conflict between persons or groups. They entail:

- a substantial degree of reciprocal knowledge and understanding of ways of life, between pupil groups of different ethnicity and between teachers and pupils – such knowledge and understanding being generated through the formal curriculum and in other ways;
- substantially shared values and attitudes concerning, for example, respect for persons, tolerance, rights/responsibilities and repudiation of racism and other kinds of unjust denial of worth, together with consistent and public commitment to such values throughout the school on the part of its management and staff;
- and (not least important) a considerable degree of positive interaction between persons and groups of different ethnicity – whether as collaboration in tasks or in social situations.

Our pilot study seemed to give modest support to a point I made earlier in this chapter: that a school which suffers from more racial incidents than another one *may* also enjoy better interethnic relationships.

What influences interethnic relationships?

I distil the following from our research and joint reflections. We have picked out these indicators but do not pretend it is an exhaustive list.

1   *The development of strategies to promote positive interaction between pupils.*   This is obviously easier said than done, but let me give just one example: I know of a school (not connected with our research) at which a comfortable social centre was set up for Bengali pupils who were second-language learners of English. The centre – for lunchtime recreation etc. – was set up to help those pupils feel more nurtured. The unexpected upshot was that, when word went round that a rather pleasant facility had been instituted, progressively more white pupils came to use the centre, and were welcomed by the Asians. The positive effect on interethnic relationships was, apparently, remarkable. I realise, of course, that the outcome could have been very different, but it was not.

2   *The development of agreed criteria for recognising racial incidents*, in particular, seeking agreement by staff that any abusive behaviour which uses racial categories as a weapon and as justification for the behaviour is unacceptable – whether the motive is racist or not.

3   *The development of agreed and, as far as possible, routine principles and procedures for responding to racial incidents.*   These would embrace: a differentiated and graduated repertoire of action to deal with the incident; lines and levels of responsibility; methods of recording; internal and external communication; promulgation by the school of its attitudes, policies and practice in this area; and the nature of possible follow-up beyond the immediate response.

4   *The extent to which school policies on interethnic relationships, racism, cultural diversity and equality in its various dimensions represent shared commitments on the part of the staff rather than impositions or tokens.*

5   *The extent to which those commitments are also understood and shared by pupils and parents;* and the extent to which the school involves parents in discussing racial incidents and interethnic relations in general.

6   *The degree of support which exists – including INSET – to enable staff to develop their knowledge, self-awareness and attitudes in this area.*   This

would include teachers' knowledge of the cultural and religious backgrounds of ethnic minority pupils, as well as their awareness of dimensions of racism and training in dealing with racially abusive behaviour.

7   *The impact of the presence of, and attitudes and expectations concerning, teachers of ethnic minority origin.*   At one of our pilot study schools, eighteen per cent of the full-time teaching staff were members of ethnic minorities. On the whole the presence of those teachers in the school was very beneficial to interethnic relationships – not least because their sheer numbers made it impossible for them to be marginalised in the staffroom.

8   *The impact of the formal curriculum on interethnic relationships.*   Although it is almost certainly true a priori that there would be high correlation between modes of curriculum delivery and the condition of interethnic relationships, our pilot research was illuminating in throwing up positive illustration of just how much difference the curriculum might make. We were convinced (to give just one brief indication) that the high level of positive social interaction at the school between pupils of differing backgrounds was reinforced by some of the work being done in the curriculum. The challenge now, of course, is to see what can be done with the National Curriculum in this context.

9   *The influence of language policies on interethnic relationships.*   It is worth recalling that, at both of our pilot study schools, one of the biggest sources of irritation to longer-established pupils was the newer arrivals speaking in their mother tongue. It is also worth noting that at neither school was there a positive policy on mother tongue teaching and learning. It is at least plausible to argue that where mother tongue is publicly valued and plays a systematic part in the curriculum of the school, the 'irritation factor' is lessened and the milder and most common forms of racial abuse become less frequent.

How should we deal with racial incidents?

My answer to this question will be very brief, since I have refused to treat the issue out of context and I have already implicitly answered it. However, I should want to state the following nine principles – again, on the basis of our limited research and reflection.

1   As far as possible, no case of abusive behaviour using racial categories should be ignored by any member of staff.
2   The degree of 'moral indignation' manifested in picking up a case of abusive behaviour should match the degree of nastiness of the behaviour.
3   There should be a clear and routine procedure for logging such incidents – the more substantial of which should be brought to senior management.
4   However, teachers should be given as much autonomy as possible in dealing with incidents – which will necessitate appropriate training.
5   Good communication with parents and the local community is essential – both in general, on what the school's policies and practices are, and in relation to particular incidents.
6   Where the incident is more serious than, say, a piece of casual, semi-humorous name-calling, the opportunity should exist for calling a case-conference, which may include not only adult representation from all relevant ethnic groups but pupil representation as well.
7   The school should decide and make public its level of response to racially abusive behaviour, so that all concerned know that the more serious cases will be punished.
8   The punishment should be clearly and publicly placed within a framework of justification which indicates that racial incidents are examples of uncivilised behaviour which, because it denies human worth, will not be tolerated by the school.
9   In the more serious cases, pastoral and educational strategies need to be devised to follow up a case after the immediate situation has been defused.

What we observed in our pilot research was in fact helpful in fixing these principles, rather obvious though they may seem. But I am wedded to the view, made clear in this chapter, that it is really the institutional context of racial incidents which matters. The overall moral climate of the school – especially the degree to which in all aspects of its life it instantiates the democratic principles which are the enemy of racism – is crucial here. Consultative management styles and procedures; a curriculum to which all have equal (if sometimes appropriately differentiated) access and which addresses issues of equality and inequality; a united commitment of all teaching and non-teaching staff to the value of respect for persons and to action to defend that value where necessary; the promotion of mutual knowledge and interaction between members of the school from different ethnic backgrounds – these are some applications of democratic values.

A school permeated by democratic values is unlikely to be completely free from conflict even perhaps from interethnic conflict. But it *is* likely to be freer from the whole repertoire of racial abuse than is a school which fails to live by democratic values because it fails to teach by example.

I began this chapter with a story, whose telling I defended on the grounds that it poked fun at all of us. Perhaps the kind of climate I should like to see in our educational institutions is one where all can understand the difference between that kind of story and a racist joke, and where the self-confidence and mutual trust exist to laugh at the one while repudiating the other.

References

Akhtar, S. and Stronach, T. (1986) They call me blacky. *The Times Educational Supplement*, 19 September

Cohn, T. (1987) Sticks and stones may break my bones but names will never hurt me. *Multicultural Teaching*, 5, 3, Summer

Commission for Racial Equality. (1988) *Learning in Terror: A Survey of Racial Harassment in Schools and Colleges*. CRE

Department of Education and Science. (1984) *Race Relations in Schools: A Summary of Discussions at Meetings in Five Local Authorities*. HMSO
  (1985) *Education for All* (Swann Report). HMSO

Epstein, D. (1989) Burnage and after. *Multicultural Education Review*, 9, Summer

Macdonald, I. *et al* (1990) *Murder in the Playground: Report of the Macdonald Inquiry into Racism and Racial Violence in Manchester Schools*. Longsight Press

Chapter 18

Resourcing the Next Generation
1 To Confine or to Connect?

Beverley Naidoo

Addressing a group of new American graduates, the political economist J. K. Galbraith spelled out a challenge. It is one which has always existed for teachers, charged with transmitting society's 'knowledge' to a future generation:

> Your real choice will be in the realm of truth. Specifically it will be in deciding whether you will be guided by sometimes inconvenient, even painful reality or by what I will call institutional truth.
>
> Institutional truth in our times bears no necessary relation to simple truth. It is, instead, what serves the needs and purposes of the large and socially pervasive institutions which increasingly dominate modern life. (Galbraith, 1989)

Even before the advent of a National Curriculum and explicit state intervention in the control of 'knowledge', have we not always been faced with this 'daily choice extending on through the years between institutional truth and truth, between the convenient belief and reality'? (ibid.)

Although perceptions may differ and we may sometimes disagree just what 'reality' is, I believe Galbraith's distinction is nevertheless crucial in assessing what we offer young people. How an educational establishment is resourced is a critical indicator of its health and commitment to real education as opposed to convenient training, with all that that implies.

Where are we now?

Where then are we, towards the end of the twentieth century, in terms of resourcing our schools for equality, justice and cultural diversity? My first response is that there is still widespread failure in this society to acknowledge that Western civilisation is the result of the created wealth of many cultures. Britain did not pull itself up by its own bootstraps. Secondly, with advances in technology, the world has shrunk and we need to have the intellectual and emotional capability to live with each other or perish.

It is over fifteen years since Bullock and his committee asked a straightforward question in their Report *A Language for Life*:

> has the school removed from its shelves books which have a strong ethnocentric bias and contain outdated or insulting views of people of other cultures? (DES, 1975, 20.5)

Bullock did not use the terms 'racist' or 'racism'. It took ten years before the Swann Committee was to do that. But clearly the reference was to racist literature. Although we might query the notion of 'outdated' as an adequate criterion for assessing such material, at least the word implied recognition that the colonial era had ended and that ethnocentric bias was anti-educational. The question is, however, all these years on, how many schools, colleges and libraries have actually carried out Bullock's very basic directive – namely to remove the most overtly racist material from their shelves? How many have familiarised themselves with the relevant criteria and begun to consider the range of issues? How many have made this area a priority for continuing discussion and action? How many are involving their students in this process? Hampshire has included some useful appendices in its document *Education for a Multicultural Society* (1987). How many schools are *actually* setting aside time to make use of them?

Of course the concept 'resources' carries a much wider meaning than just books and materials. For instance, four categories are specified in the Non-statutory Guidance accompanying *English in the National Curriculum* – people, buildings (for example available space), time and teaching materials (DES, 1990).

It is necessary to ask ourselves questions about each area in relation to the institutions we know.

People

- How many black teachers are there, especially in mainly white schools? How many are at senior management level?
- How many teachers have been on anti-racist/multicultural courses?

- How many teachers enable children to be excited about life beyond their own corner of the world? How many challenge racism?
- How many institutions have a programme of inviting in people from ethnically, culturally diverse communities, for example writers, artists, dancers?

Available space for displays

- How often is such space used for anti-racist/multicultural purposes?
- How many visual images encourage reflection about the world in challenging ways? (Not the 'Let's feel sorry for poor people in Africa' variety.)

Time

- With cultural diversity a cross-curricular issue in the National Curriculum, what *actual* time is being given to it in different areas of the curriculum?

Materials

- Have schools reviewed their stock, deciding what to do about racism in books and other materials?
- Have they developed a policy?
- Have they involved pupils in identifying racism in materials?
- What criteria are being used for selection of new stock?
- Does the school/college subscribe to a journal like *Multicultural Teaching*, and do staff read and discuss issues?

If I have to answer such questions in relation to the largely white schools I know – in an attempt to reflect truth and reality, not institutional truth or convenient belief – my own overall picture is frankly not inspiring. There are some encouraging examples – but their central feature is that those involved always seem to be working against the odds. Certainly my own responses to the above questions – in terms of what is *not* being done – lead me to concur with Stuart Hall's statement:

> Racism is as much a structured absence – a not-speaking about things – as it is a positive setting up of attitudes to race. (Hall, 1985)

Dominance and distortion

Resources for combating racism and promoting cultural diversity are still 'structured' out – missed or marginalised – not necessarily through wilful hostility, but through indifference or constantly putting other issues first. Given more than three hundred years of colonial history in which institutionalised truth upheld the right of British might, this is hardly surprising. Whenever did a dominant power pass on to its young a perspective which questioned that dominance? For generations young Britons have been taught about the Industrial Revolution as a key stage in British history. Yet how many have been taught about slavery and the wealth it produced as part and parcel of that revolution? How many have been encouraged to explore the reality behind Winston Churchill's words:

> Our possessions of the West Indies, like that of India . . . gave us the strength, the support, but especially the capital, the wealth, at a time when no other European nation possessed such a reserve, which enabled us to come through the great struggle of the Napoleonic Wars, the keen competition of the commerce of the eighteenth and nineteenth centuries, and . . . enabled us to make our great position in the world. (quoted in Thames Television programme, 1979)

How many of today's adults educated in yesterday's Britain would genuinely want to discover for themselves anything of the painful reality of slavery for the African continent or want to question the consequences for the social and economic fabric of having millions of people abducted? For generations, young Britons have been taught about colonialism as a civilising mission – a mission of 'development' not of destruction. How many of today's adults would want to explore, for instance, the historical roots of the poverty in present day Zambia: how a colony which produced huge annual profits from copper-mining for British investors was left at Independence in 1964 with merely one local secondary school (to O-level) for two million people? Yet how many adults would cite education as one of the benefits of colonialism?

I could go on, but the point is simply that the question of resources is centrally linked to what adult society finds acceptable and chooses to pass on to its young. For generations of colonial rule, schools and adults passed on to the young the justifications and rationalisations for that rule – wittingly and unwittingly, overtly and covertly, through what was said and not said.

I understand this process as an 'insider', having been brought up as a child in South Africa to accept traditional white English views and explanations. The processes I observe here in England – by which lenses are set up for young people through which to view the world – appear to me essentially the same. The ability of adults to distort children's perceptions of reality simply revealed itself much more crudely in the white South African community, placed at the very fingertips of the colonial arm.

Evidence that adults in Britain acknowledge the role of books in transmitting messages to the young was clearly provided by the furore over the little book, *Jenny Lives with Eric and Martin* by Susanne Bosche. We had questions in Parliament and it became an element in the campaign leading to Section 28. It would appear that a significant number of adults believed that showing children this diversity of family life would threaten the fabric of the society they wish to maintain.

Yet there has never been a comparable negative response to the host of materials displaying overt, gross racism, let alone to those where racism is far more subtly embedded. In fact campaigns which have attempted to address the issue of racism in materials for children have commonly been the subject of ridicule. Look, for example, at the popular response to critiques of Enid Blyton's *Noddy* books or the golliwog figure. The cry of censorship has been quickly raised and derision cast on those arguing the social implications of racist caricature.

There are of course schools and libraries which have removed racist material and initiated critical ongoing debates about 'censorship' or 'selection'. It is vital however that the issues are not dealt with in a superficial way. We cannot deal with what may be regarded as embarrassing aspects of our past through censorship, that is by simply not talking about them. We need to acknowledge our past and the heritage of racism in the present. We have to learn how to deconstruct received images and learn how to reperceive. Children need to be encouraged to identify racism in resources for themselves and to question the process of cultural transmission. For instance, what was the effect on their parent's generation of resources embedded with racism? What was the effect on white people of not having access to black views? What was the effect on black people of being denied a voice?

A commitment to questioning 'knowledge'

We need to encourage questions about our construction of 'knowledge'. If, under the National Curriculum for history, we are told that the focus must be on certain key areas, in particular on what is considered 'British' history, then we must encourage questions about what that history encompasses. Just as our understanding of the Industrial Revolution is incomplete without seeing its relationship to slavery, so does the development of parliamentary democracy necd to be placed alongside colonial domination by Parliament of other countries.

The ideals of the French Revolution need to be examined alongside the struggle of Toussaint L'Ouverture and others to realise those same ideals for the slaves of Haiti. Students of the American War of Independence need also to hear the words of the famous ex-slave, Frederick Douglass, when invited to give a Fourth of July speech in 1852 to a white audience:

> The rich inheritance of justice, liberty, prosperity and independence bequeathed by your fathers, is shared by you, not by me. The sunlight that brought light and healing to you, has brought stripes and death to me. This Fourth of July is *yours*, not *mine*. *You* may rejoice, *I* must mourn . . . What to the American slave, is your Fourth of July? I answer; a day that reveals to him, more than all other days in the year, the gross injustice and cruelty to which he is the constant victim. To him, your celebration is a sham; your boasted liberty, an unholy licence; your national greatness, swelling vanity. (quoted in Alkalimat, 1973)

If we are committed to real education and to fundamental principles of equality and justice to secure a future for us all, then we need to be bold and take courage from the spirit of those who have been engaged in such struggles before us. We need to pass on the spirit of people like Frederick Douglass and their commitment to truth as opposed to convenient belief. If we are to be real educators we have a responsibility to keep educating ourselves. Racism, like apartheid, keeps people within the same society apart in the most fundamental ways so that not only do our experiences differ – and are ranked differently – but our perceptions of our society will inevitably differ. As a white educator I have a particular responsibility. I have to resource myself first of all, to listen to voices that challenge me to reperceive and stretch my understanding beyond the confines of my own experience.

A great deal of my learning is done through resources not regarded as mainstream. I realise that so far I have quoted only men in this chapter. That too says something about the nature of our resources. Yes I read women writers, but I too have a long way to go. In her essay on Martin Luther King, 'The Mountain and the Man who was not God',

June Jordan exhorts recognition for 'the Invisible Woman whose invisibility has cost all of us incalculable loss' (Jordan, 1989). We have constantly to evaluate where we are and decide on priorities for our own learning as well as our children's.

Resources to affirm self-worth

We require resources which affirm every child's identity and self-worth, while encouraging children to explore the identities of others. It is vital to have resources which celebrate the rich variety of human experience in our thousands of different cultures, yet equally crucial to have those which support truthful exploration of painful subjects. Investigating issues like slavery and racism can be painful for both black and white children from their different perspectives.

All young children seem to have a strong sense of what is 'fair' as well as an expectation of just treatment, unless they have been emotionally scarred at an early age. We need resources which affirm that expectation into a full desire for equality and an entitlement to be free from the prejudices of the adult world. We need resources which enable young people to talk openly about the injustice of racism, past and present – but which do not overburden white children with guilt nor allow black children to feel further oppressed.

We need resources which help explain processes of cultural transmission honestly and encourage responses in terms of a shared sense of justice. The desire for justice needs to be positively nurtured and harnessed. The alternative is to propagate, if not hostility, something equally destructive – indifference. When we see children at seven eager to be part of a global, equal community and at fourteen cynical and indifferent, then we have seriously failed.

Hanging overhead are major issues of funding and overall allocation of resources within the new constraints of the Education Reform Act. I have, however, maintained my focus on our need to acknowledge – individually and collectively – responsibility for the way we resource our children's learning and its central connection to the kind of future we are enabling them to create. Resources are a vital element in the struggle to break the mental confines erected within an ethnocentric, racist society. An organisation such as the Afro-Caribbean Educational Resource Project (ACER) – an independent organisation supported previously by the Inner London Education Authority – has played a key role in developing resources not just for children of Afro-Caribbean origin but for all children. Len Garrison, former director of ACER, is well placed to describe this.

2   A Unique Contribution

Len Garrison

The Afro-Caribbean Resource Project

This is a brief retrospective account of the Afro-Caribbean Education Resource project (ACER). It includes ACER's contribution to the Inner London Education Authority's (ILEA) policy, ACER's structure, the two phases of the project's development and a critical review of ILEA's policy during the eighties. It will, however, serve as an introduction to ACER's unique contribution. Since ACER's inception in 1976 the project has contributed to the multicultural/anti-racist debate and to classroom practice well beyond the borders of ILEA. This brief account highlights some of the issues as well as the significance of the contribution.

ACER represents a unique experiment between a community-inspired initiative working in partnership with a local education authority in a climate of mistrust and lack of confidence between black parents and community groups on the one hand and the LEA on the other, over the poor representation and educational attainment of black pupils in the state education system. What made the ACER scheme possible?

Here is a written comment from a white teacher who used to teach in a predominantly black school:

> We have no colour problem. Some of our children have darker skin than others. There are no non-English cultural problems. I think making people aware of the problems often causes more problems. I believe people need protection from others who want to interfere . . . school could be called English and middle class. My previous school was in Vauxhall, London, and we had about seventy-five per cent negroid children. I could never see any point in 'remembering' who was what . . . it didn't seem to matter.

How could such persons be helped to overcome their colour-blind approach to teaching Afro-Caribbean and other children? ACER resolved towards a positive involvement of black children in British education as a way of combating their underachievement.

The background to ACER's pioneering story

Having started as a small group in a basement in Stockwell, concerned about the lack of resolution to the crisis that faced black children in schools, Paul Boateng (then a lawyer) and the author decided to take up the challenge by becoming co-founders of ACER. Our philosophy was that schools should be made to work for all pupils. Black children should not have to go outside the mainstream school to seek recognition and gain confidence in being themselves. White pupils should also learn from and about being black in a white society. Together pupils could learn to respect each other.

This mutual respect was to be achieved by a positively created multicultural environment and purpose-designed learning resources. The experiment was to challenge the assimilationist and Eurocentric model of education, more commonly called the 'colour blind' approach, which informed most educational practice. We decided to devise a major Afro-Caribbean library resource base as well as develop a programme of materials which identified the ethnic, cultural and social dimensions of the black child, acknowledging them as an integral part of learning for all pupils.

Reversal of underachievement

This programme was advanced as a community response to underachievement. It was a countermeasure against the identification of black children by the authorities as the cause of their own problem – namely, being black, being of a different culture and just being different. It came about as a result of a number of factors. One was the publication of Bernard Coard's experience and testimony as a teacher, in an Educationally Subnormal (ESN) school, in the booklet *How the West Indian Child is Made Educationally Subnormal in the British School System* (Coard, 1971).

Another was the publication in 1975 of the Bullock Report *A Language for Life* (DES, 1975), which acknowledged the need for a positive approach to tackling the questions of linguistic diversity and multi-ethnic education. The Report argued convincingly 'that a child should not have to leave its culture or language at the door of the school'.

Reaction to miseducation

Black parents, meanwhile, could not see any resolution to the problems their children faced in school in terms of overt and covert forms of racism. By the end of the seventies supplementary schools had emerged in many communities as channels to enhance black pupils' education and compensating for the lack of cultural support and miseducation in the schools. Others saw these schools as a way to make up the deficit features encountered in mainstream schooling's basic delivery which they felt was responsible for the continuing failure.

In a few schools, efforts to compensate for the deficiency in the curriculum took the form of a black studies package for black children in the lower streams, as a way of appeasing critics who saw schools as indifferent to black pupils' needs. Maureen Stone, in her book *The Education of the Black Child in Britain: The Myth of Multi-racial Education* (1981), argued that black children's culture was not the problem, racism was the problem. These refutations that the black child, family and culture were responsible for wholesale underachievement, also helped to prepare the way for ACER's schemes to correct the imbalance in the mainstream curriculum. Equally the focus on countering racism as a priority issue in combating underachievement gained currency against fierce resistance.

ACER's contribution to ILEA's policy

In 1977 when ILEA passed its first multi-ethnic policy document, ACER was included as a partnership project. The ACER scheme sought to produce learning materials, based on classroom trials, which would bring the everyday experiences of the black child into mainstream classroom activity for use by all children. It also sought to develop and gather a range of curriculum materials from various sources relating to the African–Caribbean and black British experiences into a central bank. These were to act as a reference source for classroom teachers and others pursuing a more positive approach to multicultural education. This specialist collection eventually became the largest independent collection of books and non-book resources, not only in the ILEA area, but in the country as a whole.

The philosophy and structure of ACER

The philosophy of ACER was based on the principles that racism as a process was reversible and that damage could be minimised. The definition held was that: 'Racism is neither a natural nor a permanent feature of society. It is an artificial creation devised to facilitate and perpetuate inequalities.'

The project structure of ACER and its relationship with the local authority was a unique one. Although ACER established itself as an independent educational charity, it was devised on a partnership basis between the black community and ILEA.

The management committee comprised teachers, parents, school governors and community workers representing community interests. Officers of the Multi-Ethnic Inspectorate, namely Bev Woodroffe and Mike Hussey, also played an important part in their advisory roles and in liaison between ACER and ILEA.

The first phase of development 1978–82

ACER 's primary goal in its first phase was the designing, developing and piloting of new materials, set out in its phased programme which included in-service evaluation by teachers. The materials gave schools the opportunity to start from where the children were and therefore to incorporate the multicultural content into the mainstream school curriculum in order to improve the quality of education on offer to all pupils. The core team comprised a school liaison officer, a research officer, a director, a graphic designer/illustrator and an administrative officer.

ACER publications and awards

This period saw the publication of the *Ourselves* pack – based on stories of a group of children from various backgrounds celebrating differences as a positive asset of an individual, and the piloting of *Words and Faces* – a pack to help children develop their self-perception and image, vocabulary and use of language through drawing, colouring and discussion. Both of these units were designed for middle school children (aged nine to fourteen). Once published, there was an immediate demand for the material when teachers saw the positive results.

A large part of ACER's work was a ground-breaking and pioneering role. It made remarkable achievements. Schools which had been hesitant and even resistant, began to see positive results as black children began to accept their colour before their friends and teachers unapologetically. White pupils encouraged by ACER materials began to accept difference in a positive way, and teachers began to feel less threatened when asked to treat race-related issues positively.

Alongside this work, ACER initiated the Black Young Writers' Award, now in its eleventh year, an annual competition which rapidly grew with entries from over 300 people nationally, and the Annual Awards, which draws an audience of over 500 to the presentations at Lambeth Town Hall, Brixton, London, each February.

What significance could we attribute to the role and unique contributions made by ACER to the development of resources and anti-racist educational practice in ILEA? Summing up in a paper presented in September 1985 at a Commission for Racial Equality conference on Resourcing Change, the author stated:

> The work of the ACER project has shown that pupils of the middle years of schooling can be given a more suitable start in the classroom – that learning materials do not have to be only about one point of reference. Learning can take place from and about each other while children are allowed to share their own experience.
>
> Children also show that they respect each other more when the teachers and the classroom materials support each other's point of view. The ACER learning materials have shown that they can provide an important lead in this work. (Garrison, 1985)

ILEA's multi-ethnic policy initiative

Development of the project at this stage was greatly enhanced by the fact that in 1979 Peter Newsam, the then Education Officer of ILEA, actively promoted the authority's multi-ethnic policy. Schools were asked to prioritise and take up the issues of a school policy and to translate this into practice at a classroom level. As ACER's work gained prominence, teachers, librarians and parents began to call in to see how the materials were being produced, as well as to seek advice, support and information on a wide range of related topics. At this time ILEA's prominence in the field of multi-ethnic education began to be recognised, being the first LEA nationally to adopt a policy initiative. Interest in ACER's work was not confined to the ILEA area; demands for information and advice came from many parts of the country.

The second phase of development 1983–87

In this second phase the project expanded to ten workers, culminating in 1985 with a move to larger accommodation and a base of its own in Wyvil School, Vauxhall in South London. Specially refurbished, the base was organised into a library to house about 8,000 books and a non-book collection, a graphics and print room with a complete in-house printing outfit, and a large workroom for staff.

'I'm special' – early years' material

While the team were developing packs for middle school pupils, a constant demand from parents, under-fives' workers and teachers had been for materials for the early years. The second phase therefore concentrated on producing a unit of material for this age group. An introductory pack was put together, *I'm Special: Myself*, which consisted of early-learning books with full colour photographs and a teachers' and parents' guide to assist the three- to seven-year-olds explore ideas about themselves. Again, the strength of these materials is that they are child-centred, allowing children to start learning from where they are and encouraging them to feel positive about being different. Demand for this material was equally good, requests outstripping supplies in the first year of production.

ACER video programmes

The work was enhanced by a series of videos produced by the ILEA television centre. *To School Together*, for instance, documents the use of ACER materials by pupils in the classroom. In *Anti-Racism in Practice*, Professor Stuart Hall examines the wider implications of such materials and the challenge they present, particularly to 'unthinking racist assumptions'.

The video programme *Multi-Culturalism in the United States*, in which Professor Geneva Gay discusses the parallel development in the institutions in that country, also added an important dimension to the work of ACER. These programmes played a valuable role in highlighting and popularising the work of ACER nationally.

Policy without practice

Throughout the history of ACER its independent community stance meant that it could be objective and openly critical of the lack of clear action and results from ILEA's paper policies which failed to actively challenge the serious overt and covert forms of racism experienced by black children in schools.

The author's critical review of the situation in a paper in 1985 highlighted some of the major concerns:

> There has also been a clear failure to come to terms with the various forms of racism which restrict the multicultural concept of education from becoming a reality.
>
> Failure also to come to terms with the magnitude of the situation and to evaluate work that has been carried out or effect changes in areas remain untouched. (Garrison, 1985)

In summing up the situation, we could say that the multi-ethnic and anti-racist policies as part of the recent equal opportunities initiatives have been more of a paper exercise and have not been given the base or financial commitment needed to mount an effective campaign. The paper went on to call for clarification of ILEA's policy position between equal opportunity and multi-ethnic education and practice, because of the confusion and uncertainty caused by the terms:

> Within the ILEA's equal opportunity initiatives what has not been clarified is the relationship between equal opportunity and multi-ethnic education. This new tier in the structure does not explain how the Authority intends to effect a radical policy of anti-racism and multicultural education. It does not suggest how black children's prospects will be improved within the system as it is at present. (ibid.)

Resourcing is about power

Production of well-piloted and high-quality curriculum materials is costly; ACER's work was only possible through substantial support from ILEA. Commercial production of wide-ranging materials to support classroom practice has not kept pace with the increase in demand and awareness of the fact that post-war Britain is a multicultural society. This must be reflected in common textbooks in all schools to stress an 'Education for All' for the 1990s.

The future of ACER

The demise of ILEA has shifted the primary focus of funding the work of ACER on to commercial viability in a new privatised model. There is pressure to cut down on development and research and to prioritise profit. We can only speculate at this point that the consequences of no future development in this area will be detrimental to all. What remains certain is that all children must know who they are before they can appreciate and value others. White children receive constant affirmation of the dominant values within mainstream education. That right must be extended to all, thus making cultural diversity of pupils a strength rather than a weakness in good educational principles and practice. Positive affirmation of oneself in all curriculum resources is not only imperative for every individual, it is a right.

Conclusion

Both the Rampton and Swann Reports (DES, 1981 and 1985) acknowledged the need for a positive affirmation of black children's presence in British schools, thus supporting the basic tenets of ACER's premise: challenging the content of Anglocentric resources and combating underachievement. The mid-eighties saw much debate centring on multicultural education as a token gesture; ACER's contribution has, however, further challenged that negative view of cultural diversity and led to positive curricular resources and practice. An important factor in its success nationally has been that the materials have proved equally accessible to white pupils in predominantly white schools, therefore questioning the value of Eurocentric materials with their distorted reality. With the demise of ILEA its future is uncertain.

3   Mainstream Publishing and Multicultural Education

Anne Marley

The materials produced by ACER – described by Len Garrison in the previous section – are the only ones quite of their kind on the market and represent a unique contribution. Here, however, I am concerned with mainstream publishers and, in the context of this chapter, specifically with children's publishers such as Franklin Watts and Wayland. They provide the books that are most likely to be found on the shelves of public libraries and those of schools.

Developments in mainstream publishing

How have these publishers tackled multicultural issues and, more importantly, have they been effective? To answer this we have to go back to the 1960s and early 1970s when publishing for children and teenagers was almost totally white-orientated. The only exceptions were perhaps books by C. Everard Palmer and Andrew Salkey from the West Indies, and Rosa Guy from America. Information books were totally Eurocentric in content and frequently blatantly racist. The attitude was still 'assimilate' and 'integrate'.

In the early to mid 1970s, an outcry from black groups, teachers and librarians about the paucity of books available gradually began to be heard by the publishing world. The results were not quite what was hoped for because the books now became 'tokenist' in their approach to the issue. The occasional black or Asian characters were there, but peripheral to the story or illustration. It wasn't until the 1980s that we began to see real illustrations of black children in stories; real characters taking a central role in the storyline.

So we seem to have got what we wanted, or have we? When you look quickly through the book catalogues and see the covers of the books and the sections labelled 'Multicultural books', you might think we had it made, and that the publishers had got it right at last. But sadly that is not the case. The situation has improved and publishers are looking more to representing ethnic variety in their information books and fiction, but they have still not got it right.

When statistics of hardback children's information books published in 1989 were being compiled for Hampshire County Library, it emerged that three publishers dominated approximately 50 per cent of the market – Wayland (19 per cent), Franklin Watts/Gloucester Press (17 per cent), Macmillan (11 per cent). They are all well-known and respected houses, all of whom appear to publish books with multicultural content. Indeed Wayland states in their 1989, but not in their 1990, catalogue:

> We are very aware of the need for multicultural books so we have endeavoured to introduce a multicultural element to all our books . . . [we] hope to reflect the needs of the multicultural societies found both in Britain and in other countries.

Franklin Watts (1990) say that they:

> attempt to represent a multicultural and non-sexist approach to reflect today's society.

However, given their dominance of the market, if any one of the major editorial boards were to get it badly wrong, a lot of children would be seriously misinformed. But they do not even have to get it badly wrong to give cause for concern. To a greater or lesser extent, most publishing houses are still not providing the kind of unbiased, accurate, non-Eurocentric approach we are seeking.

It is no longer the overt mistakes that most concern us but the covert, which manifest themselves in various ways. The most difficult to spot is the sin of omission, because of the fact that relevant information simply is not there. For example, in reading *Focus on Israel* by Rivka Hadary, published by Hamish Hamilton (1988), would a child understand from her account the reasons for encouraging Jewish people to live in the new towns being built in politically volatile areas?

Many books are guilty of giving a very negative impression of certain countries and people by omitting vital information. For instance, in *Food or Famine* by Christopher Gibb (Wayland: Gibb, 1987), why is practically the only form of mechanisation shown in Africa an army tank?

Another sin is that of misinformation – one that is very easily committed simply by the manner in which information is expressed. In Wayland's *Growing Up in the Fifties* by Jeremy Pascall (1982) – now thankfully out of print although still on library shelves – one reads:

> Poor conditions and unemployment in their countries caused them [immigrants] to flock to Britain . . . Before long there were too many immigrants for the homes and jobs available. (Pascall, 1982)

The major fact omitted from this episode in British and Commonwealth history is that these immigrants were *invited* by the British Government to do the jobs that post-war British people could not or would not do.

One of the most common faults in mainstream publishing is the author's use of language, which often condemns a group of people by value-laden terms such as 'primitive'; or by the use of emotive language as in the example above of people 'flocking' to Britain.

Illustration is the most powerful medium for children because they read a book first by its pictures. The visual impression often remains long after the words have faded from the memory. An example of this is an otherwise excellent book from Wayland, *Farming in the Twentieth Century* by Graham Rickard (1988), which is *saying* all the right things about farming in the developing world. However, a pair of illustrations completely belie this written image by actively encouraging the reader to compare rice *planting* (manual) in the Philippines with wheat *harvesting* (by machinery) in the USA. What kind of comparison is this between two quite different processes? Yet children will probably remember this and not the text.

What can be done?

So what should we do about this type of error by very positive publishers, as well as others like Jonathan Cape who, at the time of writing, do not feature a single multicultural title on their otherwise admirable children's list, except for folk tales?

A good publisher is always open to constructive suggestions from concerned teachers and librarians, so it is essential to do something rather than expect the publisher to be automatically aware of current educational thinking.

1   Write to the publisher if you find something objectionable, but also write to let them know if there are books which are positive.
2   Contact groups like the Librarians Anti-Racist Strategies Group (c/o

Mary Briggs, Education Library Service, Pendower Hall Education Centre, West Road, Newcastle Upon Tyne NE15 6PP) which aims at promoting anti-racist resources for children and young adults. Let them know if there is new material felt to be offensive or inaccurate.

3   Encourage pupils to discuss books and other resources they are reading. Encourage them to think about the content and the appearance of what they see so that they don't accept everything at face value. They can do this from a very early age – it is often too late by the time they get to secondary school age; the damage has been done.

4   Evaluate the material. Learn to look for errors and encourage students to do the same.

It would be very unfair only to highlight the negative side of children's book publishing. There are many well-thought-out books, well researched and beautifully produced, like the *Threads* series from A & C Black, as well as the *Friends* and *Celebrations* series, which present good, useful, accurate information for the primary school.

The Way We Live series from Hamish Hamilton/Evans Brothers, plus the *People and Issues* and *In Her Own Time* series, have on the whole been providing sound and informative material for secondary schools, though each book should be evaluated in its own right. It is worrying though that no new titles in the *In Her Own Time* and *People and Issues* series seem to have been added to the list.

On the fiction side, both Andre Deutsch and The Bodley Head have good positive stories both for children and teenagers which reflect our multicultural society. One thing that would be appreciated though is the continuation of the dual language story book into the newly independent readers' stage. There is a need for this type of book, although the problems it would create for the publisher are obviously quite difficult to overcome.

Books which reflect our multicultural society accurately and without bias are crucial for children growing up in the world today. The need is greater in predominantly white areas, like Hampshire, where they do not necessarily have the advantage of first-hand knowledge and experience of the richness of different cultures. It is crucial, therefore, that we as teachers, advisers and librarians are aware of the content of what is being served up to our children, and that we do something positive about it before it is too late.

References

Afro-Caribbean Education Resource Centre. (1981) *Ourselves.* ACER, Wyvil School, Wyvil Road, London SW8 2TJ
  (1983) *Words and Faces.* ACER
  (1984) *To School Together* (video). ILEA/ACER
  (1985) *Anti-Racism in Practice* (video). ILEA/ACER
  (1986) *Multi-Culturalism in the United States* (video). ILEA/ACER
  (1987) *I'm Special: Myself.* ACER
Alkalimat, A. (1973) *Introduction to Afro-American Studies: A People's College Primer.* Twenty-first Century Books and Publications
Bosche, S. (1983) *Jenny Lives with Eric and Martin.* Gay Men's Press
Coard, B. (1971) *How the West Indian Child is Made Educationally Subnormal in the British School System.* New Beacon Books
Department of Education and Science. (1975) *A Language for Life* (Bullock Report). HMSO
  (1981) *West Indian Children in Our Schools* (Rampton Report). HMSO
  (1985) *Education for All* (Swann Report). HMSO
  (1990) *English in the National Curriculum.* HMSO
Franklin Watts. (1990) *Catalogue*
Galbraith, J.K. (1989) In pursuit of the simple truth. The *Guardian*, 28 July
Garrison, L. (1985) *Resources for Education in a Plural Society: Policy to Practice.* ACER
Gibb, C. (1987) *Food or Famine.* Wayland
Hadary, R. (1988) *Focus on Israel.* Hamish Hamilton
Hampshire Education Authority. (1987) *Education for a Multicultural Society.* HEA
Jordan, J. (1989) 'The Mountain and the Man who was not God'. In *Moving Towards Home.* Virago
Multicultural Teaching, Trentham Books, Stoke on Trent, Staffordshire
Pascall, J. (1982) *Growing Up in the Fifties.* Wayland
Rickard, G. (1988) *Farming in the Twentieth Century.* Wayland
Stone, M. (1981) *The Education of the Black Child in Britain: The Myth of Multi-racial Education.* Fontana
Thames Television. (1979) *Our People* programme
Wayland. (1989) *Catalogue*

PART 4: The Management of Change

Chapter 19

The Role of Local Education Authorities

1 Shire Authorities and Hampshire's Policy

Alec Fyfe

Policies

If we look back over the 1980s we witness a substantial formal recognition by local education authorities of the need to respond to cultural diversity issues. In 1979 only the Inner London Education Authority had a policy; while Berkshire's policy, adopted in 1983, was a landmark for shire authorities. By the end of the decade 80 out of 115 LEAs in England, Wales and Scotland had adopted multicultural/anti-racist policies. Most of these had been passed with all-party agreement in largely Tory controlled authorities.

The Swann Report (DES, 1985) laid great stress on the need for policies by both LEAs and institutions, but recognised the real danger that they might be viewed as the beginning of the end, rather than the end of the beginning. Chris Mullard has remarked that most LEA policies:

> are rag-bags of good intentions, bits of ideology, strips of anger and cotton wool balls of love.

This seems both ungenerous and to miss the point that the balance of one's energies should go into implementation rather than the chimera of ideologically pure policy statements.

The all-white context post-Swann

For Swann, a pluralist perspective was even more needed in 'all-white' areas, but the Report fell short of actually suggesting the strategic preeminence of shire authorities in any national movement. The Report, paradoxically, helped make that unity less attainable by alienating the vociferous on both the extreme Left and Right. One side saw it as a sell-out to the establishment, the other as a subverting of traditional values and an assault on national identity. Clearly the field needs to come together and to begin to think and act on a national plane. This will require a redefinition of the 'front line', away from multiracial areas to the mainstream, largely all-white shires. Strategically it needs to be recognised that though the battle for multicultural/anti-racist education can be lost in the inner cities it can never be won there. The case nationally can most persuasively be made, on educational grounds, in rural areas where the sole *raison d'être* is not the physical presence of black pupils and students. The need is all the greater there and the impact of success will be all the more significant too.

The role of LEAs post-ERA

The Education Reform Act 1988 (ERA) has of course radically altered the relationship between LEAs and their institutions. LEAs must now adjust to a culture change in which they cease to be service providers and move instead towards an enabling and evaluation function. This still gives LEAs considerable room for influence. LEAs' statements on the curriculum, which are a legal requirement, offer an opportunity to embed a commitment to multicultural education as part of the whole curriculum. Interestingly, the field continues to attract central government funding – for bilingual pupils under Section 11 and Travellers Education Grants – which lies outside financial delegation to schools and therefore provides one of the few financial levers now available to LEAs. To this must be added funding for European awareness via the Central Bureau and the European Community.

The monitoring role is now strategic, and if LEAs build this concern into their Inspectorate's *aide-mémoire*, a major step forward will have been taken in institutionalising a commitment to multicultural education. LEAs still have a legal requirement under the Race Relations Act 1976 to promote racial equality and have through governor training a major vehicle to secure this. Reports of the demise of LEAs' influence, like Mark Twain's death, seem somewhat exaggerated.

The Hampshire Policy

In June 1986 Hampshire adopted a policy, *Education for a Multicultural Society*, which is set out below:

> Against the background of the Swann Report and as a development of the County's statement on the curriculum, the following policy was adopted on 10 June 1986.
>
> The Hampshire Education Service should prepare pupils and students for life in a multicultural society by developing an ethos and a curriculum which:
>
> a   reflect and value cultural diversity and turn it to advantage in enriching pupils' and students' experience and understanding of the world in which they live;
> b   recognise and counter racial prejudice;
> c   foster racial harmony and understanding amongst all in society; and
> d   offer all pupils and students equality of opportunity and an education for life in a culturally and racially plural society.
>
> This policy should permeate the whole curriculum and find expression in all aspects of school and college life.
>
> *Implementation*
>
> In order for this policy to be fulfilled, all educational institutions in the Authority should:
>
> a   review both the context and content of their curriculum and the books and other materials used in the light of the broad statement of principles outlined above. The review should involve all areas of the work of the institution and lead to a plan of action;
> b   regard multicultural education not as an added aspect to the curriculum but as a perspective which permeates their thinking in all subjects;
> c   establish ways of dealing with both implicit and explicit manifestations of racism.

A specialist adviser was appointed in April 1987 and within six months, in collaboration with colleagues, had produced county guide-lines (up-dated in October 1988). These were issued to all institutions, and on the back of this a series of ten conferences for all headteachers took place between November 1987 and March 1988. Following these, from June to November 1988, there was a similar cycle for further education and adult, youth and community education. This was a necessary 'top-down' phase, with a good turn-out and team support along the lines of Swann's notion of a 'shared enterprise'.

Since summer 1988, as a consequence of this programme, there has been a perceptible take-up in professional days devoted to the issue. Many institutions are forming working parties and developing policies, finding help from support groups across the county.

But, like most LEAs, we have failed to undertake any research exercise which would gauge accurately the qualitative as well as quantitative impact of our policy. Neither have we adequately addressed the issue of the 'laity' and in particular the need for governor training. Nevertheless, we intend issuing guidelines for dealing with racial harassment, which will have implications for governor training. Finally, as part of our own *perestroika* we have adopted the concept of intercultural education to embrace the traditional concerns, with the addition of the European dimension. The medium is often the message and we believe this redefinition of the field, as part of a more international approach, will add significantly to what has to be a broad and long-term strategy.

Indeed, one is tempted to echo the reply of Premier Chao Enlai when asked what had been the impact of the French Revolution: 'It's far too early to tell,' might equally apply to all LEA attempts at policy implementation in this field.

2   Working for Social Justice: Laying the Foundations in Cumbria

Clare Brown

A description of Cumbria

How might one describe Cumbria? Perhaps, simply, as a piece of land nearly 100 miles from north to south, the sea to the west, the Pennines rising to the east, Scotland, more and more clearly another country, to the north and Lancashire to the south. The M6 corridor the length of the county brings, perhaps increasingly, people who may incite young Cumbrians to acts of macho nationalism but rarely those leaders, black and white, who would challenge our ideas of ourselves.

Less than half a million people live within these 'frontiers'. Around five thousand of them are black and other minority ethnic group people. They live dispersed in isolated family groups throughout a country willing to accept their contributions to the economy but rarely, if ever, ready to take responsibility for the occasionally savage, and always harmful, acts of racism to which they are subject. The working-class communities along the west coast are struggling to forge a life for the 1990s out of a past of coal, iron and steel into a future dominated by the nuclear industry. The central fells shelter strongly traditional farming communities whose relationship to the land is being questioned by considerable changes in agricultural and rural policy. The gentrified villages of the Eden valley and south lakes have recently seen an almost wholesale 'offcomer' takeover of the space which only fifty years ago had a distinct Westmorland rural identity. The two largest towns, Barrow and Carlisle (small by national standards), sit uneasily at opposite ends of the county, one dominated by employment in the shipyards and still feeling like industrial Lancashire, the other, the border city, the administrative centre of the county but in no sense its identifiable capital.

Multicultural education in Cumbria

And so to the Local Education Authority. Working within the political context of a hung council where issues of opportunity and equality rarely appear on agendas, spending much of its budget on transporting children to its 380 or so schools, many of them with three teachers or less; involved in the relentless struggles of tiny villages to retain their schools, its apparent concerns are very different from those of, say, Bradford or Brent. How did a multicultural education project come into existence and function in this seemingly unfavourable climate?

In 1984 a small group of teachers came together on the basis of their interest in widening the cultural experiences of children and, in some cases, because of their commitment to working for race equality. When education support grant (ESG) money became available, the LEA bid successfully and Cumbria's multicultural education project worked throughout the LEA from September 1986 to March 1989.

To try to establish something of the views of teachers on issues deemed to be 'multicultural', the project conducted a small-scale survey in early 1987. What we discovered was what we had already guessed: the great majority of teachers saw little or no relevance for a multicultural project in Cumbria – 'no problem here!'

Next we tried to gather evidence on racial harassment in and out of school. Although a number of black people were prepared to relate their experiences to project workers, they had little confidence that any authority would be prepared to take action which would not hurt the victims more than the perpetrators.

In 1987 the project worked with a group of about fifteen teachers on the writing of *Curriculum Paper No. 14: Education for Life in a Multicultural Society*. The writing of these twenty-one pages involved the curriculum group in a series of lengthy debates. The ideas which grew out of these have formed the basis of the approach to work in INSET sessions with teachers and other LEA staff and with children, usually in primary schools.

Some of the tentative conclusions of the group were:

1   A 'cultural diversity' approach (just add on, as Salman Rushdie is reputed to have said, saris, samosas and steelbands!) may have a degree of success if it exposes children to the everyday experiences of individuals and thus challenges stereotypes, but must ultimately be unsuccessful if it fails to make real to children that the most oppressive form of prejudice is that which, coupled with power, results in racism.

2   The notion of 'culture' as applied only to black and other minority ethnic groups may be itself racist. Is there an assumption that 'they' have a culture while 'we' have civilisation? (See Khan, 1982.)

3   The very term 'multicultural' as applied to British society post-1950 is problematic. As Raphael Samuel pointed out in his critique of the 'new history' (Samuel, 1989), the story of Britain can always be read as the struggle of oppressed groups to gain economic power and to have their cultural expression validated. To accept 'multicultural' as only applicable to some cities where there are visible expressions of black experience is to imply that there is a cultural homogeneity in the rest of Britain, which ignores such vital factors as class, gender, geographical location and others.

4   Even if we accepted multicultural education as simply an apprecia-
    tion of the cultural experience of black and possibly other minority
    ethnic groups, we would still need to take the cultural experiences
    of white children in any area such as ours very seriously. Cross-cul-
    tural approaches, such as those suggested in *Issues and Resources*
    (AFFOR, 1983), require a careful consideration of, for example,
    family structures or homes in the children's own community.

5   For many if not most white children, large parts of their cultural
    heritage are rapidly becoming invisible as the mass media and
    other standardising influences distance them from their own com-
    munity's traditional language forms, styles of life and sense of
    themselves. If children are to genuinely value, for example, the oral
    tradition of some black British communities they need to under-
    stand how similar traditions may have existed in their own
    communities. The issue of the cultural deprivation of large sections of
    the British population is one which must inform our teaching.

6   If, however, we are to go beyond a cultural diversity approach and
    work for race equality, and if we accept that education must be gen-
    uinely child-centred, then we need to lay strong foundations in
    terms of a child's own felt experiences so that eventually children
    may have the emotional and intellectual tools to see the connec-
    tions between their own experience, as more or less empowered
    people, and that of black people.

Some concepts, skills and attitudes

Fig. 1, from *Education for Life in a Multicultural Society* (Cumbria LEA,
1987), suggests ways of looking at cultural identity and some issues for
multicultural society. Below we suggest some concepts, skills and attitudes for school and curriculum development. (The distinction
between skills and attitudes is not always an easy one to make: some
may fit equally well in the other category.)

Concepts

VALUES AND BELIEFS

. . . understanding other people's values and beliefs. May help explain
differences as well as reasons for conflict . . .

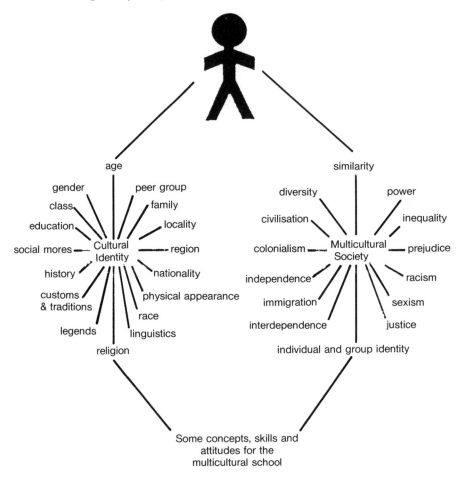

Fig. 1   Living in Cumbria . . . living in Britain . . . living in the world (© Cumbria LEA)

SIMILARITIES AND DIFFERENCES

. . . everyone has the same basic nature . . . the same physical needs and similar wishes and hopes, for example for friendship, love and happiness . . . We need to understand what we have in common as well as the differences.

SOCIAL CHANGE

. . . while change is normal and necessary, social change can have wide-ranging and complex outcomes not all of which are desirable . . .

CONFLICT

People continually disagree and often fight with each other but the resolution of a conflict can bring people together and generate new ideas.

POWER AND INEQUALITY

People or groups are able to influence what happens in the world . . . this affects people's freedom and welfare . . . power is often distributed unequally . . .

INTERDEPENDENCE

People depend on each other in many ways – from caring emotional support to the exchange of goods and services.

FUTURE

. . . aspirations, hopes, possibilities, probabilities . . . responsibility for creating a fair and just world . . .

Skills

COMMUNICATION SKILLS

People should be able to describe and explain their ideas about the world in a variety of ways: in writing, in discussion and in various art forms, and with a variety of other people, including members of other groups and cultures.

CO-OPERATION

People need to be able to relate to each other through play and work, giving mutual support by valuing the contributions that each can make.

ENQUIRY

People should be able to find out and record information about world issues from a variety of sources, including printed and audio-visual, and through interviews with people.

POLITICAL SKILLS

People should be developing the ability for decision making at local, national and international levels.

EVALUATION

People need to be able to stand back and attempt to consider the situation objectively.

OPEN-MINDEDNESS AND CRITICAL THINKING

People need to be prepared to consider views and issues with an open and critical mind. They should explore the relationship between fact and opinion before making judgements and be prepared to compromise and change their minds as they learn more.

POSITIVE SELF-IMAGE

People need to value themselves as individuals of worth. Without valuing oneself, a positive image of others is impossible.

Attitudes

HUMAN DIGNITY

People should have a sense of their own worth as individuals, and that of others, and of the worth of their own particular social, cultural and family background.

CURIOSITY

People should be interested to find out more about issues related to living in a multicultural society and an interdependent world.

EMPATHY

People should be willing to imagine the feelings and viewpoints of other people, particularly people in cultures and situations different from their own.

JUSTICE AND FAIRNESS

People should value genuinely democratic principles and processes at local, national and international levels and be ready to work for a more just world.

APPRECIATION OF OTHER CULTURES

People should be ready to find aspects of other cultures of value to themselves and to learn from them.

RATIONAL ARGUMENT

People need to be able to put forward reasoned arguments and evidence for the point of view they hold.

The ideas described above have, over the last few years, been further explored in INSET sessions with teachers, advisers, officers and clerical and administrative staff. Some of the work with children is described in *A Spanner in the Works* (Brown, *et al.*, 1990). Although approaches in classrooms clearly vary with the ages of the children and the attitudes of the teachers, most of the steps below are part of a process common to all the thirty to forty classrooms on which the book is based.

- Encourage children to value themselves. Challenge cultural views which, for example, only have positive language for certain physical attributes.
- Explore with even the youngest children similarities and differences. Use the children's natural curiosity about their peers and others they see around them to challenge ideas of 'normal'.
- Create a culture in the classroom which allows the children to express what they honestly feel – about themselves, the treatment they receive from others, their everyday conflicts and national and international situations. Work on strategies for resolving conflict at classroom, playground and street level.
- Help children to discover aspects of their own culture, particularly those which help them to locate themselves historically (for example language forms and oral traditions, movements of people, stories about individuals or groups who have taken control over their own lives).
- Use everyday situations to analyse which people have power and influence and what the 'victims' can do to protect their own rights.
- As children develop, help them to recognise which groups in society are oppressed economically and culturally by using the tools of analysis they have developed about their own experiences.

Cumbria's ESG-funded project ended in March 1989. In the report sent to the DES, INSET sessions were enumerated as were schools who had had any involvement with the project. A qualitative evaluation was not, however, attempted. If the aims can be described as being a process where teachers and children begin to ask the questions which link their own experiences with those of an oppressed black minority group, then it is certainly true to say that some people are using everyday life in the classroom to give children the tools to try to understand something of what it is like to be black and British. The extent to which that process will continue and genuinely empower young people to challenge the racism of the structures and situations around them will, of course, depend much on the 'official' and hidden agendas of the DES and LEA as well as on influences outside school.

It is, however, important to say that, with the exception of schools in Cumbria twinning with those from other LEAs, none of our work involved large material resources. (If talking, however, is expensive then our project was hugely overspent!)

A broader approach

In March 1989 Cumbria's education committee approved a small sum to continue the work of the multicultural education project for another year, under the title 'Equal Opportunities in Education'. By taking this broader title we try to make even more explicit our conviction that practical school classroom work towards social justice and equality needs to address itself to the way that class, gender and race are all crucially important determinants for educational outcomes and for the development of the whole person. There is, of course, a danger in this umbrella approach. Gender issues can swamp work specifically on race and ethnicity where vocational, as opposed to liberal, education initiatives, such as the Technical and Vocational Education Initiative (TVEI), perceive it as important to 'get girls into the labour market'.

The all-pervasive, if rarely acceptable, factor of class underlies all issues related to equality of opportunity. Outcomes for fifth-year students in terms of GCSE results vary dramatically: 51 per cent of the students in a small market town in south Cumbria with a relatively affluent community achieved five or more passes at grades A–C (92 per cent achieved five or more GCSE passes at grades A–G), while only 8 per cent in a school with a largely working-class catchment area finished five years of secondary schooling with five A–C GCSEs (56 per cent A–G passes) – a reasonable passport into higher education or well-paid employment. If schools are not seen as important in affecting the outcome, at least in formal examination terms, for working-class students, then how seriously can we expect national and local authorities to challenge the racism so clearly evidenced in even government reports?

The debate about education for life in a multicultural (and unequal) society will continue in the 'white highlands' (how apt this is for Cumbria!) whether or not there is future funding for special projects from local or national sources. The experience in Cumbria suggests that that debate will bear fruit as long as we continue to explore how children can themselves generate from their own experiences the knowledge and the will to challenge racism and other inequalities.

3   The Derbyshire Post-Swann Curriculum Project

John Evans

The nature of the project

The Derbyshire post-Swann curriculum project has been resourced, since Easter 1987, on the basis of whole school approaches to education for all in a multiracial society and countering racism. The project has aimed to address both the perceived educational disadvantage of black pupils and racist attitudes in white schools.

The intended outcomes of the project are:

1   to ensure whole school curriculum development which reflects our multiracial and multicultural society, to develop classroom materials and methodology, and to improve educational outcomes for all pupils;

2   to counter racism by identifying and eradicating racist structures and practices wherever they are found in schools, such as in pupil placement and allocation;

3   to facilitate new methods of personal and professional development for governors, headteachers, teaching and non-teaching staff of the school in responding to the multiracial nature of their school and/ or society; and to involve a wide range of agencies in these developments, such as the careers service;

4   to involve minority ethnic communities in the activities and developments of their schools and to respond to the aspirations of the

community for the education of their children – community liaison groups might be appropriate;

5   to review, evaluate and monitor regularly the developments in project schools and to disseminate good practice throughout the education service and other agencies, both locally and nationally.

Over half the LEA's secondary schools made bids for inclusion in the project, from which were chosen six multiracial comprehensive schools from the city of Derby (Bemrose School, Derby School, Homelands School, Littleover School, Merrill Community School and Sinfin Community School), and six schools from predominantly white communities situated throughout Derbyshire (Anthony Gell School, Wirksworth; Glossop School; Granville School, Swadlincote; Middlecroft School, Staveley; Swanwick Hall School, Swanwick; and Woodlands School, Allestree).

The schools represented a range of sizes and included both eleven–sixteen and eleven–eighteen schools. The proportion of ethnic minority children in the multiracial schools ranged from seventy to fifteen per cent.

The project was led by a small central team which consisted of a project director, appointed at senior adviser level, two project leaders (equivalent to Head Group 7) and a clerical assistant. Each project leader was responsible for supporting the work of six project schools. Each school's staffing establishment was enhanced by 0.5 fte (full-time equivalent) to reduce the teaching commitment of a school co-ordinator and to enable the release of teachers for preparation, planning and training. For each school there was also a small addition of clerical time, an opportunity to bid each year for additional funding for materials to support curriculum development and support for travelling expenses.

The project recognised the need to allow each school to identify its own starting-point and determine its own direction and rate of development, with project staff acting in a consultancy role and seeking to engender confidence and trust between themselves and teachers. The network of schools would be mutually supportive and would enable work to continue as extra support from the LEA reduced after two to three years. Regular meetings of school co-ordinators, sometimes with headteachers, were held by project leaders to share experience and meet the emerging needs of the co-ordinators themselves.

To support and advise schools and project staff in achieving the agreed 'intended outcome' of the project, a community support group and a professional support group were established. The community support group comprised elected members, representative governors and staff from project schools, representatives of minority ethnic community centres and groups, the Commission for Racial Equality and industry/commerce. The professional support group included representation from project schools, the police and the main agencies of the education service in the county. In addition to supporting the work of the schools, it was envisaged that the support groups would facilitate wider communication of the project's aims and achievements and would provide a monitoring and evaluation role.

School co-ordinators were responsible for monitoring the use of resources and developments in their schools, reporting termly to project leaders. Project leaders also supplied each school with a short, written assessment of progress made in the school each year. It was envisaged that the main form of evaluation would comprise a three-year action research programme involving a group of LEAs and managed through a higher education institution. Unfortunately this programme received insufficient support from LEAs nationally and contributed only to the early stages of the project's development. Project schools have been involved in HMI visits, a major national research project and a survey in three of the 'white' schools by the LEA's advisory service.

The experience of one school

Glossop School is an eleven–eighteen co-educational comprehensive school with 1,000 students on roll and a teaching establishment of seventy staff. Glossop is a small industrial and commuter town of 27,000 people situated on the edge of the Greater Manchester conurbation in the extreme north-west of Derbyshire. The school serves the town of Glossop and a large rural area on the edge of the Pennines. Only one per cent of the school population is from minority ethnic groups. Glossop School was one of the schools included in the LEA survey and is illustrative of the development of the project in the 'all-white' schools.

In the two years preceding the project there had been successful work involving an advisory teacher seconded under the Education Support Grant for Education in a Multi-Ethnic Society. In addition, a deputy head and the head of history had participated in a Technology Related In-Service Training project out of which developed a school working party. When the LEA's post-Swann project was announced, the then headteacher decided to bid for inclusion. The head of humanities was made post-Swann co-ordinator, with the head of history chairing the multicultural working party. This group was widely representative of subject departments and was attended by members of the school's senior management team.

In the autumn of 1987 the working party produced a short school policy statement on 'Education for All', which was intended for publication in the school prospectus and staff handbook. The policy statement was discussed at a staff training day in the autumn of 1988 but was not developed further and no code of practice or plan for implementation resulted from it. In 1989 it was agreed that incidents of racist behaviour should be reported to the post-Swann co-ordinator who would maintain a record and be involved in subsequent counselling, though there remained considerable latitude in the interpretation of 'racist behaviour'.

In the first year of the project a good deal of time was spent in seeking agreement on philosophy and approach within the working party. It was felt that staff awareness and confidence regarding multicultural education needed to be raised before anti-racist approaches could be tackled. There were visits by staff to schools, religious centres and multicultural education centres in Derby and Greater Manchester, a theatre group worked with students in English and pupils visited a synagogue in Manchester. There were also displays at parents' evenings, a Parent–Teacher Association event and regular reports to the school governing body. The multicultural working party sought to widen its active membership with invitations to representatives of parents, non-teaching staff and governors.

The pace of staff and curriculum development activity quickened in the second year. A whole school closure in the autumn term was judged by staff to have been useful in raising their awareness of the issues involved and giving the project a higher priority. There was also attendance at a series of subject-specific, one-day courses organised by the LEA's central project team and at courses on 'Black Writers' and 'Jamaican Culture'.

A series of 'focus events' in which the combined arts faculty had a central role also contributed to a greater awareness of cultural diversity among staff, students and parents and involved departments in working collaboratively to exhibit their work. These included a 'Chinese Event', an 'Afro-Caribbean Event', which formed part of a multicultural festival with other schools in the area, and an active learning project, instigated by one of the LEA's advisory teachers and developed from a Sanskrit poem. An important result of the Afro-Caribbean and Sanskrit projects was the involvement in the school of black artists, supported by funding from North West Arts. The active learning project culminated in a county presentation by all the project schools involved and demonstrated work from all areas of the curriculum.

Over the course of the project there has been significant development of the curriculum in humanities and in personal and social education. A multicultural perspective is evident across the humanities curriculum in the work of all students in their first three years. Resources acquired by the use of project funding to supplement departmental allowances have accelerated the development of new courses and reflect a strong concern to promote positive images of black people and a balanced presentation of the 'Third World'. There is work on ancient world civilisations, festivals, migration, human rights, development education, world faiths and South Africa.

In the fourth and fifth years, the pluralist perspective is maintained in geography, religious education (RE) and history options. GCSE groups in RE take a multifaith option, and in history, modules on the American West and Ireland examine cultural values, prejudice, propaganda and racism. This perspective is reflected in displays of students' work and is supported by learning strategies which encourage students to share and explore their attitudes and values and those of other people.

A module on 'Prejudice and Racism' is experienced by all fourth-year students in personal and social education (PSE). This originated through co-operation with another project school but has been further developed by Glossop staff. The course uses drama, discussion, video and media extracts to raise the issues of prejudice, stereotyping, racism and life in a multicultural society and to encourage students 'to formulate and question their own values'. A complementary RE module also incorporates a multifaith approach.

In English, notes of guidance for staff have been produced on the use of mini-sets of books by black writers or on multicultural themes. There is work on prejudice in the second year and all teachers include a multicultural perspective in their GCSE work. The department has contributed to focus events and has involved theatre groups in interactive work with students. GCSE drama groups have developed work on 'Disadvantage', which was followed up in PSE and Assembly, and on 'People and Culture'.

There has been a commitment in home economics to a whole department approach based on the systematic review of schemes of work and on building in a multicultural context. In addition, cross-curricular focus events and projects on 'Festivals', 'Poverty' and 'Action Aid' have been supported. The department has catalogued an extensive range of materials which are readily accessible to students.

The project at Glossop was initially perceived by many staff as primarily of concern to the humanities, a view reinforced perhaps by the appointment of successive heads of humanities faculty as post-Swann co-ordinator. Nevertheless there has been wholehearted backing from many colleagues, especially from the members of the multicultural working party which, although less representative that it was, has continued to play a prominent role in supporting developments. An enhanced awareness among staff of issues of stereotyping, prejudice, language, ethnocentricity and cultural diversity has been developed, and there is broad support for the promotion of a pluralist curriculum perspective. Some subject areas have found it easier to respond than others and there is still a cautious attitude towards the implementation of overtly anti-racist policies.

Science staff have been anxious to avoid 'tokenist' approaches and the presentation of negative images. Departmental resources have been reviewed and, as part of the development of balanced science for the Technical and Vocational Education Initiative (TVEI) extension, modules are being produced on 'Water' and 'Energy' which incorporate historical and global contexts and the concept of appropriate technology.

In physical education there has been work on politics in sport and posters depicting successful black athletes have been displayed. The special needs department has been able to influence resources and promote positive attitudes through its support role across the curriculum and there has been some review of library stock, but there are still areas of curriculum which have been barely touched by the project.

Although the project aimed to promote whole school approaches, much of the development at Glossop has originated from personal initiatives or within individual faculties. The post-Swann co-ordinator, who has been an important stimulus to and support for development, has recorded areas of curriculum development and resource acquisition, but the monitoring of pupil experience and evaluation of the effectiveness of initiatives is only beginning. Whole staff involvement in sharing experience and setting targets for development, and active involvement of parents and non-teaching staff, have been limited but there is regular liaison with local primary schools.

The project in Glossop School has enabled the school to promote significant change in the curriculum and to raise awareness of and create positive attitudes to education for cultural diversity among staff. During the project, the school has changed headteachers and post-Swann co-ordinators. The implementation of the Education Reform Act, TVEI extension and the process of amalgamating with a neighbouring school with effect from September 1990, have resulted in pressures on staff. Against this background, it is testimony to their commitment and, in particular, to the effectiveness of the current co-ordinator that the project has maintained its strong profile in the school. The appointment at senior level in the new Glossopdale Community College of an Education for All co-ordinator reflects a determination to continue and extend its work.

Review of the project

During the course of the project there have been changes in key staff in schools, and seven of the schools hve been involved in major reorganisations. Inevitably these changes have had an effect on the coherence of the project and on its ability to achieve all of its ambitious objectives.

The project has demonstrated that schools are generally more comfortable with subject-focused rather than whole school development. The importance to any development of establishing an appropriate organisational climate and structure, clear targets and good communication has been evident. The role of the co-ordinator in the school and the support and status accorded to the post-holder have been crucial to the progress of the project. It is clear that awareness-raising activities, while important, are not enough. They lead to the emergence of strong feelings and complex issues which need to be worked through. They also identify the need for further training and support for the management of change and for implementing practical classroom strategies in all curriculum areas. Less progress than was hoped for has been made in involving parents, teachers, governors, non-teaching staff and ethnic minority communities in Derby.

There have been interesting developments in individual schools covering almost all curriculum areas and, inevitably, some differences between all-white and multiracial schools, but generally there has been encouraging development in humanities, PSE, the arts, home economics and English. Schools have tended to be apprehensive about establishing a clear anti-racist stance and implementing a code of practice. The project has demonstrated that, given a modest enhancement of resources in materials and time, access to relevant, good-quality training and a supportive framework, schools can make real progress in developing a curriculum appropriate to a multiracial society and has provided valuable lessons to be carried forward by the Education for All service in its work with schools.

References

All Faiths for One Race. (1983) *Issues and Resources: A Handbook for Teachers in the Multicultural Society.* AFFOR

Brown, C., Barnfield, S. and Stone, M. (1990) *Spanner in the Works: Education for Racial Equality and Social Justice in White Schools.* Trentham Books

Cumbria Education Authority. (1987) Curriculum Paper No. 14: *Education for Life in a Multicultural Society.* CEA

Department of Education and Science. (1985) *Education for All* (Swann Report). HMSO

Derbyshire County Council. (1987) *Towards the 1990s: Proposals for Public Consultation. An Action Programme for Education for All People in Derbyshire.* Matlock, DCC

(1988) *A Derbyshire Approach to the Curriculum for 5 to 16 year olds.* Matlock, DCC

Hampshire Education Authority. (1987) *Education for a Multicultural Society.* HEA

Khan, V.S. (1982) The role of the culture of dominance in structuring the experience of ethnic minorities. In C. Husband (ed.) *Race in Britain.* Hutchinson

Samuel, R. (1989) History's battle for a new report. The *Guardian*, 21 January

Chapter 20

Managing Change in Schools

Alec Roberts and Ian Massey

Two Hampshire schools – strategies for change

In this chapter we will discuss two schools in Hampshire, each at varying stages of commitment to developing multicultural and anti-racist education. These are Frogmore School, Yateley and Bohunt School, Liphook. Each school employed different strategies to bring about change and, from these, seven important processes can be identified as turning-points for change.

We begin by stressing the following:

1 *The formation of a group* or working party within the school. This will often be driven forward by enthusiastic commitment to the key issues. However, in order for the group to develop in confidence and take the ideas and the commitment outside, it will need to:

2 *clarify the concepts* within this field. Understanding the basic historical, sociological, religious and philosophical implications of anti-racism and multiculturalism, and using its language, can be an empty exercise unless it becomes tied to one's own teaching and learning experience. This involves teachers in:

3 *focusing on their own institution*. Gathering evidence of racist behaviour in a class in their school or college, looking at an area of the curriculum or giving an assembly could be seen as a one-off activity and thus might merely give the impression that significant change was occurring. Purposeful change does not usually occur until the group starts.

4 *Seeing their institution as a whole*. When they begin to consider the full implications of multicultural/anti-racist education in terms of the whole school structure, ethos and curriculum, the group is ready to plan an INSET day for the whole staff. The planning, delivery and evaluation of an:

5   *in-service training (INSET) day* is dealt with as our fifth turning-point for change. We have compared the two very different approaches.

Following the INSET day or days comes:

6   *The generating, drafting and redrafting of the school policy.* We feel this should involve consultations with a much wider group than just the teaching staff of the school. The governors and the parents need to know that the policy is evolving and taking shape. Our final turning-point is:

7   *Monitoring the school policy's progress.* This implies keeping a constant eye on the workability of the policy and a willingness to change and adapt it, should it prove problematic.

We need to state from the outset that our expertise lies in managing change in schools which are virtually all white, in one part of south-east England. The validity of our ideas may bear little relevance to an inner city school containing children from many different cultural and ethnic backgrounds. However, each of the two schools we deal with is very different.

Frogmore lies in the semi-rural north of Hampshire and takes in children from a wide social background. Indeed it might be said to have a truly comprehensive intake, with a balanced number of children of all abilities. About one per cent of the children are from ethnic minority backgrounds.

Bohunt is situated in rural east Hampshire. The catchment area, although wide (children are bused in from surrounding villages), does reflect a tendency towards middle-class values. The overall academic ability levels are skewed upwards. About two per cent of the children are from ethnic minority backgrounds.

Formation of a group

Forming a group gives shape and purpose to ideas.

The title of the group reflects how the group regards itself, how it wants others in the school to regard it and the group's awareness of the wider political context outside school. For Frogmore, the title 'Multicultural Education Working Party' (MEWP) was used because that is what the head and senior management team (SMT) wanted. Their definition came from the top. At Bohunt, the group called itself the 'Racism Awareness Group' (RAG) and from the very start the title provoked a clash of values. ('Why did the word "racism" have to be used?' and so on.)

That the group perceived itself as tackling racism and the rest of the staff did not, caused a degree of friction and misunderstanding but what was most significant about the group's identity was its sense of purpose. Holding on steadfastly to the word 'racism' meant that the group was able immediately to enter territory which dealt with slavery, colonisation, imperialism and racist language and behaviour. Had the group not at that time (September 1983) called itself RAG, then the field of discourse would have been narrowed considerably. By keeping the title the group kept racism and racist issues on the agenda of every meeting.

Such a purist stance allowed the group a degree of intellectual freedom, but perhaps the way it alienated not only itself but other important levels of responsibility *and* closed down possibilities for early cross-curricular initiatives were too high a price to pay. However, the stance was necessary to avoid tokenism.

The Frogmore MEWP originated from a small group of staff concerned about the extent of racism among pupils. This concern was voiced to the head who shared their anxieties. Although Frogmore began very much like Bohunt, in that each group had little idea of where they were going or how they were going to get there, a significant difference was the early support of the headteacher. Just prior to the publication of the Swann Report, when national and county interest was being focused on these issues, the head instigated a formal working party, supported by the SMT. It was made explicit that members of staff in positions of responsibility would be asked to participate. These people were head-hunted by the leader of MEWP on behalf of the head. From its very inception this group was given legitimacy by the SMT.

At Bohunt RAG began with a brief report by a colleague on a course dealing with racism-awareness training. Staff were openly invited to attend this and subsequent meetings. There was no sense of coercion, only a genuine and perhaps naive desire to bring staff together to explore this vast and complex area called racism.

Clarifying the concepts

Once a group starts to play with the key concepts, another turning-point in its development has been achieved. This will come after much initial input from the group leaders (videos, articles, speakers, cassettes). Playing with the concepts involves understanding the links between personal feelings and the needs of the school; sets of ideas and the needs of the school. For example, it is one thing to state boldly that the school will eventually have a policy on anti-racism and multi-culturalism, but it is quite another to convince the group members of the potential content of that policy.

In both schools those leading the groups were aware that policy formation would be part of their group's role, but most of those taking part had little understanding of what is meant by racist, multi-culturalism, institutional racism, anti-racism or even policy. Clarifying these concepts is crucial and once the group becomes clear about them it will begin to play with them with confidence.

For the working party and group members in both Bohunt and Frogmore one of the most successful ways by which these concepts were clarified was by using a simulation exercise based on different models of school. Groups were asked to devise a racist school model and then a subtly racist model. This encouraged colleagues to apply the terminology to their own real-life situations. The moments of deepest insight occurred when colleagues realised that there were similarities between their own school and the racist school.

Focusing on your own institution

A significant point in a group's development occurs when they turn their attention towards their own institution. No longer are the issues 'out there' but from this point onwards there is an implicit understanding that this *does* make sense for us, here, at *our* school.

At Bohunt this moment was reached when a couple of group members complained that too much attention was being paid to the experiences of black people in the inner cities and not enough thought was being given to the 'pikey' issue. 'Pikey' was an extremely hurtful insult used by pupils within the school. Roughly translated it meant travelling person. Its derivation has probably something to do with living on the road and stopping at turnpikes.

A number of children from one village had relations who were travelling people and these families were often victimised. The term was also used of other children in the school who had no such relations. One member of RAG volunteered to carry out a small piece of research involving a few written responses by children, and this revealed the strength of the negative feeling associated with this one term. 'Pikey' meant dirty, smelly, badly clothed, ugly, unintelligent, greasy-haired, without car or telephone. It became evident to the group that when the time came for a policy to be drafted, the 'pikey' issue would have to be included. It was something particular to *their* school.

At the same time two members of RAG carried out similar research to help them gauge the opinions and attitudes of the pupils. This involved a cassette-recording during tutor/registration time. Each of the three group members carried out the work with their own tutor group, children they knew well and they knew would be more likely to give honest points of view. Here is a short extract from one recording of three boys in the fourth year. It was made in February 1984, only a short time after the inception of RAG.

> *B*   The Pakistanis have intruded our country and as soon as somebody says 'Pakistani', I automatically think of market and the way they 'con' us because they think they are so cool and . . .
>
> *A*   The stupid red dots on their heads.
>
> *B*   The little Paki mushes, the Pakistani mushes think they are so cool, I will punch one in the head.
>
> *C*   If you say, if you say 'Pakistani' to me I think of turbans and horrible sort of . . .
>
> *A*   And the way they build their temples and pray their religions in *our* country.

Contrast the above recording (made without the presence of a teacher) with the following made during the same week. This one involves third-year boys and girls.

> *Teacher*   Um when I say black people who do you think of? Do you think of anybody who is coloured or what?
>
> *A & B*   Yeah.
>
> *C*   I don't usually.
>
> *A*   Michael Jackson definitely.
>
> *B*   Yeah.
>
> *C*   Michael Jackson?
>
> *A*   I mean most black singers are the best singers in the world.
>
> *C*   Yeah Michael Jackson and what's his name? What's her name? Diana Ross.

> B   Like the lady who sings . . .? They are good singers. My
>   mum prefers any black person singing.
>
> A   So does my dad.

Both recordings reveal a limited and racist view of black people. The first with its violent undertones and sense of threat caused the most concern. Earlier on in the recording these boys actually agreed to the suggestion that all people who are not white should be segregated and placed in a separate part of Britain. ('Yeah, give 'em Ireland, we'll have the Irish people.') Such dangerously misinformed perspectives by children who, within a year, would be leaving school, made it very clear to the group how important its work was. The second recording exposed clearly the issues involved in stereotyping based on media-read images and attitudes – and the need to take parents' attitudes into account.

At Frogmore the focus upon the institution was carried out within the context of planning for the INSET day. The group collected evidence from both staff and pupils. A questionnaire was issued to staff on multiculturalism and anti-racism. The results revealed a significant number of sympathisers and many who considered the initiative irrelevant. Pupils of different ages were asked in many different lessons by staff (some not in the group) to write down opinions on a variety of topics (not problems) of which ethnic minorities was just one. A significant number of hostile remarks were received. Here is an illustration from a third-year who has acquired the language of tolerance but still holds on to prejudices on race and discrimination. The child wrote:

> I think that black people get all the rotten jobs because of their bias, white employers. And I think they should be treated the same as white people.

But when writing about immigration, the same child wrote:

> I think that Pakis, black people and Chinese people should not be allowed into Britain. Because some people in Britain need houses more than foreigners. They should go back to their own country.

The following was written by a fifth-year student:

> I hate the Pakis because they are so dirty and they work all the hours that god sends and send all the blood money back home to Grandma in the mud huts back in India.

The material collected was used as a basis for all the planning of the INSET day.

Whereas Frogmore saw the evidence-gathering as a natural part of the movement towards staff INSET, Bohunt's group kept the two processes separate. Consequently the opportunity of using evidence already gathered by the group as a mirror upon which the whole staff might reflect, was lost. The Frogmore MEWP was also very aware of how previous examples of change (for example profiling, GCSE) had been managed. They attempted to learn from the mistakes and draw upon the successful approaches. Focusing change around INSET had been successful. It was therefore adopted by the group as an important strategy.

Seeing your institution as a whole

When a group begins to start thinking not only about the attitudes of staff and pupils within its own school but also about the school's struc- ture and ethos, another significant turning-point is reached. Real progress from this point onwards depends upon the group's flexibility in thinking towards whole school matters. This necessitates breaking out of the bunker mentality encouraged by narrow-minded heads of department. It also means accepting a degree of responsibility for every- thing that takes place within the school. For example, if members in the group question the implicit messages transmitted to both staff and pupils during school assembly and if, as was the case at Bohunt, it was considered to be almost exclusively Christian in its outlook, the group must begin to do something about it.

At Frogmore the working party planned a number of visits to schools with existing policies. This not only highlighted to them Frogmore's need for a policy, but it also enabled them to view themselves from a distance and see those areas within the structure and life-blood of the school which should form the foundations of a future policy. These included: ethos, curriculum, abuse, language, staffing and community links.

By September 1985 Bohunt had just made important structural changes to its curriculum by putting personal and social education (PSE) into a more central position. But although a quarter of staff were involved in teaching PSE in the upper school, those who were not were kept at a distance and thus the central ideas about racism in our society, in our language, in our media, in our sport, were never at this stage explored or agreed upon by the whole staff. Racist views held by pupils were left unchallenged in some PSE lessons. The staff who felt confident talking about racism and multiculturalism tended to be members of RAG; there were others who were teaching about the issues and then coming to members of RAG for guidance and support. There were others who openly stated their hostility to PSE and its handling of 'dangerous' issues.

INSET day(s)

Planning and delivery

The approaches to planning for the first INSET day adopted by the two schools could not have been more different. Bohunt's day was put together too quickly and it was forced upon the staff at a time when the school had not been fully prepared to discuss these concerns. This approach made the group's work just another 'issue' to be talked about and then forgotten, whereas they should have been thinking about where the whole school might be going in the future. RAG had by that time realised that there was a problem in the school (evidence had been gathered), but instead of looking for legitimisation within the school, the group brought in an outsider from the BBC to help explain the rationale behind anti-racism and multiculturalism. He spoke well and illustrated his arguments admirably by use of video extracts but many staff members considered that he was referring to issues 'out there' and that it lacked relevance to their part of Hampshire. This was one fault of poor planning.

Another was that they tried to cram several months' work into a morning. Any actual or potential stimulus for change was dissipated by the lack of time for colleagues to discuss ideas. RAG leaders had agreed in the planning to the head's request that the day combine an examination of anti-racism with anti-sexism, the former in the morning and the latter in the afternoon. Consequently the school placed the speaker from the BBC in a false position, expecting him to address staff without providing time for immediate small group follow-up in which staff digested and made sense of the arguments explored. More to the point, the school placed *itself* in an impossible position because it failed to provide a forum in which ideas and feelings could have been expressed on aspects of human behaviour which demand great understanding and sensitivity. The backlash from that day was unpleasant for many months.

Frogmore's planning for the day had really started when the working party was first set up. Their approach was much simpler and home-based. Small groups were asked to agree on meanings of concepts like 'prejudice' and 'racism'. It was during these discussions that the pupils' views and other materials were fed in. Consequently all staff were left in no doubt about the status and legitimacy of this day. It was not just an 'issue' but a major turning-point for the school. It was considered crucial on the first INSET day that there should be a clear blend of formal and informal sessions. The working party went to great pains to ensure that all staff had ample opportunity to express themselves and approach the ideas in their own ways.

INSET days dealing with anti-racism and multiculturalism must involve *time* for everyone to express thoughts and feelings. At Frogmore this time was built into the day and, although there was not enough time, many members of staff expressed how pleased they were to have had a forum in which to communicate anecdotes about racist incidents in the school. The Bohunt day had had too broad a focus.

Evaluation

No better indication of the poor planning of the Bohunt INSET day could be found than the absence of any evaluation. This meant that colleagues were left without a record of the day and no opportunity to voice their views and opinions about the content of the day. Frogmore had outlined to all staff that the points made on this day would help in planning future whole school INSET. All staff, particularly newer members, were encouraged to participate fully. The reporting back produced the following points: surprise and horror at the racist views expressed by pupils, the possibility of developing a school policy, requests for guidance on approaches to curriculum change, the need for sexism to be addressed in the school and more discussion over the terminology in this field.

The evaluation report to staff was designed in such a way as to undermine the vocally negative minority who had strongly expressed the view that all this work was irrelevant. The Frogmore working party decided to concentrate upon the positive developments already occurring in the school and suggested by colleagues on the INSET day. They had introduced the whole school to some of the terminology, they had given an opportunity for everybody to become immediately involved if they wanted to, and they had also made it clear that eventually everybody would have to become involved. The next stage for the working party was to work on examples of good practice which could be held up to the rest of the school.

By contrast, the Bohunt day pushed RAG back into its corner and almost killed it off. It made the group think about different tactics. They shifted their focus to the curriculum and concentrated upon PSE, English and history.

Generating, drafting and redrafting a policy

Within the group/working party

For Frogmore the emergence of a policy came formally out of the evaluation of the INSET day. The group were given a mandate by the staff and the senior management team to proceed towards policy creation. The working party concentrated on making it belong to the school by basing it upon the key points which had arisen out of the INSET day. They also made a point of writing it in clear and simple language so that it could easily be understood by everybody, staff (teaching and non-teaching), pupils, parents, governors and the local community.

As one of the working party was at that time attending a DES course on multicultural education, there was a direct line available to experienced professional advice. Contact with and advice from black professionals in this field opened up the group's deliberations in a new and sometimes critical way. This helped in the initial drafting stage. The SMT also kept a watchful eye on the policy construction.

Bohunt's first draft was written by two members of RAG and brought to the rest of the group, rather than everybody in the group saying what they thought should have been included. This was hardly conducive to creating a sense of ownership, but it still has to be remembered that these events occurred in 1985 when there was very little happening (either locally or nationally) which offered any support to a group taking an anti-racist stance in all-white schools in Hampshire.

Presenting draft policy to the senior management team

The SMT at Bohunt was surprised and slightly worried by the first draft of the policy statement. This reaction contrasts strikingly with the similar stage at Frogmore, where the SMT was expecting to be presented with a discussion document. The head of Frogmore supported the work of the working party and welcomed their efforts.

At Bohunt a number of blocking tactics were employed to hold or slow down the process. One of the main ones can be summed up by the argument: 'There are too many other very important issues to be tackled, leave this until a better time.' Of course, the truth is that there is never a better time than the present to challenge racism.

Presenting the policy to staff, governors and pupils

Frogmore regarded the draft statement as a live and working entity which had to grow *out of* staff awareness and discussion. Some staff called for another INSET day to examine alternative resources and develop different approaches. However, the hidden agenda for the next INSET day was the emergence of a school policy and its acceptance by all. The presentation of the document to the governors was regarded as a mere formality, a culmination of the work that had been carried out over the past two years.

Bohunt's policy appeared before the whole staff at a staff meeting, after receiving cold acceptance at both the head of department meeting and the senior tutor meeting. There was a lack of urgency by many of the middle management to accept the work carried out by RAG.

That the draft policy eventually appeared on the agenda of a staff meeting was the result of continual questioning by the group and the growing commitment of the head. A few racist incidents had occurred in the school which had shocked and disturbed him. He understood that a framework for dealing with such incidents was emerging in the school and he put his authority behind it. He was also impressed by the quality of materials being used in PSE and the breadth of curriculum change that had started in such subjects as history and English.

The formal presentation before the whole staff and the question and answer session that followed was probably the most important turning-point in whole school change at Bohunt. At last everybody knew what was being asked of them. Equally important was the stamp of approval given by the head.

Presenting the policy to the governors involved much patience and planning. To coldly put before them a statement without any explanation would have been insensitive. The head's advice was to contextualise the policy within a short paper. This set back the progress of the statement by a term (the group did not feel confident enough to request a special meeting of the governors to discuss this single item) but it was worth it, because the group were able 'to take stock' and go to the next governors' meeting properly prepared. In February 1987 the policy was welcomed by all the governors.

The Bohunt model was not so sudden and jerky as it might seem, because most members of RAG also taught PSE and at least one other subject. Consequently ideas about challenging racism and making the curriculum more attuned to the needs of our multicultural society were permeating planning and teaching. This was reflected, for example, in the choice of books being bought for the library and the topics selected for whole school assemblies.

Frogmore's presentation to their governors did not require the same degree of preparation and orchestration employed at Bohunt. As the Frogmore working party involved members of the governing body in their INSET day, there was no mystery behind their work. The head regarded the policy to be of such importance that he requested a separate meeting of the governing body. The presence of governors who had attended the INSET day was effective in that they could describe what had happened and the positive effects it was having on the school and on them personally.

Both Bohunt and Frogmore focused almost solely upon teachers and governors in bringing about change. What about the pupils? In 1987, through the PSE lessons in the fourth and fifth years, the Bohunt RAG was able to evaluate the module 'Living in a Multicultural Society' by looking closely at pupils' views, not only on the course content but also on the recently adopted school policy. The majority of pupils were resentful about not having been consulted or involved in the process of devising. Their views were collated and used as a basis for further discussion. This resulted in the rewriting of another parallel statement in language which all pupils could understand. Frogmore had made no attempt at any stage to involve pupils in the policy making and implementation, and MEWP recognises that as a major flaw in their development work.

Monitoring the school policy's progress

For Frogmore the policy is a continual reflection upon the positive achievements of the INSET days. Ideas that were thrown up by the staff as being important to the school are still being worked through.

But at Bohunt, once the policy was in place, the next steps were erratic and illogical. RAG had no clear idea where to go and how to set about implementing the policy. The senior management team adopted an unhelpful attitude, which can be summed up as: 'Now you've got what you wanted, what else is there to do?'

The group made determined efforts to take the policy into the main-stream consciousness of the school, but there did not seem to be any coherence in the implementation. As the group later discovered, the majority of pupils did not know anything about it. How to release it to pupils and the wider community became one of the prime concerns of the group.

It was a fortunate coincidence that during this time (November 1987) the BBC education department decided to make a series of schools' programmes involving Bohunt: *Getting to Grips with Racism*. Local press coverage, a letter home to parents and an assembly by the head about his abhorrence of racism all gave the school policy greater prominence and exposure.

Two models of change

The ways in which both these schools reached the stage of implementing policies are very different.

The head's stamp of approval

They both exemplify the importance of a central requisite for success-ful change – the headteacher's backing. Bohunt's RAG was driven along for over three years by the commitment of a few members but they would never have been able to take their ideas further to the whole staff if the head had not added his full weight and support to the draft policy.

Frogmore's working party had the support of the head from the start. Throughout their development they had to counter those within the school who considered their work of less significance than national high-status issues. Without the solid support of the head, the working party would not have been able to overcome barriers to change pres-ented by other staff.

INSET day

Both schools approached in-service training in very different ways. Bohunt jumped in head first without preparing the ground. The day was shared with the equal opportunities/gender issue and involved no follow-up or evaluation.

Frogmore's working party tried to involve as many colleagues as possible in the INSET sessions. They achieved success on their INSET days by using three separate sessions (two-and-a-half days in all), comprehensive preparatory and evaluation documents aimed at guiding all colleagues forward in their thinking and using members of the working party as group leaders/facilitators during the sessions. Frogmore's working party also used evidence gathered from the school itself as the basis for much of the school's INSET work. Bohunt did not.

People need time to work things out

Accepting that there will be a degree of hostility and resentment to the changes discussed is another factor which needs to be considered. The Frogmore sessions, especially one which involved a black educationalist talking about her personal experiences of racism, involved a degree of argument and emotion. The crucial point is that such dialogue must be carried on in a safe and carefully structured situation which allows for dissension and disagreement but which also indicates that the school is moving towards developing a policy.

The school policy

Both schools recognised the significance of a policy. Bohunt's RAG saw this as its long-term goal right from the start but they were unable to break through into the policy-forming senior management team until the head shared their need for a policy.

From its inception, Frogmore's working party was charged with the responsibility of developing a school policy. At that time (1986) Frogmore was responding to national and county-wide documentation.

Bohunt, in 1983, had very few national or local directives to add legitimate support to their work.

Curriculum change

Bohunt's eventual success owes much to the close link between PSE and RAG. The group members, at a very early stage, realised that PSE provided an ideal opportunity for real curriculum innovation without affecting any examination classes in the upper school or cutting across colleagues' planning within their departments. PSE was rethought in order to incorporate a dimension on living in a multicultural society. This triggered off change within large and significant areas: English, humanities and science. Each of these departments agreed to reassess their aims in the light of RAG's work.

At Frogmore the lever for curriculum change came from the second INSET day which looked at resources and called upon colleagues to consider change within their own curriculum areas.

The effects of the change within both schools

Just as collecting evidence about your own institution is a fundamental part of developing the process of multicultural/anti-racist change, so too is monitoring that change. The effects on the two schools were as follows.

Bohunt

1   Over the years 1988-90 staff have become less hostile to RAG and the group has gained increasing respectability (especially since the publication of the county policy) as it received praise for its work from the head and the SMT.
2   There has been a growing involvement with the wider community. For example, a special leaflet for parents explaining the developments was produced and closer contact was established with feeder schools through the formation of a pyramid multicultural education group.
3   The annual 'One World Week' event has been used to foster curricular developments and cross-curricular links.
4   The school's policy has been incorporated into the staff handbook and the chairperson of RAG is involved in the induction of new staff.
5   The policy has been rewritten in language accessible to lower school pupils. It is introduced during personal, social and health education lessons.
6   RAG ensures that the stated INSET needs of the school include anti-racist multicultural education.

Frogmore

1   Each department has submitted details of how they plan to incor-

porate anti-racist/multicultural approaches in their curriculum. This has resulted in significant development in many areas.

2 A new referral system has been established to deal with the handling of incidents which might involve racist issues. If an incident is racist it is dealt with immediately, treated seriously, involves counselling of victim and perpetrators and where necessary the school's usual disciplinary sanctions are applied.

3 The number of pupils with hard-core racist attitudes is noticeably smaller and their tendency to dominate class discussions has also been tempered. Pupils with positive views now feel supported, not only by the teacher but also by the school and they tend to speak out more confidently.

Staff have also commented favourably on pupil reaction to curriculum initiatives especially in maths and home economics. Some have noticed how there seems to be a greater knowledge among pupils of other cultures and their contributions to the sum of human knowledge.

4 The School Aims and Objectives have recently been rewritten through a process of negotiation between staff and governors and contain statements which include 'a commitment to promote equality, correct prejudice and discrimination on any grounds and to prepare pupils for life in a multicultural society'.

They also pledge 'to offer teaching which positively reflects the various cultures of Britain and the rest of the world'.

5 To get parents involved it was decided to run an evening of workshops which needed the participation of first-year pupils and would show examples of good practice. This evening was a success. (For further details see Massey, 1990.) (The Macdonald Report on the events at Burnage High School endorsed a wider and more open involvement, at an early stage, in the child's education.)

6 One of the feeder schools has been involved in a school twinning project which has led to some multicultural developments and a growing recognition of the need to address continuity and progression in this area as well as in the National Curriculum subjects.

7 An examination of staff views revealed that most felt not only that they had more favourable views on multicultural education but that they had become more conscious of racism at a personal and professional level.

Into the 1990s – what Bohunt and Frogmore hope to be doing in the future

1   Increasing the awareness and involvement of governors, especially in the context of Local Management of Schools.
2   Continued induction of newly qualified teachers into the basic philosophy of multicultural/anti-racist education.
3   Continued open dialogue between staff and pupils over the re-enactment of the policy. This will lead to more school-based staff development work.
4   Continued permeation of the policies' philosophies into the local community beyond the school gates.
5   Developing an effective monitoring and evaluation procedure.
6   Implementing the County guidelines on combating racial harassment.
7   Ensuring the permeation of the multicultural dimension within the framework of the National Curriculum.

References

Macdonald, I. *et al.* (1990) *Murder in the Playground: Report of the Macdonald Inquiry into Racism and Racial Violence in Manchester Schools*. Longsight Press

Massey, I. (1991) *More Than Skin Deep: Developing Anti-racist Multicultural Education in All-White Schools*. Hodder & Stoughton

Roberts, A. (1988) *Gaining Commitment: Developing Anti-Racist Multicultural Education in Bohunt School*. Hampshire Education Authority

Chapter 21

A National, Nationalistic or Transnational Curriculum?

Alec Fyfe

An international dimension

> The most universal quality is diversity. (Montaigne)

We are introducing something quite new in our history - the implementation of a national curriculum. The National Curriculum represents an educational revolution which has coincided with the political revolutions of Central and Eastern Europe. Only time will tell whether a generation of children and teachers will echo Wordsworth's sentiments of the 1790s and exclaim: 'Bliss was it in that dawn to be alive, but to be young was very heaven.' As we enter the 1990s there are real danger signals, both educational and political – indeed they are interrelated. As the political map of Europe starts to revert to that of the 1890s, with heightened racism and nationalism, will education play its part in managing this growing pluralism, or will it simply cling on to those vestiges of educational nationalism derived from the 1890s?

What is striking about the current state of multicultural education in Britain is its parochialism. Paradoxically the field appears to be a symptom of the problem for which it claims to be the cure. If as Banks (1989) claims, multicultural education is an international reform movement, then there appears to have been little attempt to learn from Western Europe, North America or Australia. Yet another paradox, in an area which should emphasise similarity, has been the failure to grasp the links with other curriculum reform movements, such as development education, human rights education, peace education, environmental education and global education. As Lynch (1989) points out, such a failure of the 'family' to unite, has resulted in fruitless competition over increasingly scarce curriculum time, during a period of growing racism and educational conservatism.

Multicultural education is then incomplete without the incorporation of the reverse side of the coin – an international dimension. Swann recognised this clearly:

> In our view an education which seeks only to emphasise and enhance the ethnic group identity of a child at the expense of developing both a national identity and indeed an international global perspective, cannot be regarded as in any sense multicultural. (DES, 1985)

Education for cultural diversity must operate at three levels:

1   the local community
2   the national community, and
3   the international community

Ultimately its goal is the forging of a sense of identity within young people of themselves as citizens of these interlocking communities. But to work successfully towards such an ideal will require an appreciation of cultural diversity and the legacy of Empire reflected in contemporary educational nationalism.

Cultural diversity – the presence of different cultural, linguistic, ethnic or religious groups – has been the normal state of affairs for most societies for most of the time. There is no such thing as a monocultural society. But the recognition, particularly in Europe, that we belong to multicultural societies, is relatively new. It is really only since the 1960s that educational policy makers have been forced to respond to this reality. Indeed for much of the last century, as well as this, nation states have tried to suppress cultural and ethnic identities, in part through the use of education. Such attempts at assimilation, into one dominant national culture and language, were never wholly successful. The political map of Europe was in many cases as arbitrarily drawn (ignoring ethnic groupings) as was the case in the colonial carving up of Africa, and we can now witness similar reactions in terms of the over fifty ethnic revitalisation movements across the continent. The Soviet Union, as the last great multi-ethnic empire, is the classic case, with sixty million people living outside their ethnic homelands.

Europe is one of the most culturally diverse continents in the world. The mix has simply been added to since 1945 by labour shortages, which encouraged immigration from the poorer south of Europe into the most prosperous north, and from the ex-colonies. Britain, along with France and Germany, now has a significant black population, and 1992 will result in even more mobility and cultural diversity. The landmark of 1992 is yet another reminder that holding to a pure and absolute notion of national sovereignty is increasingly mythical in a world which now resembles a global village. The gap between our education systems (still not free of the imperial legacy) and the real world of growing pluralism is one of the critical time-lags and crises in contemporary education.

An appropriate curriculum

It was in 1977 that the DES stated that:

> the curriculum appropriate to our imperial past cannot meet the requirements of modern Britain.

Nevertheless, Tomlinson (1989) questions whether public consciousness, or the curriculum, have been completely divested of those beliefs and values characteristic of British imperialism. The notion of the British identity and heritage harkens back to the end of the Victorian era, a time not only of the height of Empire but of the development of mass education. Multicultural education has then not only failed to make comparative links with other places, it has similarly failed to engage with the historical dimension.

Tomlinson states that from the 1890s:

> imperial values become strongly reflected in school textbooks and these values have been extremely resistant to change. It was also a period when a single ideological slant was introduced to all school texts particularly in history and geography books. (ibid.)

Mackenzie (1984) suggests that:

> the values and beliefs of the imperial world settled like a sediment in the consciousness of the British people.

How to dislodge that sediment, with a National Curriculum which in part reflects the ideology of a return to traditional standards and values, is the major task ahead of us. We must establish a framework (see fig. 1, p. 70) for both interpreting and intervening in the National Curriculum so that it promotes those values, attitudes and skills needed for citizenship in the twenty-first century.

The foundation subjects and religious education (or the basic curriculum) are not intended to be the whole curriculum as outlined in Section 1 of the Education Reform Act. A balanced and broadly based curriculum is for the first time an entitlement established in law for all pupils. It must be a curriculum which as Section 1 states:

a promotes the spiritual, moral, cultural, mental, and physical development of pupils at the school and of society; and
b prepares such pupils for the opportunities, responsibilities and experiences of adult life.

Within the emerging framework for the whole curriculum now being developed by the National Curriculum Council, education for a multicultural society features as a cross-curricular dimension (with take-up also in the five major themes because there are important content issues) which helps to enrich and integrate the whole curriculum. Strategically, the field must start to view itself as a key fulcrum of the whole curriculum, given the gap between the aims of Section 1 and the subjects of the National Curriculum. Multicultural education then permeates the basic curriculum and through its process-orientation could help to provide the necessary value underpinnings for the whole curriculum.

The effective school

What will this mean for the individual institution? It may well be that a more oblique and broadly based focus on what constitutes an effective school in a multicultural society, rather than a head-on quest for racial equality, is ultimately more likely to be successful.

An effective school in a multicultural society will be led by an informed and enlightened headteacher who will involve all staff, as well as pupils, parents and governors, in the negotiation of a whole school community policy on multicultural education. The effective school recognises that 'the medium is the message', and consequently the process-dimension is placed at the heart of its strategy. Process issues have, as Lister (1983) points out, been traditionally left out by British educational reforms, whose targets have tended to be content and access concerns. In education for cultural diversity, process is of equal if not more significance than content, hence the need to stress participation, co-operation, relationships, ethos, teaching and learning styles, approaches to discipline (including racial harassment), the community etc. Multicultural education then does not raise new concerns in education, it simply illuminates underlying issues and therefore provides a key opportunity to improve professional practice and quality.

The effective school will view multicultural education as a whole curriculum issue which can be articulated both as a dimension and as a theme. The aim should be to develop within pupils and students both a systems and cross-cultural perspective. This means providing opportunities to view the world as an interrelated system of local, national and global events and communities. Such a systems view needs to be complemented by the acceptance and appreciation that the world-view of one's own culture is not the sole, or necessarily superior, one and this means challenging what is a natural ethnocentrism. The corollary is an expanded and liberating notion of cultural heritage and citizenship, which can initially be expressed within a European context. Citizenship at the level of the local, national, European and international community, is a cross-curricular theme which opens up the potential for developing a human rights dimension.

Human rights education

Lynch (1989) views human rights as the core of a global approach to multicultural education. It is an issue which links back to content and process debates. The Universal Declaration of Human Rights adopted on 10 December 1948, the European Convention on Human Rights of 1950 and the United Nations Convention on the Rights of the Child adopted on 20 November 1989, all have implications for educational practice. Collectively they provide the moral framework for education which transcends the partial interpretations drawn from religious and political traditions, in that they embody universal principles and entitlements. These rights in one sense transcend cultural diversity in stressing common humanity, whilst at the same time affirming the right to cultural expression and equal opportunities for all. The UN Convention on the Rights of the Child in particular deserves to be widely known within the profession, particularly articles 28 and 29 on the aims of education and article 30 on the rights of minority groups to cultural expression.

Human rights education can provide a key integrating mechanism for a more global multicultural education, as it operates at all levels and links both the planned and informal curricula. It must be viewed as a central component of all pupils' personal and social development as expressed by Section 1 of ERA. There needs to be a stress on exploring values and beliefs – a moral education about the ways human beings behave towards each other in the family, in groups, in their community, in their nation and globally. Education for cultural diversity, with human rights at its moral core, is essentially education for effective citizenship. Educators will find additional endorsement of an international approach to citizenship education in the UNESCO Recommendation of 1974 and the more recent Resolution from the European Commission (1988) concerning the European dimension in education, both adopted by the British Government. And of course in Curriculum Guidance No. 8 (NCC, 1990).

These issues clearly have staff development implications, the most prosaic of which is the general lack of knowledge within the profession concerning the facts of cultural diversity, the nature and extent of racism, global interdependence and of human rights instruments. Staff development will need to be delivered sensitively as part of a gradual approach to whole school policy development and implementation. The focus will need to be on researching the institution, and building on the positive developments and competencies. There needs also to be a variety of approaches and an opportunity to learn from other teachers. In a field which appears threatening because it exposes at all levels (personal as well as professional), there need to be opportunities for participants to explore their own values, attitudes, self-image and professional practice. An effective school will also grasp the resource implications of such a process.

Conclusion

To sum up, the real potential weakness of the National Curriculum is its very designation 'National', as all schools should be international schools. Education for the twenty-first century will need to be global; and if any curriculum is a selection from a culture, there are at least two implications. Firstly, that education can never be value free, and secondly that our notion of cultural heritage needs extending. All schools in a global age are multicultural as a statement of fact, but need to be intercultural in their celebration and response to this fact. This provides an opportunity but also a fundamental dilemma. How does one reconcile diversity with a need for unity? What are the core values of British society which all groups can contribute to and share, and what are the areas over which we can agree to disagree? Schools should be the places where this debate is begun, where connections are attempted between supposed opposites. It is a never-ending debate – a journey best begun with an intention of travelling hopefully, rather than an expectation of final arrival. On that journey it is best to avoid those terrible simplifiers who have the magic answers to questions of race and education, and are therefore impatient with the pace of change.

Such a harnessing (or appropriation) of the National Curriculum would make it a tool for internationalism and help bridge the gulf between the growing economic and political reality and the education systems of Europe. Perhaps the logical next step is a European core curriculum. This may appear fanciful, but the argument has already been advanced that all education systems will need, post-1992, to respond to the twin demands of rationality and interculturalism (McLean, 1990). Though many of our European partners appear better equipped to prepare students for the new high-technology labour market, few have a tradition of creatively managing cultural pluralism, which will be accentuated after 1992 with free labour mobility.

The real challenge ahead is for educators to work (perhaps informally rather than waiting for governments) towards a universal respect and creative response to cultural diversity, so that education systems can move from being part of the problem, to being part of the solution to disharmony, inequality and injustice.

References

Banks, J.A. and Banks, C.A.M. (1989) *Multicultural Education: Issues and Perspectives*. Boston: Allyn & Bacon

Department of Education and Science. (1977) Green Paper: *Education in Schools*. HMSO

(1985) *Education for All* (Swann Report). HMSO

Education Reform Act 1988

Lister, I. (1983) Alternatives and the mainstream and the humanisation of education. Paper presented to the National Organisation for Initiatives in Social Education

Lynch, J. (1989) *Multicultural Education in a Global Society*. Falmer Press

Mackenzie, I. M. (1984) *Propaganda and Empire: The Manipulation of British Public Opinion 1880–1960*. Manchester University Press

McLean, M. (1990) *Britain and a Single Market Europe: Prospects for a Common School Curriculum*. Kogan Page

National Curriculum Council. (1990) Curriculum Guidance No. 8: *Education for Citizenship*. NCC, November

Tomlinson, S. (1989) The origins of the ethnocentric curriculum. In G. Verma (ed.) *Education for All: A Landmark in Pluralism*. Falmer Press

United Nations Children's Fund. (1989) *The Convention on the Rights of the Child*. New York; UNICEF (copies available from UNICEF (UK), 55 Lincoln's Inn Fields, London WC2A 3NB)

United Nations Educational, Scientific and Cultural Organisation. (1974) *Recommendation Concerning Education for International Understanding, Co-operation and Peace and Education Relating to Human Rights and Fundamental Freedoms*. Paris: UNESCO

Index